Released into Language

COLLEGE SECTION COMMITTEE

Tilly Warnock, Chair
University of Wyoming

Lil Brannon
SUNY at Albany

Doris O. Ginn
Jackson State University

Brenda M. Greene
Medgar Evers College, CUNY

Linda H. Peterson
Yale University

James F. Slevin
Georgetown University

Joseph F. Trimmer
Ball State University

Art Young
Clemson University

James Raymond, ex officio
University of Alabama

H. Thomas McCracken, CEE Representative
Youngstown State University

Janet Emig, Executive Committee Liaison
Rutgers University

Released into Language

Options for Teaching Creative Writing

Wendy Bishop
Florida State University

National Council of Teachers of English
1111 Kenyon Road, Urbana, Illinois 61801

For Morgan and Tait—my own best resonators and fearless language learners

Staff Editor: Robert A. Heister

Cover Design: Carlton Bruett

Interior Book Design: Tom Kovacs for TGK Design

NCTE Stock Number: 39884–3020

Library of Congress Cataloging-in-Publication Data

Bishop, Wendy.
Released into language : options for teaching creative writing / Wendy Bishop.
p. cm.
Includes bibliographical references.
ISBN 0–8141–3988–4
1. English language—Rhetoric—Study and teaching. 2. Creative writing—Study and teaching. I. Title.
PE1404.B55 1990
808'.042'0711—dc20 90–48879
CIP

Contents

Acknowledgments vii

Introduction ix

1. Writers in Motion 1
2. Writers and Researchers on Writing 15
3. Options in Design 39
4. Generating Writing 62
5. Ten Inventions and Variations 84
6. Collaborative Composing and Imitations 116
7. Responding and Revising 131
8. Evaluating and Responding 157

Appendix A: Response Protocol Sheets 177

Appendix B: Teaching Creative Writing—A Selected, Annotated Bibliography 183

Works Cited 217

Index 227

Author 233

Acknowledgments

First, Katharine Haake has talked writing and shared writing with me for eleven years. We have experienced the ephemeral pleasures of writing conferences, maintained the lifeline of a long correspondence, and valued rare visits, filled with Scrabble and popcorn and serious talk and white wine. She has helped more than she may realize. Also, sharing ideas with Hans Ostrom always reminds me that sensitive teachers, both male and female, are providing important support to their sometimes marginalized undergraduate writing students.

I need to mention Peggy Schumaker, who shared her own and her graduate students' discoveries concerning invention several years ago. Ken Waldman was especially generous in teaching me his well-conceived invention activities, and he also provided tutoring-that-mattered for my undergraduate creative writers for several years. When I conducted a seminar in creative writing pedagogy for the English department at the University of Alaska–Fairbanks, the enthusiastic and professional response of M.F.A. graduate student-teacher-writers in that class contributed enormously to the development of this book. I remember fondly those arctic evenings with Steve Bailey, Scott Herzer, Carolyn Kremers, Trecie Melnick, Ellen Moore, Peg Peoples, Jill Robinson, and Terry Wike. Their work and thoughts and collaboration appear often in these pages.

These days, graduate teaching assistants at Florida State University are sharing the results of their own transactional creative writing workshops, and I work with an English department faculty that provides solid support for and expertise in creative writing instruction.

My own ideas have been refined within articles published by receptive journal editors. I want to thank the following editors and journals for permission to adapt or reprint material from my previous publications and those of my former students: Suzanne Bratcher and *Arizona English Bulletin*, for material used in chapters 2 and 4; Charles Duke and *Exercise Exchange*, for material in chapters 5 and 6; Ray Gonzalez and *The Midnight Lamp*, for material used in chapter 5; Nell Ann Pickett and *Teaching English in the Two-Year College*, for material in chapters 6 and 7; and Roseanne De Fabio and *The English Record*, for material in chapters 7 and 8. I would also like to thank Peg Peoples, Ken Waldman, and Terence Wike for allowing me to reproduce material from their unpublished manuscripts.

I am indebted to Michael Spooner, senior editor for publications at NCTE, who has supported *Released into Language* from the original proposal onward; I have greatly valued his encouragement. In addition, reviewers Charles Duke and Joseph Moxley and the members of the NCTE Editorial Board offered me insightful, challenging, and always relevant revision suggestions. Bob Heister of NCTE helped immensely with final editing and production. These individuals are responsible *only* for the successful results of their contributions.

Most often, though, my thoughts go to my undergraduate creative writing students. Their writing appears with their permission and with my appreciation. As always, their classrooms have been crucibles for my learning.

Introduction

Due to the steady movement of American writers into lifelong academic careers, today "colleges are where most of our writers can be found" (Stegner 1988, 51). Since the late 1930s, most creative writing professors have been publishing authors who teach graduate students about the world of contemporary letters. In Master of Fine Arts (M.F.A.) programs—and more recently in English Ph.D. programs offering creative dissertation options—many promising apprentice writers gather to craft poetry, prose, or drama and share it with peers and with their master-writer/mentor-teacher in a workshop setting.

However, it often seems that creative writers have moved into the mainstream of English departments without understanding or reviewing their own history—as part of a changing academic discipline called English studies—and without reconceptualizing graduate *and undergraduate* creative writing programs. Creative writing teachers are, of necessity, implicated in questions of theory and practice, primarily because they now teach large numbers of students at the undergraduate level. And these students vary widely in their needs and interests.

For instance, students in *elective* undergraduate creative writing classes may be more similar to students in *required* composition classes than they are to the graduate students many academic writers would prefer to teach. Undergraduate students may possess little knowledge of writing processes or writing products. Especially problematic, many of these students come from different cultural backgrounds than their teachers and have acquaintance with and value for a range of noncanonical literatures—from popular romance novels to oral storytelling to rap poetry to religious texts to television sitcoms—and enjoy those literatures in a variety of languages and dialects.

This book examines the undergraduate creative writing workshop. To do this, I begin here with a brief review of the history of college writing instruction as I have been able to glean the details from sources in three areas: writers about institutional history (Arthur Applebee, Terry Eagleton, Gerald Graff, and Robert Scholes), creative writing history (George Garrett, Wallace Stegner, and Stephen Wilbers), and rhetorical history (James Berlin, Robert Connors, and Anne Ruggles

Gere). The difficulty I have experienced trying to trace these sometimes overlapping, sometimes widely diverging historical strands suggests that more of us should be examining the ways our institutional pasts inform our teaching presents.

During the early nineteenth century, a college education in America meant primarily a classical, *undergraduate* education—the study of Latin, Greek, math, history, logic, theology, and natural science—and was reserved for the nation's all-male elite, aspiring doctors, lawyers, and, especially, ministers (Graff 1987, 22–23). Theirs was an "oratorical culture," in which classical texts were anatomized, memorized, and recited. The English language and English texts were not considered proper subjects for rigorous intellectual study.

The study of English literature, as we practice it in the late twentieth century, began in British universities in a slow and piecemeal manner, and for many reasons that seem surprising today. Early on, the study of English literature was a proper undertaking *for women,* who were beginning to enter the university system, and for working-class men attending "Mechanics' Institutes." Literature was valued not in the college lecture hall but on the popular lecture circuits and within informal study groups (Eagleton 1983, 27).

In his book *Literary Theory,* Terry Eagleton's reading of the invention of what we now call literature studies is made from a British and, admittedly, Marxist viewpoint. "Literature," he says, "in the meaning of the world we have inherited, *is* an ideology" (22). In England, the eventual canonization of certain texts was socially expedient, and he suggests the growth of English during the late nineteenth century is a not unexpected result of the failure of religion. Over time, there has been a narrowing from a broader field—which once included essays, sermons, histories, letters, journals, poetry, and novels—to a literature which includes only what we now term "imaginative"—poetry, drama, fiction (Eagleton 1983, 1–16).

In America, the study of literature and the development of our familiar English departments occurred with the displacement of the existing oratorical, classical culture. The effectiveness of the classical college education was challenged on many fronts, but it clearly disappears during the last quarter of the nineteenth century with the development of administrative "departments" of language and literature and the creation of graduate programs. At this point, the classical college becomes the new university.

Graff attributes much of this change to secularization and the rise of a scientific educational model as American colleges began to reform themselves, taking after the German universities, and assuring that the study of English would acquire a philological and linguistic emphasis. The drive for professionalism resulted in *graduate* programs which commenced "in the image of the great European universities" (Graff 1987, 57). Johns Hopkins instituted the first effective graduate school model, which was imitated by Harvard, Yale, and the University of Chicago. The developing graduate programs of the late 1870s, in turn, reinforced a new vision of academic professionalism by calling for programs in which instructors "could not become so 'absorbed in routine' that they would be 'forced to spend their strength in the discipline of tyros,' as they were doing in the old college. Instead, they 'should have ample time to carry on the higher work for which they had shown themselves qualified' " (Graff 1987, 57).

Equally important, during the 1870s, the new university evolved from the classical college because undergraduate education was now being offered to any student who could "meet the entrance requirements (a growing number, due to the new free high schools), offering upward mobility through certification in such professions as agriculture, engineering, journalism, social work, education, and a host of other new professional pursuits" (Berlin 1987, 21).

English department stratification—graduate programs for the professional scholar and undergraduate programs for the mass of new college students—was supported by the implementation in 1874 of "a test of the student's ability to write in English as a part of the Harvard entrance requirement" (Berlin 1987, 23). Such testing assured that the burden of writing preparation would be returned to (or blamed on) the developing free high schools which were producing these large new ranks of undergraduate college students. Earlier in the century, rhetoric (proficiency in oratory *and* writing) had required years of upper division coursework. When rhetoric was no longer viewed as the necessary acquisition of and finishing touch for the best educated minds, rhetoric was delegated to freshman composition and soon wished upon high school teachers. Where formerly expertise in writing assumed a student's long apprenticeship, the writer in the late nineteenth century was suddenly perceived of as needing to acquire a set of surface-level skills that could be applied by teachers-as-technicians.

The freshman composition sequence was started at Harvard in 1874. The development of such a course represents a "devalorizing of the writing course in the curriculum." Devalorization was to continue for the next one hundred years (Berlin 1987, 20). The newly designated "freshman composition" teacher became the overworked, undervalued member of the developing English department, correcting untold numbers of themes for a newly visible body of seemingly underprepared students (21).

The history of composition instruction during the twentieth century is complex but worth reviewing briefly. Current-traditional rhetoric, an objective (scientific) view of instruction which assumes that "reality [resides] in the material world, in the material objects of experience" (Berlin 1987, 6), came to dominate the classroom. This view of writing instruction narrows classical rhetorical aims from invention, arrangement, style, memory, and delivery down to arrangement and style, placing an unnatural emphasis on "the patterns of arrangement and superficial correctness [as] the main ends of writing instruction" (9). Not until the 1960s was this pedagogy successfully challenged, resulting in subjective (expressionistic) and transactional (classical, cognitive, and epistemic) theories of writing instruction.

Meanwhile, of course, Americans were still writing "imaginative" literature outside of the academy and within it. Nonacademic writing groups flourished as early as 1753 (Gere 1987, 14). These groups developed in most university communities, including the Universities of Wisconsin and Iowa. And purely "imaginative" writing entered the curriculum: "Iowa's first course in creative writing, entitled 'Verse-Making Class,' [was offered] in the spring of 1897" (Wilbers 1981, 20).

The development of creative writing courses at the University of Iowa provides the archetypal story of the development of creative writing within the discipline of English studies, although programs developed, also, at other institutions. Wallace Stegner notes the concurrent rise of conferences like the Bread Loaf Writers' Conference, but the primary influence on American creative writing programs remains the *graduate* writing degrees like those instituted at Iowa. There Norman Foerster began the "School of Letters," allowing the first M.A. creative theses and dissertations from 1931 onward (the M.F.A. degree was first conferred in 1941). Foerster's justification for this program reflected a movement away from the scientific, philological roots of English studies toward a more scholarly professional view of the discipline. It reflected a desire among practicing writers (and some students of literature) to include living authors in the literary canon. In fact, these courses adopted the methods of nonacademic writers' groups and included visits by "famous" living authors, the sharing of and responding to each member's work, and so on—the workshop approach.

Those who created and nurtured the Iowa workshop in its first year believed:

> [T]hat "no university could undertake to turn out writers as it produces physicians, lawyers, chemists, and teachers." He [Wilber Schramm, first director of the Writers' Workshop] observed that a man [*sic*] cannot be taught "to write, or for that matter, to practice any profession," but that "the teacher directs, aids, encourages; the student learns by his own effort." The necessary program for the university, then, was simply to "open the riches of the university to the young writer. . . ." (Wilbers 1981, 62)

This description reflects an essentially romantic, subjective view of literary creation and writing instruction; writers can be nurtured but not really taught. In his own writings, Norman Foerster warns us away from pedagogy:

> And let us not create an elaborate system of courses in imaginative writing, but rather keep the relationship as simple as possible. The "teaching" of writing, as has already been suggested, is essentially a relationship of apprentice and master. The most important requirement is that the "master" be a wise man [*sic*] who has been or is a practicing artist and has learned to read with an artist's eyes. (1941, 210)

In these views, *teaching* is a relatively unnecessary area of concern for graduate writing programs. These perceptions have held steady for many years in the world of academic creative writing.

In the Iowa model, the best young writers in America were to enter the academic system at the top—through graduate programs. And, from the late 1930s on, these programs flourished. Creative writing programs were at first vitalized and then transformed, though, by an influx of students. Due to the financial support of the GI Bill, colleges and universities were filled by "millions of young Americans, back from the wars, who wanted to read the literature of their own age, and who demanded it" (Garrett 1989, 49). In the 1950s, the GIs helped change the study of literature and swelled the ranks of creative writing programs.

The Iowa program produced many fine, publishing authors. In *Midland: Twenty-Five Years of Fiction and Poetry from the Writing Workshops of the State University of Iowa*, workshop director Paul Engle celebrates them in a sonorous roll call. In his own roll call of successful *graduates* of the Iowa Writers' Workshop, Stephen Wilbers intentionally notes those writer/alumni who have gone to other universities and colleges to start graduate *and undergraduate* programs in creative writing. Undergraduate workshops had been instituted at Iowa as early as 1949, while course offerings were broadened in 1957 to help the "many graduate students [who] were handicapped in their attempts at creative writing by a poor background in literature" (Wilbers 1981,

97). However, as graduates from the writing programs moved into other universities, they would not have academic positions unless they could generate an interest in undergraduate instruction in creative writing. By instituting undergraduate workshops, M.F.A.-trained writers, though, were increasingly faced with more varied students drawn from a broader set of open-admissions applicants.

From the 1940s to the present, "professional" writers have remained in English departments for various reasons. More and more, they stay because the situation is familiar and English departments represent—relatively—friendly territory, these writers having themselves come of age in writing programs. "The combination of modest academic salaries plus the incremental additions that were potentially available through grants, fellowships, prizes, awards, and, above all, public readings added up to a kind of precarious security for writers . . ." (Garrett 1989, 53).

As the numbers of graduate *and undergraduate* creative writing programs increased, the need for a professional organization became apparent; in the 1960s R. V. Cassill organized the Associated Writing Programs (AWP). Interestingly, successful graduate programs like Iowa did not rush to become charter members of AWP (Garrett 1989, 55). This period coincides with a burgeoning undergraduate enrollment in most American colleges, an enrollment that also revolutionized the teaching of composition. It is in the 1960s, then, that the intersection of creative writing and composition studies becomes especially important; teachers in these areas began, regularly, to teach the same undergraduates.

Professional organizations for composition teachers had developed much earlier than did AWP. The National Council of Teachers of English (NCTE) began in 1911. The Conference on College Composition and Communication (CCCC) formed as a special interest group of that organization with its first meeting held in 1947. In the 1960s, members of AWP were responding to the marked growth of their profession and to the complicated issues engendered by such growth. That is, it was not until creative writing blossomed into a graduate *and undergraduate* system that professional management through AWP seemed called for in order to serve the many degree-holding writers who were (re)turning to the university for academic employment. Currently, membership in AWP is still increasing, representing a greater number of programs and writers each year.

This already long, brief introduction to the history of writing instruction in America cannot encompass a full discussion of English studies in the 1960s. The rise of alternative critical theories challenged the dominance of New Critical methodology and has been described in Graff's *Professing Literature* (1987). During the same period there occurred a surge of professional growth in composition studies, which is best understood by reading James Berlin's *Rhetoric and Reality* (1987); essentially, current-traditional rhetoric was challenged by subjective theories of instruction that were not dissimilar to those promulgated in graduate creative writing workshops. Writing was advocated as a medium for self-knowledge and self-expression; models for instruction were varied and experimental, including a workshop approach as well as the " 'happening,' an art form distinguished by its making the audience part of its very existence" (Berlin 1987, 150). Published in 1973, Peter Elbow's influential book *Writing without Teachers* both results from and illustrates the changes in pedagogical thinking of the period. In its most idealistic manifestation—power to the writer as well as power to the people—writing instruction was revisualized; it should serve students and no longer be utilized as a way to discriminate against students.

Working against student empowerment, in many senses, has been the dominance of literature studies and, perhaps, an overvaluation of the importance of graduate scholarship and research. Over the last two hundred years, literature has moved from its place as a product for popular consumption to a property of the scholarly elite. Not everyone is allowed to write imaginative literature. "We may consume 'literature,' which comes from outside our classrooms, but we cannot produce literature in classes, nor can we teach its production. Instead, we teach something called 'creative writing'—the production of pseudo-literary texts" (Scholes 1985, 5). The dominance of "literature" is maintained by having an Other—both creative writing and composition—with which to compare itself favorably. In a similar way, creative writing has an Other—composition— to which it feels superior. Writers of modern imaginative texts have had a long-standing desire to align themselves with privileged texts (literature) and have preferred to see themselves as having little in common with teachers of a further debased type of text—composition or "pseudo-non-literature" in Scholes's hierarchical description. In this sense, *writing instruction* has lived an artificially divided life within English studies.

Today, in English departments, lively controversies are afoot. There has been a rapid growth in literary theory and practice, feminist and Marxist critiques of English studies, and composition research and theory (including a movement from expressionist rhetorics to a more sophisticated model now called transactional, with variants termed social-constructivist and epistemic [see Berlin 1987]). These developments are changing English studies, and thinking in these areas has helped me inform this text although this text cannot in any manner do full justice to the work being generated by such exciting (and often contentious) academic growth.

Released into Language

> At the bedrock level of my thinking about this is the sense that language is power, and that, as Simone Weil says, those who suffer from injustice most are the least able to articulate their suffering; and that the silent majority, if released into language, would not be content with a perpetuation of the conditions which have betrayed them. But this notion hangs on a special conception of what it means to be released into language: not simply learning the jargon of an elite, fitting unexceptionably into the status quo, but learning that language can be used as a means of changing reality. What interests me in teaching is less the emergence of the occasional genius than the overall finding of language by those who did not have it. . . . I too am most interested in helping students find language.
>
> —Adrienne Rich, *On Lives, Secrets, and Silence: Selected Prose 1966–1978*

It is my belief that academic creative writing has not been responsive enough to theoretical and pedagogical changes now going on in literature studies and composition studies (not to mention cultural studies, feminist studies, and linguistics). For instance, not enough questions have been asked about how we can (re)form graduate creative writing workshops and (in)form undergraduate workshops, composed as they are, increasingly, of multicultural students. Even though some of us are offering critiques (see Haake, Alcosser, and Bishop 1989; Moxley 1989b; Ostrom 1989; Shelnutt 1989; Stewart 1989; and others), we need to move beyond critique and begin to institute more productive practices. Both Stewart and Ostrom, for instance, suggest that creative writing courses might become core requirements of a newly fashioned undergraduate English degree.

Composition *and* creative writing instruction in American colleges are affected by concerns of both the undergraduate and the graduate curriculum. But it is no longer effective to remain tied to hierarchical ways of thinking about such instruction. We should not assume that "basic" writing instruction should take place at "lower levels," while upper-level classes exist merely to sort "best" writers into smaller and smaller cadres. Instead, teachers need to look at their beliefs, goals, and pedagogy for each of these levels and to dismantle artificial "class" boundaries that have been formed, mainly, by a relatively unstructured historical progression. George Garrett suggests that our "distortions of the past derive from the simple and familiar error of working backward from our present state of things, comfortably imagining that somebody planned or intended things to be the way they are now. . ." (1989, 47). I am hopeful that we can begin to bring our past experiences to bear on a more responsible present.

In this book, I attempt to reduce some of our hierarchical thinking and to reweave the currently separate strands of college-level creative writing instruction and composition instruction in the belief that developments in these perhaps artificially severed areas can and should enrich the other. In design, this book should serve the students in creative writing workshops to the extent that it asks their teachers to consider new ways of approaching their academic subject.

To perform my reweaving, I have had to make claims about our current understandings of writing and reading processes—what we know about writers, texts, and readers. In combining fields, knowledges, experiences and understandings, I hope to help redefine what I now, for convenience, call the traditional undergraduate creative writing workshop. I point out directions, options, and possibilities that will help concerned teachers develop a fuller view of the creative writing workshop. To do this, I have called the model I am advocating the *transactional* workshop. By naming this model, I am not merely seeking to discover new (and perhaps necessary) terminology. More simply, I want to distinguish between one pedagogical vision/reality and another—I hope more comprehensive—pedagogical vision/reality.

Intentionally, I have filled my text with the traces of my research. I have tried to share the knowledge and advice of the best writer/educators in the several fields I consulted. Since I view this text as a sourcebook, as well as an argument with illustrations, I have included references to readings that influenced me or that say in greater detail what I am trying to say. I hope that first-time readers will ignore the necessary distraction of parenthetical sources. I also hope that readers will return and dip into the text and its contributing texts more than once.

Finally, this book is ambitious but, perhaps, not ambitious enough. Although I have not focused my discussion on the secondary or elementary creative writing classroom or on the graduate creative writing workshop, I should mention my belief that much of the material covered here is applicable to writers and teachers in those classrooms (and there is much that I owe to writers and teachers in those classrooms). It is my hope that this book will encourage *all* creative writing teachers to join in conversation. It should also encourage more research and thoughtful introspection on issues of concern to academic teachers of creative writing.

Released into Language

1 Writers in Motion

> Of course we have to define creative writing. Like most writers I detest the term. Its connotation seems to imply precious writing, useless writing, flowery writing, writing that is a luxury rather than a necessity, something that is produced under the influence of drugs or leisure, a hobby.
>
> —Donald Murray, *Learning by Teaching*, 1982

Professional writers are notoriously opinionated, but most would agree with a simple observation: writers are people who write. Students who enroll in undergraduate creative writing classes sense this. Students begin a writing workshop hoping to learn many things about themselves. They may be trying to decide if they should become zoologists or historians or English majors. They may be trying to find out if their writing promise, identified by a favorite high school teacher, really exists. Student writers may have published work in the high school newspaper, done well in English classes, and garnered reputations for being creative. Some undergraduate creative writing students are loners, and they find important outlets in writing extremely personal, songlike lyrics which they have never shared with anyone before. A few may be shopping for an easy class. Others believe that writers have more fun, for apocryphal anecdotes portray writers as driven creatures who take drugs, drink, commit suicide, and still, or because of such dubious habits, create lasting works of art. And many students are interested readers who want to learn what it feels like to write.

College writing teachers want to conduct workshops for as many reasons as students want to enroll in their classes. Some teachers are practicing and publishing writers who hold Master of Fine Arts (M.F.A.) degrees. Some teachers have specialized in literature and composition studies but are also writers; they publish journalism, or an occasional poem in a literary magazine, or share elegant letters with their acquaintances. A few teachers have less than honorable reasons for deciding to teach creative writing classes. They imagine teaching creative writing will be less demanding than lecturing about literature, or they long for any alternative to what feels like a constrictive composition teaching load.

Most often though, teachers of undergraduate creative writing find real rewards through their involvement with student writers. An involved teacher, as Donald Murray observes, "will find that he has entered into an exciting and productive relationship with his students. He will not be a teacher, he will be a senior learner, what a teacher ought to be" (1982b, 138).

When varied students and varied teachers meet, however, curricular questions arise. What is the most productive form and content of an undergraduate creative writing workshop? How should activities in this workshop be sequenced? What is the teacher's role on the continuum from senior learner to master writer? How should the teacher grade students' creative work? What happens in a mixed genre workshop; can students actually learn much about writing prose, poetry, *and* drama in nine or fourteen weeks? Are there models for instruction that writers, as teachers of other writers, have found useful?

To explore these questions, I'll look at three areas: students' expectations, English department expectations, and current writing workshop models.

Students' Expectations

Creative writing students want to know, overall, if they can write. They can, of course, but like many of us they are unsure of themselves and driven by some myths about writing: that creative writing is something done by a few geniuses; that good writing proceeds inevitably from good ideas; that good writers compose nearly perfect drafts, often at a single sitting; that writers pack one overriding theme into a text to be construed later by a well-trained reader; that writing is a rather magical, solitary occupation; and that writers are more interesting than other people (see Bishop 1988b; Crowley 1989; Moxley 1989b; Ostrom 1989; and F. Smith 1981).

Linda Brodkey (1987) calls one of these primary myths the "scene of writing." In the modern scene of writing, the artist is locked into a garret, writing masterpieces alone. Writing is an arduous and highly individual process. Brodkey warns of the danger of this romantic devotion to the image of the individual writer: "[T]hose who teach as well as those who take composition [and all writing] courses are influenced by the scene of writing, namely, that all of us try to recreate a garret and all that it portends whether we are writing in a study, a library, a classroom, or at a kitchen table, simply because we learned this lesson in writing first" (397).

Certainly there are ways to deconstruct this overwhelming image. It can be done when teachers design innovative classes. For example, Valerie Miner (1989) designed a seminar for advanced writers entitled "Social Issues in Publishing," which includes theoretical and practical discussions on literacy, publishing economics, and minorities and publishing. In addition, students "follow a book from author's conception to reader's bookshelf" (228) and participate in a publishing internship. The seminar was not designed to commercialize a writer but to allow a writer to understand the forces that are already at work in the publishing world and so enhance understanding of the "society" the writer wishes to enter, someday, as a professional. Robert Scholes argues for new curricular directions in his influential book *Textual Power* (1988). He suggests that teachers at all levels can help students reverse what has become almost a worship of Literature—"the attitude of the exegete before the sacred text" (16). Scholes feels that we should help students to replace worship with a "judicious attitude: scrupulous to understand, alert to probe for blind spots and hidden agendas, and finally, critical, questioning, skeptical" (16).

Before undertaking ambitious classroom agendas, however, it is important, first, to see that prejudices, myths, models, and culturally determined practices drive us *and* our students. Not surprisingly, the image of "solitary genesis," as Miner calls it, coupled with years of New Critical reading instruction, has resulted in close readings of poems and fiction in classrooms at all levels. Undergraduates naturally tend to rebel against such readings since, for years, they have been forced to battle with texts, to hunt and peck for overriding symbols or monolithic themes. Their varied and confusing experiences often turn them away from a seemingly dense and unfriendly "Literature."

Even while students rebel against canonized texts, they enroll in creative writing classes, hoping to find out from the teacher if *they* are among the anointed few who can escape to a garret and reappear hours later with a soon-to-be-acknowledged masterpiece. The role of author is seductive. And the conflicting impulses experienced by student creative writers as they move into the author position can be seen in their journals. In this example, a freshman creative writer, John, was asked to discuss those writers he reads and why:

> I like several different writers. I think my favorites are Stephen King and J.R.R. Tolkien for the simple fact that their writings are entertaining, and not meant to be anything else, and George Orwell for his economical writing style; he does not include extraneous B.S. in his writing.
>
> In addition to simply entertaining writing (such as Tolkien's or

> King's), I like writing that makes one think, such as Orwell's. *1984* was one of my favorite books because after I finished reading it, I thought about all the ideas that were floating around in the story. I especially like Orwell's writing because I didn't have to *dig* to figure out what he was saying; his thoughts and values were all up front.

In this journal entry, John is letting me, his teacher, know that he likes writing which engages ideas, but he suspects "extraneous B.S." and dislikes digging for hidden messages.

John's class journal taught me a lot about a writer's development, and I quote from it several times in this book. Although he was responding to his experiences in an introduction to creative writing (poetry) class, his experiences are quite representative of any novice writer who is exploring his or her creative potential. John's opinions are similar to opinions expressed by beginning fiction writers and dramatists in my writing classes.

For instance, here is John describing why he enrolled in a creative writing class:

> I think the first time that I realized that I enjoyed writing was about 5 years ago in ninth grade. I was taking a class where we read a lot of Shakespeare and Hemingway, and (sort of a strange combination . . .) although the aim of the class was to instill some sort of literary appreciation into our ninth grade heathen minds, the way the teacher did so was perhaps a bit unconventional. Mr. Givens would have us read the material and then would let us respond to it through projects. For example, for "Romeo and Juliet," my friend and I made a 16th century newspaper, *The Verona Enquirer*; it had articles about "rumbles" between the Montagues and the Capulets, articles about two certain youths who killed themselves in a bizarre suicide pact, and so forth. For "Old Man and the Sea," the same friend and I made a slide presentation about the life of Hemingway. I can honestly say that not only did Mr. Givens give me a sense of literary appreciation of the books we read, but he also showed me how much fun creative writing could be.
>
> You may notice that I have not mentioned any poetry. You know why? Because there weren't any poetry classes to take. Beyond learning rhyme patterns and Joyce Kilmer's poem about trees, there simply was not much in the way of poetry at my school.

John explores his own reasons for enrolling in a writing class, similar to those I mentioned earlier. Overall, John had positive experiences during high school in an active literature class—one that did not privilege the author, the text, or the reader. In this class, John was allowed to write new, creative material in response to literature; he was not simply asked to explicate texts. Also, in this high school class, John was allowed to collaborate with a friend on his projects, and he sensed that his teacher, Mr. Givens, enjoyed literature *and* creative writing.

At the same time, John is almost surprised at himself for choosing to enroll in my college-level poetry writing class since he felt he had never encountered poetry as a subject in high school (although he seems to have encountered it as punishment when he had to learn the rhyme patterns in Kilmer's poetry). Luckily for John, his teacher, Mr. Givens, had looked beyond the text-centered approach of New Criticism and the romantic, author-centered approach of traditional creative writing instruction to develop a broader view of writers and readers.

W. Ross Winterowd, in an introduction to Sharon Crowley's *A Teacher's Introduction to Deconstruction* (1989), describes three current models which inform writing (and I would argue reading) instruction: "It is defensible (though hardly neat and incisive) to say that composition theories and practices can be classed as text-centered, author-centered, or transactional. The images are clear: that of pages in an open book; that of the lone writer producing text; and that of a writer on one side, a text in the middle, and a reader on the other side" (xi). During high school, John was given the opportunity to participate in a transactional approach to reading and writing, and John found much to engage him in this instructional model.

Then John carried into the classroom what he had gained from Mr. Givens's approach. In undergraduate creative writing, John challenged received myths concerning the "proper" subject for poems and the "ideal" identity for a poet. In his journal, he explains:

> I wrote the poem as a reaction to a lot of the poems I've read lately, which are usually gushy love poems, or death or other things that the good sensitive poet should write about. Call me unsentimental, insensitive or whatever, but I haven't seen much humor at all in the poetry I've read lately. I guess I don't take a whole lot seriously, but [my poem] "Doin' Da Funky Chicken" is my answer to all the spurned lovers, suicides, etc., that are popular subjects with poets. Not only that, but I hope it was an enlightening description of what chickens *really* do at night. . . .

John was typical of a new college student who wanted to explore a subject area that had started to interest him in high school, but he was somewhat atypical in his humorous questioning of received wisdom. He saw himself as a novice, but he was a pleasantly skeptical one.

Some freshman writers, though, already view themselves as "writers" and enroll in creative writing classes for the structure such a class can offer them. In doing this, the individual begins to submit to a writer's discipline while trying to maintain the very high standards posed by his personal images of writing and writers. Freshman writer Paul, who had never before written poetry, says: "Okay, I admit that my poems suck, but so did Shakespeare's first three or four poems (so it's okay)." Paul has very high standards indeed for his first works.

Other student writers crave the discipline of class assignments but worry (rightly) about their ability to be self-disciplined after the class is over. At the end of an introduction to creative writing-fiction workshop, Sharon says:

> My only complaint is that your not hard enough. I think that there were times that you could've nailed us [to complete assignments] and probably should have. I know there are times that I need that push. I still need to learn to discipline myself. This summer will be the real test. I'm just glad that I had this course to fall on to. It has definitely helped me as a writer by teaching me critiquing techniques, style, and it has given me hope, believe it or not.

As writers, Paul and Sharon are already exploring their own scenes of writing and images of themselves as authors. Paul imagined himself a budding Shakespeare, emulating the best work in the canon, and Sharon, who already considered herself a lifelong writer, had plenty of projects and hoped to test herself in the summer following our class, seeing if she could write regularly.

Other students come to undergraduate workshops with much more hesitation. These individuals have only recently developed a need to share their work; they are looking for readers. In a study of college-level writers, Gene Krupa and Robert Tremmel (1983) found that college students produce an enormous amount of what the researchers call "underground writing," that is, personal letters, journals, and exploratory writing that reviews the writers' own feelings and helps them deal with the ideas they are encountering in college. Students often enroll in an undergraduate creative writing workshop as a first step in learning to share writing of this sort, whether or not they have intentions of becoming professional writers.

The workshop provides a first audience, yet it is rarely easy for these novice writers to share their work publicly, even with receptive peers. At first, underground writers do not understand just how cryptic their writing can be. For instance, they may have to translate their own mysterious, almost hidden, thoughts into a readable format. Paul describes how he "used to keep a journal and write in a very personal, spur-of-the-moment fashion that I thought was so personally me no one else would ever understand it, and I didn't care. The thing was, when I read it now *I* can't understand it because it was too personal to the moment which has long passed. It's written in a foreign language and I can't derive what life was like back then by reading it." Paul came to value audience by the end of the semester. He writes: "I am more conscious of audience—something I completely forsaked in the very beginning—I've become more aware of public, or typical, interpretation, and I understand more that if I'm really going to write all for myself then there's no purpose in learning, is there?"

Sharing personal writing can help student writers understand and develop an awareness of audience. Exploring audiences' expectations, in turn, helps these novice writers better understand academic conventions. This sequence was illustrated by an entry in Ginger's fiction writing journal. Near the end of the semester, she says:

> I have gotten better in critiquing stories. I know more of what to look for and what more there needs to be. I find a spot I didn't enjoy in the story and I try to figure out why and then I tell the person how they might improve that section. I used to never be able to pick things out as right or wrong and what could be better. Everything sounded good to me. Now I know better. I have read things in my English class that were pretty good stories. I saw how they developed the characters and how information was packed into the words without telling what it was right out. The story I liked the best was *Good Country People* by Flannery O'Connor. You could tell so much about the characters just from the reading. How the characters acted and talked told everything the reader needed to know about them.

While Paul found that the workshop helped him to move into an acceptance of public sharing, Ginger found that the workshop helped her to segment and differentiate what had previously seemed like a uniformly competent literature ("Everything sounded good to me").

Writers also enroll in single-genre creative writing classes to explore a less familiar genre. This was true for Paul, who wrote in his poetry journal, "I am a writer of prose and I don't know how unusual it is for someone who has written prose all his life to completely ignore verse, but I have, at any rate. So, this is my introduction to the subject (this class, I mean)."

The creative writing workshop provides a student writer with a community, and the community also contributes to the writer's developing sense of audience. A writing community helps writers discover readers' tastes and explore the effects of stylistic experimentation. A writing community also provides the student writer with a forum for trying on the *personality* of a writer. The creative writing workshop provides an important, primary, peer community, but that community disbands quickly at the end of most class meetings. The teacher offers mentoring and insider's knowledge about writing. But often the teacher is busy or so much older and more experienced than the students that he or she cannot comfortably be considered a colleague.

Yet student writers, like writers anywhere, need others with whom they can just talk. John, in his poetry writing journal, discusses the usefulness of an extended community, the campus writing center. Students in John's class could visit a writing center where they were tutored by M.F.A. program teaching assistants. The tutors provided an important alternative audience. John explains the value of these tutors: "Just hanging around with Ken on Mondays and Wednesdays and talking about poetry has really been helpful. It's nice to have someone just to talk with about poetry. The Writing Center does this for me, because none of my friends really understand what poetry is about. They don't have a problem with the fact that I am taking a poetry class (which some people do, if you're a guy at least), but they just don't KNOW anything about it." In this instance, at the writing center with other writers, John could say he was writing poetry without risking what seemed to be the stigma of female behavior, and he could talk to an insider in the system, an M.F.A. student, someone whom he respected as "KNOW"-ing something.

Student journal responses like these show that novice writers enroll in creative writing classes for many reasons. They may approach their learning by valorizing the text (product), author (writer), or reader (audience) viewpoint, or they may already be willing to consider the interactive nature of all three positions. The undergraduate creative writing workshop can be a turbulent place, filled with shallows and crosscurrents and exhilarating rapids. Students are seduced by the image of becoming "great" writers and repelled by the demands of craft. They are weary of experiencing their insights alone, yet terrified of sharing them with an unknown audience. They have some habits, or bad habits, or no habits. They have spontaneity and enthusiasm, and the ability to work hard, almost doggedly, when the creative writing workshop offers them opportunities to move more deeply into language.

Departmental Expectations

Most English departments today offer courses in literature, in critical theory, in composition (sometimes rhetoric and advanced professional writing), and in creative writing. Over several decades, the creative writing course has been inducted into existing, predominantly literature-based curriculums because there were academic writers eager to teach such courses. In turn, English departments were interested in boosting enrollment and developing readers through these popular elective classes. In workshops, students were encouraged to learn to read critically, to write, and to discuss their own and model writers' writing in a workshop conducted by a "professional" creative writer.

Several problems exist with undergraduate creative writing workshops and programs in this version of their development. First, the field divisions of course offerings that I have mentioned above are value-laden (see Emig 1983; Graff 1987; Scholes 1985). In many departments, literature courses, as "content" bearing courses, are considered much more valuable than writing courses, which may be viewed as contentless craft courses, or worse, as therapeutic (see Ostrom 1989). Department divisions fragment what should be interrelated reading-and-response and writing-and-response activities (see Moxley 1989b).

At the most practical level, literature and writing fight for status and department funding. In this fight, creative writing classes may function as "bait" to lure students to enrollment in literature classes, and creative writing students are not valued for themselves, for the learning they hope to achieve. In such an English department, only the best creative writing students are strongly supported and encouraged (in direct proportion to the slots available to them in the department's graduate program in writing, if it has one). Students of creative writing, then, in general, are viewed as future readers of literature or as students who may be converted into enrollment in literature studies. These students do develop as readers and do change majors to English, and some of them do continue their careers as writers through enrollment in graduate programs. But undergraduate creative writing students, as seen in the journal entries that I shared above, have important reasons of their own for taking English department workshops; they do not exist primarily to swell the rosters of English departments.

Graduate and Undergraduate Writing Workshops

Just as there is tension between strands of study in college English departments—literature, criticism, composition, and creative writing—there is disjunction between the goals of graduate and undergraduate creative writing programs. Graduate programs work to find the undergraduate genius and to recruit him to the graduate M.F.A. program where he will study with a master writer and fit himself for a "writer's life." Recently, there have been indications that such a life is less exhilarating than it may seem. Eve Shelnutt (1989) claims that creative writing programs have intentionally stunted their own intellectual development, in part, by becoming isolated within the discipline of English studies, by engaging in a workshop method that assumes students already know how to write, and by placing M.F.A. students in the untenable position of producing "publishable" work while learning the traditional canon of literature and undertaking heavy composition teaching loads. At the same time, M.F.A. students are not being encouraged to write academic prose; Shelnutt finds M.F.A. students feel untutored in academic and scholarly writing due to a lack of critical theory in their programs and coursework. She critiques the traditional graduate workshop, "most teachers of creative writing find the workshop format effective because it is the only format they know" (16), and suggests that in such a workshop students are not pushed to take risks, to experiment, to "produce awkward work on the way to a broader understanding and polishing of forms" (18).

This type of graduate program pedagogy transfers poorly to the undergraduate workshop. In spite of this, the dominant teaching model in graduate *and undergraduate* courses remains the traditional workshop. In this classroom, the master writer or mentor discusses drafts of student writing in a near-finished state. Students work through the semester to write a piece they feel "safe" sharing in public, and have their moment of glory or dismay when the entire class, under the direction of the mentor, responds in detail to their work. Overall, at the undergraduate level, this model is limiting rather than empowering. Mentors can only work with the few, not with the many, and are, by the nature of their goals—to find, train, and support the "best" new writers in the country—only partially attentive to the average or underprepared student. In addition, students in a mentor-model class rarely write informally or share consecutive drafts or, as Shelnutt reminds us, take risks or learn from publicly shared experiments.

Creative Writing before College

Just as problematic, at the precollege level, creative writing instruction takes place in a different, but equally unreceptive, environment. Studies of writing in secondary schools conducted in the last decade indicated that students may write ten minutes a day or less *overall* and direct their compositions exclusively to a teacher-as-examiner. In addition, students are allowed few opportunities to explore their worlds and expand their thinking through imaginative writing (see Emig 1983; Moxley 1989b). Professional poets and prose writers teach at the elementary and secondary levels under the auspices of national and state arts councils or with the support of groups like Teachers and Writers Collaborative in New York City, but their effect on student writers is regrettably fragmented. These professional writers work with too few students and for only a short time. Therefore, the best precollege creative writing experiences, of necessity, occur through the intercession of sensitive elementary and secondary teachers, like the Mr. Givens mentioned in John's poetry journal. These teachers allow students to explore literature by reading and writing, and by sharing their reading and writing.

In spite of the occasional Mr. Givens—and the growing influence of teachers trained in writing theory through national, writing-teacher training projects (see Daniels and Zemelman 1985)—there seems to be a significant gap between the goals and practices of the precollege teacher and the graduate creative writing professor. Too often, the elementary or secondary teacher is viewed by those at higher grade levels as being mired in record-keeping and practical, uncreative, day-to-day concerns. The secondary teacher, in turn, may become skeptical of the graduate-level English professor who seems irresponsibly lax in the classroom and who appears engaged in rarefied and irrelevant battles: Can creative writing really be taught? Or which is the appropriate terminal degree for a graduate program, the M.F.A. or Ph.D.?

Misunderstandings arise in both directions. Academic creative writers are always working to legitimize their "pseudo-literary" activities in increasingly theory-dominated English departments. Those individuals, in turn, scorn any art-as-therapy tendency in the public schools. For instance, John Ciardi (1974), at one point, seems to blame precollege teachers for all the ills of the college writing classroom:

> I worry about one thing in the public school classroom. I don't have an answer. There seems to be a need to praise the young, no matter what they've done—at least the public school system is dedicated to this. It starts when you have them put their grubby little fingers into finger paints in kindergarten, and then you tell them how wonderful their smear is. You don't point out to them that it's impossible to do bad fingerpaint and therefore it's impossible to do a good one. I don't know the balance in this, but there's also a need, it seems to me, if we are going toward the arts, to begin to develop criteria much sooner than they appear in the public school system. I think it's lack of criteria that sends freshmen into the college illiterate. (64)

These remarks represent Ciardi's thinking in 1974, and perhaps his feelings changed, or perhaps his remarks are best received by remembering the cultural upheaval of the late 1960s and early 1970s. But Ciardi's words highlight familiar prejudices that still can be found on the elementary to graduate school continuum.

The journal comments of my undergraduate creative writers reflect the tensions a novice writer experiences when she tries to move along this academic tightrope. Sometimes she is encouraged to "express" every thought freely and extensively, and sometimes she is castigated for not having better basic skills or critical insights. Equally, a student feels mounting confusion when her creative writing teacher at a later time distrusts or downgrades the professionalism of her previous teachers or writing instruction performed at other educational levels.

Writing Workshop Models

Not too long ago, the creative writing workshop was held up as a model for composition classrooms. In 1978, Randy Freisinger described a productive creative writing workshop in this manner:

> Creative writing classes usually establish a workshop atmosphere. They are places where students write and talk about their writing. The writing process is more important than the product, in that students' stories and poems are never really finished. How these pieces were written, what problems were met along the way, what themes and stylistic effects were attempted—these are the issues that dominate creative writing classes. The teacher is a writer/friend who is there to offer advice, but generally not to dictate. (85)

However, recent observers feel that today influences are moving in the opposite direction. Writing teachers have begun to question whether such a benign workshop model ever really took hold in most departments. In fact, some writers feel that undergraduate creative writing classes have remained pedagogically static or become more conservative, even as composition studies and rhetoric have experienced a theoretical and practical renaissance. Virginia Chestek (1986) claims that "at a time when lower-level composition courses are increasingly process-oriented and devoted to teaching students rhetorical mechanisms to generate, focus, and organize their ideas, creative writing courses tend to stress final products only. Class time is devoted first to a study of the final products of published writers, and then to the final products of class members. The processes by which creative writing students initially develop their ideas and assemble them into these final products are largely ignored" (16–17).

Don Bogan (1981) also feels that the creative writing workshop can become too static, and he advocates a version that places more emphasis on reading like a writer and gives attention to process by using imitation, guided assignments, and other exercises that illuminate writers' activities of generation, arrangement, and revision.

Reviewing undergraduate creative writing courses as she and colleagues teach them, Doris Betts (1984) suggests that teachers of such workshops usually follow one of two models. In the first, what she calls large-scale teaching, the teacher avoids line-by-line criticism and requires that students write a lot before looking at particular issues of craft. In the second, unnamed model, Betts sees instruction moving from parts to whole, that is, scene to story or line to poem. Teaching success, she feels, depends not on method but on teacher and student seriousness of undertaking, while Bogan feels that students in the effective workshop will be learning to become writers rather than simply learning to produce writing (see Brooke 1988, who holds a similar view for composition students).

Similar to Betts's models of parts-to-whole and whole-to-parts creative writing instruction, Patrick Bizarro (1983) reviews poetry teaching practices and finds three main approaches: models, activities, and models *and* activities. Not content with these rather simplistic definitions, Bizarro argues that, rather than follow a single teaching approach, teachers should teach creative writing in a manner that is consistent with the way they themselves compose. Bizarro's suggestions propose a creative writing teacher who is familiar with writing research and the field of composition studies and who is, also, a practicing, self-reflective writer.

Virginia Chestek also advocates a composition-studies-derived, process-writing approach that emphasizes four elements: (1) recognizing the use of emotion in writing and defining audience, that is, student investment in writing equals better writing; (2) teaching students to control such emotion by focusing on a question raised by personally relevant writing; (3) balancing personal and emotional investment with informal research; and (4) working extensively with analogy. Chestek's advocacy of using student emotion in writing echoes work mentioned earlier, that of Krupa and Tremmel, who suggest that students' "underground" writing offers a strong starting point for writing teachers and writing students.

Several of these teacher-writers suggest that composition studies, defined here simply as the study of writers writing, has much to offer the creative writing teacher. They suggest that creative writing teachers must broaden the focus of their workshops to include analysis and discussion of students *as writers*. This, in turn, requires that teachers should understand and share their own writing processes and products. Several feel more class time should be devoted to invention—helping students *begin* their writing projects—since the traditional creative writing workshop focuses on revision, and others suggest looking at ways to integrate oral performance or publication into the workshop.

In essence, these teacher-writers advocate transactional creative writing workshops. Workshops that put writers in motion. Workshops that allow students to understand and to develop texts within contexts and to discuss what Robert Scholes, Nancy Comley, and Gregory Ulmer (1988) call "intertextuality," the ways in which individual writers borrow, adapt, steal from, acknowledge, and are consciously or unconsciously influenced by other texts they have encountered. These teacher-writers understand that students do not come to undergraduate classrooms simply to be harvested into M.F.A. programs, to learn about their own emotions, or to become better readers of Literature with a capital L. Students come for all these reasons and for other reasons as well. Writing students have complicated writing histories and different energy levels and degrees of commitment. Because this is so, creative writing teachers will be looking for methods to optimize each student's potential while keeping in tune with complicated and changing English department perceptions about this portion of the curriculum. The chapters that follow describe how such difficult harmony might be achieved.

2 Writers and Researchers on Writing

> I want to underline the fact that a good essay or biography requires just as much creativity as a good poem; and that a good poem requires just as much truth as a good essay. . . . It's not good giving creative writing a monopoly on the benefits of intuition or giving nonfiction writing a monopoly on the benefits of conscious awareness.
>
> —Peter Elbow, *Writing with Power*, 1981

As creative writers, we know we have writing processes. We may guard them, worry about them, nurture them, or wrestle with them, but the novice writer knows little about the composing issues that practitioners take for granted. Our knowledge has been gained through years of hard work, and, as teachers of creative writing, we must commit ourselves to sharing our knowledge with our students. By looking at our own processes and by studying current writing research, we can build a foundational understanding of composing that will help us to choose and evaluate our own pedagogy.

Teachers need to realize that it is possible to hold unexamined or conflicting theories and to be resistant to theoretical and practical changes. Sharon Crowley describes the teacher who does not pursue pedagogical self-knowledge. He is "liable to confuse his students in fundamental ways. For example, if a practitioner accepts recent lore concerning 'process pedagogy,' but has not altogether rejected traditional composition theory, it will be difficult for him to discern whether his particular combination of the two pedagogies entails contradictions or confusions" (1989, 28).

Not only may a teacher implement conflicting pedagogical practices, she may overapply a model, which leads to classroom conditions that are just as restrictive as the ones she has abandoned. Anne Martin

---

Portions of this chapter have appeared in somewhat different form in Bishop, Wendy. 1990. "Learning about Invention by Calling on the Muse." *Arizona English Bulletin* 32 (2): 7–10. Used with permission.

(1989) explains: "It is not surprising that in many classrooms of teachers newly converted to 'the writing process,' the suggestions and recommendations gleaned hastily from workshops and books are followed to the letter with excessive zeal and punctiliousness, far beyond what was intended originally by the pioneers in the field. The result can be a reformed program just as rigid as the one discarded, though presented with currently approved language and trappings that give the appearance of enlightened change"(1).

Concerned writing teachers cannot afford to be hasty or to glean activities from every sourcebook and then insert activities into an ongoing, and possibly ineffective, classroom model. Teachers do not really experience atheoretical classrooms—having teaching practices, of necessity, implies that they have models of teaching—but they may avoid the serious thinking about an *entire* curriculum that will lead to a more informed writing workshop.

Useful sources for thinking about curricular change can be found in professional writers' stories, anecdotes, aphorisms, and other forms of self-report; in write-aloud protocols and model building and testing as it has been reported by cognitive researchers in composition; and in discourse systems, the authors of which compete to develop comprehensive taxonomies of written texts. By reviewing these sources, I hope to show creative writing teachers why it is worth examining their workshops, from the practical surfaces to the theoretical bedrock.

Writers' Self-Reports

Writers' stories and observations have long provided a highly engaging, yet fallible, source of information about the creative writing process. For instance, throughout his essays and books, Donald Murray shares hundreds of professional writers' observations about writing. These quotes offer moments of insight into the writers' composing processes as well as frustrating contradictions about what writers actually do. During interviews, writers will tell the story of their composition habits *as they wish this story to appear* and are liable for certain amounts of self-deception and mythmaking.

For instance, John Berryman claims, "Writing is just a man alone in the room with the English language, trying to make it come out right." Berryman's statement reproduces the "scene of writing," that I mentioned in chapter 1, by ignoring the physical and emotional support systems required to place and to keep that writer in a room of his own. And Berryman, I'll hope unintentionally, limits writers to men.

Berryman holds some prejudicial views, yet his words also ring true to many writers' experiences as he evokes a writer writing hard to perfect "his" craft (authors' quotes here and following are taken from Murray's works—especially Murray 1989, 1982a, and 1968—unless otherwise noted).

Elizabeth Bowen observes, "I am dead against art's being self-expression. I see an inherent failure in any story which fails to detach itself from the author." In her claims, Bowen seems much less invested in the scene of writing than, say, Berryman. And she also differs markedly from Ray Bradbury, who says, "Writing is continual surprise." Bradbury's observation conjures up some of the self-expression that Bowen's words denigrate. A more pragmatic view of writing-as-discovery comes from Ann Sexton: "Craft is a trick you make up to let you write the poem" (Packard 1987, 17).

In a similar manner, Joyce Cary offers a matter of fact, "Inspiration is another name for knowing your job and getting down to it." And we find him in some agreement with Sinclair Lewis's claim, "Writing is just work—there's no secret. If you dictate or use a pen or type or write with your toes—it is still just work." In these authors' views, the writer is *agent*, whereas in Friedrich Nietzche's claim, "The author must keep his mouth shut when his work starts to speak," the writer is *vehicle* for inspired expression.

Sometimes writers contradict themselves in the same interview. At other times, they offer intriguing yet often opaque messages, like Wallace Stevens's, "It is not every day that the world arranges itself into a poem" (Madden 1988, 10) or W. Somerset Maugham's, "There are three rules for writing the novel. Unfortunately, no one knows what they are" (Madden 1988, 2).

It is not a surprise that writers fall into the trap of offering rules, sometimes seriously, sometimes with a clichéd tongue in cheek. These rules can be expected to help in *certain* situations but certainly not in all; for instance, Winston Churchill's observation that "the short words are best and the old words are best of all" might cramp the writing style of Virginia Woolf or James Joyce, while the romantic view of F. Scott Fitzgerald, that "to have something to say is a question of sleepless nights and worry and endless ratiocination of a subject—of endless trying to dig out the essential truth, the essential justice," could lead to life-threatening habits for some of us.

In the reports of creative writers on their own writing processes, there is some unison, much contradiction, and a wealth of unsubstantiated yet intuitively accurate knowledge. A novice writer certainly gains from reading through collections of writers' wisdom. However, such words should also be read with the understanding that each writer is telling us, primarily, about his or her own writing process as he or she understands it *at that moment*. That process will change and those understandings will alter as the writer moves through a lifetime and a writing career.

The difficulty involved in trying to understand these complex interactions that result in written texts may be summed up in W. H. Auden's observation: "The relationship between life and art is so obvious that nothing need be said and so complicated that nothing can be said" (Packard 1987, 5). Still, it is worth looking into these writers' complicated and semi-obscured writing processes, for writers' knowledge can illuminate why some writers succeed at their art.

Useful collections of writers on writing include those by Berg, Bartlett, Bunge, Murray, Packard, and Plimpton (and Waldrup for compositionists talking about their writing processes). Writers' observations about composing can be used in class to augment and encourage sharing of students' own, self-observed, writing-habit anecdotes as they are solicited during in-class writing sessions, collected in journal entries, or shared during class discussions. Additionally, these writers' insights can be joined to composition research and theory to further clarify what it means to be a writer and have a writing process.

Research on Writing

In composition studies, cognitive research on writing processes begins with Rohman and Wlecke's 1964 model of writing, which includes three stages: prewriting, writing, and rewriting. However, this model is linear and derives from products—written texts—rather than from the observed process of writing, writers at work. By 1971, Janet Emig had conducted her influential study *The Composing Process of Twelfth Graders*. Emig expanded Rohman and Wlecke's categories of prewriting, writing, and rewriting. For instance, in the writing stage she observes that writers exhibit silences and hesitations. She further subdivides the rewriting stage into correcting, revising, and rewriting (which for her purposes means stopping and starting over). One of Emig's most important discoveries involves the recursive nature of the composing activity—writers plan in the prewriting *and* the writing stages, and so on.

Soon, researchers confirmed empirically what many professional writers knew intuitively, that the composing process is much more complex than had been commonly thought. Writers' self-reports concerning revision often illuminate such complexity. For instance, during an interview Anne Sexton claims that "I've revised as much as three hundred times on one lyric poem. . . . I showed it to Robert Lowell after I'd rewritten it fifty times. He said the ending wasn't right. . . . He said the dead don't speak. The more I thought about it, the more I agreed with him, and that's when I turned them into stone" (Packard 1987, 15). But, cognitive researchers moved beyond writers' self-reports to observe writers as they composed. This research proved that a great deal can be inferred about writers' cognitive activities, and more questions for study grew from these projects. Specifically, what are the differences between basic and expert or professional writers, what are the steps in the revision process, and what keeps certain writers from becoming more successful in their composing?

Mina Shaughnessy's 1977 study explores the problems of basic writers. Basic writers, writers with inadequate or unproductive composing processes, she finds, are usually working within a rule-governed system. Their mistakes are often the result of misapplying or overapplying rules in their writing. This is why rules like Churchill's, quoted above—that writers should use only short and old words—can be destructive. And when Theodor Seuss Geisel (Dr. Seuss) offers guidelines—"No dependent clauses, no dangling things, no flashbacks, and keeping the subject near the predicate. We throw in as many fresh words as we can get away with. . . . Virtually every page is a cliffhanger—you've got to force them to turn it"—he may be offering advice that has been profoundly effective in producing his own, well-loved children's books. The advice would be disastrous, though, if applied by novice writers to every type of writing occasion. The basic writer too often tries earnestly to apply the expert's "rules." In the creative writing classroom, the experts are the textbooks and the teacher, so teachers need to ask themselves to what extent the texts they employ and their own writing "rules" are culture-, genre-, and context-based.

After Shaughnessy, researchers began to study the differences between basic writers' composing strategies and the strategies of traditional college students or experienced professional writers. Researcher Sondra Perl (1979) finds that basic writers often stop and scan and correct their papers at the sentence or word level. This self-imposed interruption keeps the students from achieving any type of global development in a piece of writing.

Perl also finds that more efficient writers participate in projective structuring (worrying about audience—think of Anne Sexton's attention to Robert Lowell's remarks, quoted above) and retrospective structuring (checking the text so far in order to guide future development). Perl finds that successful writers listen to what she terms a "felt sense" that helps them negotiate the demands of their text in process. Felt sense appears in creative writers' discussions. They talk about listening for direction or being taken over by the text. For instance, Nietzche's author works to keep his mouth shut; Updike claims that "writing and rewriting are a constant search for what one is saying"; and Faulkner observes "it [writing the novel] begins with a character, usually, and once he stands up on his feet and begins to move, all I do is trot along behind him with a paper and pencil trying to keep up long enough to put down what he says and does."

Nancy Sommers (1980) and Lillian Bridwell (1980) each studied revision. Sommers finds that basic writers rely on two main types of revision—addition and deletion—neglecting substitution and reordering. However, experienced writers use all four types of revision techniques. Experienced writers also have a metacognitive awareness of—an ability to articulate—their revision process, while student writers, on the other hand, speak of "cleaning up" their writing and have underdeveloped revision strategies.

Professional writers make constant observations regarding the need for scrupulous revision. These observations range from Ernest Hemingway's claim that he rewrote the ending to *A Farewell to Arms* thirty-nine times because he was working on "getting the words right," to James Michener, who observes, "I can never recall anything of mine that's ever been printed in less than three drafts," to Sydney Smith's more facetious, "in composing, as a general rule, run your pen through every other word you have written; you have no idea what vigor it will give your style." Anne Sexton observes bluntly: "How do I write? Expand, expand, cut, cut, expand, expand, cut, cut. Do not trust spontaneous first drafts. You can always write more fully," and she adds, for good measure, the encouragement that: "The beautiful feeling after writing a poem is on the whole better even than after sex, and that's saying a lot" (Packard 1987, 17).

The work of researchers like Bridwell and Sommers was extended when Linda Flower and John R. Hayes (1981) developed a full-scale, cognitive model of the composing process. They divide composing into generating, translating, and reviewing. In their model, the composing process is also dependent on the text so far and the rhetorical situation (audience demands, and so on) and is limited by the capacity of the writer's long-term memory. In this case, memory is linked to metacognitive and metalinguistic ability—abilities to talk about thinking processes and language processes—which are developed through previous writing experiences. The taxing reality of metacognitive and metalinguistic demands is echoed in many writers' observations. Stanley Kunitz explains that "in the very act of writing a poem one is playing with language, playing with the capacities of the mind to hold together its most disparate elements. The object of the game is to fuse as many of one's contradictions and possibilities as one can" (Packard 1987, 23).

Finally, and most important to the Flower and Hayes model of composing, writers are influenced by self-developed goals. Flower and Hayes found that successful writers rely on a hierarchy of sub-, mid-, and higher-level goals which take them from sentence-level to global concerns, and back. Less successful writers seemed to lack mid-level goals and became stuck at the sentence level (picking and choosing a word when more pressing difficulties exist with content or organization) or on more global concerns (perhaps for creative writers, planning but never executing the great American novel).

Professional writers often discuss similar complexes of writing goals, from sentence-level clarity (Ben Burman: "My goal in everything I write is simplicity. . . . I revise, revise, revise, until every word is the one I want.") to more global concerns, including those of audience (Joseph Conrad: "My task . . . is, by the power of the written word, to make you hear, to make you feel—it is, before all, to make you see.") and meaning (Alberto Moravia: "One writes a novel in order to know why one writes it. It is the same with life—you live not for some end, but in order to know why you live.").

A few other studies are especially important to help teachers understand problems that arise in the undergraduate creative writing workshop. In these classes, students may actually be basic writers, or have underdeveloped writing processes, and/or be blocked in spite of their strongly stated desires to write. Mike Rose has studied blocked and unblocked writers. He finds that blocked writers are often applying inappropriate, algorithmic rules to their writing, a characteristic of basic writers. On the other hand, unblocked writers have flexible planning and composing strategies which allow them to write in a variety of situations for a variety of audiences. John Daly and Michael Miller (1985) developed a survey to assess writers' apprehension which, while it does not predict individual writing performance, does illuminate writers' avoidance and hesitations when faced with writing tasks.

The work of researcher Robert Boice (1985) suggests that behavioral techniques—writers learning to set their own system of deadlines/ demands and rewards—will best help writers overcome blocking behaviors. Some of the writers Boice studied underwent the interesting constraint of not allowing themselves to take a daily shower until writing tasks were completed, and so on. Anecdotes from professional writers support a contingency-management view; writers during interviews often explain that completing a set number of writing hours in the morning allows them to feel they have *earned* and may enjoy the rest of their day.

Linda Flower (1981) discusses writer-based prose. Writer-based prose, she claims, is generally narrative and associational in structure, internal, expressive, and intended by the writer to explore a situation. Nonetheless, many writers have trouble moving from the useful medium of writer-based prose to the more public medium which Flower terms reader-based prose. Reader-based prose is expository in nature and organized with the reader in mind. Flower's observations are echoed in John Ciardi's words: "The last act of . . . writing must be to become one's own reader. It is, I suppose, a schizophrenic process. To begin passionately and to end critically, to begin hot and to end cold and, more important, to try to be passion-hot and critic-cold at the same time."

Given such complexity in the act of composing written products, it is no wonder the demands of the writing workshop are so great. Cognitive research helps writing teachers understand the basic writer as someone who is rule-governed (generally inappropriately so), who has trouble imagining audiences other than herself, and who has inflexible revising and writing strategies and an underdeveloped sense of the composing process. Successful writers are much more closely aligned to the Flower and Hayes model—able to decide upon audience and to tailor the developing text to audience demands and rhetorical demands. The successful writer not only has flexible composing and revising strategies but also has a wealth of successful, previous writing experience to draw upon, enabling her to make and adjust writing goals to suit a particular writing situation. And it is this fluency, flexibility, and sense of a writer as someone who writes that can be highlighted in the creative writing workshop.

It is worth noting a few critics of cognitive research to understand that, for a teacher's purpose, it is important to weave together research *and* writers' experiences as I have started to do here, for neither cognitive research nor writers' memories appear to be totally reliable guides. For instance, theorists like C. H. Knoblauch and Lil Brannon (1984) claim that breaking down the writing process into stages (like prewriting, writing, and revision) greatly misrepresents the composing process and encourages teachers to take a smorgasbord approach to writing instruction—picking and choosing those stages or those models they wish to emphasize—and that such an approach will lead to misinformed instruction. They prefer to emphasize a holistic approach to the teaching of writing.

Expressive theorists have made valuable contributions to composition instruction. They suggest that we start where the student is, use student-centered classrooms, and help students develop as individuals as they develop as writers. Additionally, a new outlook for composing theory comes from the social theorists. Structural social theorists like Pat Bizzell (1984), Marilyn Cooper (1986), and Kenneth Bruffee (1984) insist that neither cognitive models nor expressive models are complete, for composing does not occur only for an individual (expressive) or in the head (cognitive) but also in complex social settings which affect the ways in which both basic and professional writers write. And ethnographic studies of writers (see Heath [1983]; Harste, Woodward, and Burke [1984]) let us see that composing is transactional, negotiated by writers within households, schools, and communities, and that social/biographical factors also affect the writing of any individual (for more on these theories and theorists see Faigley 1986 or Berlin 1987, 1984).

More recently, writing teachers are asking students to provide insight into their *actual* processes. Certain students only *appear* to learn writing process methods; for class purposes, they will use "ideal" models of composing, participating in invention exercises leading to several drafts of a paper. In their own school composing, however, many students revert to previous composing habits which include a great deal of procrastination and last- minute single-drafting (the first draft is the final draft). Students may normally have a low investment in writing projects leading to nonproductive writing behaviors, or they may disbelieve their teachers' models (see Brooke and Hendricks 1989; Nelson and Hayes 1988; Ronald and Volkmer 1989).

Providing students insight into composing, then, is only the *first step* in helping students develop as writers. They will need to participate in classroom activities that nurture metacognitive awareness (writing process journals, peer group discussions of writing, invention activities, in-class writing and discussion of that writing). This awareness should result in more fluent texts and longer ones, as creative writing students begin to write more freely and for longer periods.

Fluency and freedom are goals equally desired by well-known writers; as William Hazlitt notes, "the more a man writes, the more he can write." This will be true for women writers, too, and all students will appreciate having teachers who help them set reasonable writing goals and deadlines, who provide them with real audiences, such as supportive writing work groups to encourage the transition from writer-based to reader-based prose. As they invest in their own writing, students will want to write for their groups and their workshop because they have expectations of change, through experimentation and self-analysis, and experiences of writing success.

Combining Writers' Self-Reports and Research on Writing

Several composition researchers have an equal interest in creative writing. These individuals have begun to study creative writers' processes (as opposed to studying composition students and professional writers such as journalists or writers in business settings). Barbara Tomlinson (1986) reviewed the published interviews of over 2,000 creative writers and discovered the metaphors they used regularly to discuss the writing process in general and the revision process in particular. Tomlinson finds four major metaphorical stories used by creative writers to discuss their composing. Writers compare the writing process to cooking, mining, gardening, and hunting. Tomlinson observes that each "story" of writing predicts a writer's attitudes toward writing and highlights certain elements while excluding other elements of the process. For instance:

> WRITING IS COOKING presents a unified conception of the writing process by describing it as a process of mixing ideas, transforming them through ardor and inspiration, and waiting for the transformation to be complete.
>
> WRITING IS MINING makes writing process activities coherent by emphasizing the search for valuable, buried ideas; backbreaking labor is required to find, obtain, and refine the ideas.
>
> WRITING IS GARDENING creates a coherent structure for the intricate reality of composing by implying that ideas are organic and capable of independent growth and transformation; nurturance and time for growth to take place are required for the ideas.
>
> WRITING IS HUNTING OR FISHING provides structure to conceptions and representations of the writing process by stressing the elusiveness of ideas and the need for the writer to wait quietly to trap them. (1986, 74)

Tomlinson's work reminds us that every model leaves out parts of the process, and it is possible to see that some models are grounded in different "myths" of writing or prejudices than are others. For instance, the metaphors of *writing is cooking* and *writing is gardening* are craft oriented while *writing is fishing* and *writing is mining* are more inspiration driven. Here is writer James Dickey choosing and exploring the *writing is mining* metaphor. In this example he focuses on revision and emphasizes his belief that writing and revision are hard work:

> If I have one principle, rule of thumb, I guess you could say, as a writer, it's to work on something a long, long time. And try it all different ways. . . . [L]et me see if I can come up with a metaphor or analogy—on the principle of refining low-grade ore. I assume that the first fifty ways I try it are going to be wrong. I do it by a process of elimination. No matter how back-breaking the shoveling is and running it through the sluices and whatever you have to do to refine low-grade ore, you just have the dubious consolation that what you get out of it is just as much real gold as it would be if you were just going around picking up nuggets off the ground. It's just that it takes so damn much labor to get it. (Packard 1987, 119)

I find it significant that the authors of creative writing texts naturally use extended composing metaphors. In *Writing Poems,* David Kirby (1989) uses the comparison of writing as a walk to introduce students to poetry writing. Unfortunately, such metaphors are not as prevalent in the composition texts I have examined recently. Once a teacher starts to look for a writer's composing metaphors, he finds them, and often they vary from the ones analyzed by Tomlinson. Novelist Janet Burroway (1987), for example, compares writing to child-rearing, and the writing of her novel-in-progress as being—at the time of that particular interview—at the toddler stage.

A study of metaphors by Lakoff and Johnson (1980) asserts, in the book's very title, *Metaphors We Live By,* that metaphorical language and concept mapping may represent the primary way we have for understanding the world. In that case, further research by Tomlinson (1988)—which shows writers comparing the revision stage of writing to refining ore (as in the Dickey example, above), casting and recasting, sculpting, painting, sewing and tailoring, tying things off, fixing things, and cutting—can help to amplify our understanding of the writing process. By looking at these writers' metaphors, we add linguistic and analogic insights to cognitive research.

Teachers may use students' journals or direct class discussions in a way that elicits students' metaphors. Asking students to tell us what writing is *like* for them can give us insights into their composing strategies and writing blocks. I have heard students compare revising to housework, to diluting a brew, and to giving birth to the same child a second time (see chapter 3). Teachers and students will find it worthwhile to add their own observations to those collected from professional writers. Writing teachers I have surveyed compare their composing to driving down a foggy highway, bowling, throwing pots, spelunking with no light, running, or trying to build a boat while already in the water. And writing students have told me they find it reassuring to find that writing teachers have such interesting—humorous and humane—images for composing.

Additionally, we will want to ask questions about the writing population that Tomlinson's studies analyze—are enough women and other minority writers represented? For instance, in one feminist studies class that explored women's writing processes, students came up with very different images and metaphors than the ones Tomlinson extracted from published interviews with writers (as did my students mentioned above):

> One student imaged her writing process as putting together a jigsaw puzzle; another said it was similar to finding an old chair in a garbage pile and slowly and lovingly refinishing it; a third saw it as birthing a child. One woman wrote: "Each time I am assigned a paper I suck in my breath as if I had to move a hundred-pound stone from the entrance to my apartment in order to go on living." (Annas 1987, 10)

The point of sharing writing metaphors with novice writers will be to enlarge each student's understanding of her own process and to see where her experiences intersect with the experiences of other writers (not to slavishly try to change our metaphors—a predictably doomed task, anyway). Additionally, metaphors can offer insights into composing difficulties and problems, as they clearly do for the woman, quoted above, who sees writing papers as equal to the task of moving a hundred-pound stone. For this student, writing apprehension must be overcome in order for her to go on living, and writing (see Tobin 1989).

Students do not *always* choose different metaphors from those of professional writers, pointing to the cultural prevalence of many of the metaphors that Tomlinson's research uncovers. For instance, after reading her research, I happened to review John's poetry writing journal and came across a metaphor I had not, previously, noticed. John, like many professional writers, chooses "sculpting" as a way to describe revision. He says:

> I don't revise too much while I write. I may read the sentence I've just written and change a word or two, but I save the real revising until I've finished. I sort of look at writing like sculpture; my first aim is to get my ideas on paper (the rough form of a statue) then I change paragraphs, ideas or whatever (carving the

head, extremities, etc.) and then change inappropriate words or word order (carving the hair, fingernails, etc.).

Not only had John developed an operative metaphor for revision, but he also had explored it and worked out the conceit. Retrospectively, I need to acknowledge that John must have had a fairly sophisticated sense of himself as a writer even as he enrolled in my introduction to poetry writing course, calling himself a novice. Yet his early class journal entries made it clear that John did not know and trust himself *as a writer* in spite of his metaphorical understanding of his process. Workshop metacognitive and metalinguistic discussions take place to help students to make these connections—*to come to know what they know.*

It is worth mentioning another piece of research that takes place at the intersection of composition and creative writing studies. Cheryl Armstrong (1984) has studied poets' revision processes to find that they have habits similar to those of the writers mentioned in cognitive composition research, but she also found that poets revise for purely aesthetic reasons—because they are users and lovers of language and have strong linguistic interests in wordplay and analysis. W. H. Auden observed this impulse in his own writing when he said: "I have two things working—some kind of theme, and certain formal problems—metrical structure, diction. The language looks for the subject, and the subject finds the language" (Packard 1987, 3). Research like Armstrong's starts to map creative writing processes from the base material of cognitive research but also starts to explore what it is that, particularly, makes creative writing different from, say, essay writing (realizing, also, that in many ways all writing is similar, as pointed out in the Peter Elbow quote which opens this chapter).

Theories of Writing

Discourse theorists seek to understand the varieties of writing through an examination of texts and the ways texts interact. In composition, the theories of Kenneth Burke, James Moffett, James Britton, James Kinneavy, and Frank D'Angelo are the most well known, and a good review of each is found in David Foster's *A Primer for Writing Teachers* (1983; see also Coe 1988). In my opinion, the two systems that offer the most to creative writing teachers are those of James Moffett (1968) and James Britton (1975). Theories of discourse are worth considering because they help pose questions of the greatest interest to creative writing teachers: What types of writing should occur in a creative writing workshop? And what is the most effective sequence of writing activities for learning writing? While teachers can study these theories to explore such questions, it should always be remembered that discourse theorists base their understandings on text analysis. Text analysis can only provide product-based understandings. The process of writing is more dependably examined through cognitive and context-based studies of writers at work.

James Moffett has developed a scheme of discourse that distinguishes distances between the writer and listener or audience (the I-You scale) and the distances between the writer and the writer's subject (an I-It scale). He suggests that the relations between the writer and audience change with movement along this scale from (1) reflection which is intrapersonal (writer writing for the self); to (2) conversation which is interpersonal (speech with an intimate listener); to (3) correspondence which is also interpersonal (writing for an intimate audience); to (4) publication which is impersonal (writing for a general audience). He also scales types of writing along a continuum: from drama to narrative to exposition to (what he calls) logical audience.

Although not intended for classroom application—rather, Moffett attempts a description of writers and their relationships to texts—his ideas have been used to help organize classroom sequences. For instance, the composition teacher often asks students to write reflections and then move to informal correspondence and then to seemingly more public forms of writing like expository or argumentative essays. In "Moffett and Point of View: A Creative Writing Assignment Sequence," Stephen Wilhoit (1986) adapts Moffett's work to the fiction writing workshop. He suggests a sequence based not on imagined difficulty of writing activities but on the I-You scale, increasing the distance between the narrator, narrative, and audience. He does this by asking students to write interior monologues, followed by correspondence, dramatic monologues, diaries, detached autobiography, memoir or observed narration, and ending with four types of biography, each with a different point of view. Looking at Moffett's scales, it is easy to see how this teacher developed a classroom writing sequence by designing assignments that moved along those scales.

Personally, I find James Britton's taxonomy of discourse useful for both creative writing and composition courses. In the early 1970s, researchers for the London University's Writing Across the Curriculum Project studied the writing of British schoolchildren and validated a theory of discourse from their findings. Student writing was categorized as either transactional, expressive, or poetic (see Britton, Burgess, Martin, McLeod, and Rosen 1975). Most of the work done in both

British and American schools is of a transactional nature, short essay answers, lab reports, book reports, and term papers; writing is used *instrumentally* to get things done. Little attention is given to the other two types of writing, poetic and expressive. Poetic language is closer to what we think of as *creative* or *imaginative* writing, language artfully shaped. Poetic writing includes fiction, songs, and so on, and is rarely used outside of English classes.

The final category of language use included what the researchers call expressive writing. Britton and his colleagues found that expressive writing was used in schools far less often than transactional writing. A writer uses expressive language when keeping learning logs or writing drafts. Expressive writing is an *exploratory* and *learning medium* closest to speech, which develops in an author a strong sense of audience. The nearness and comprehensibility of audience is an important aspect of expressive writing. Nancy Martin (1975) and other researchers found that not only were students using mainly transactional writing in school, but they were most often writing to a distant audience, a teacher-as-examiner, which kept them from exploring and learning through writing.

Expressive writing for these researchers was seen as the base from which transactional and poetic writing naturally develop. They also found it to have a heuristic effect. It helps students explore concepts and focus learning. Many writing across-the-curriculum programs now call for the use of more expressive and poetic writing tasks.

Britton and his colleagues' discourse taxonomy helps me to understand the division of writing labor as it now exists in English departments, and why, somewhat backwardly, we divide writing instruction by types of written products. As well as discussing genres (poetry, short fiction, drama, the novel) with creative writing students, I find it useful to discuss the differences between expressive, transactional, and poetic (creative) writing. For instance, three major types of English classes require distinctly different proportions of each of these kinds of writing. To avoid confusion with the term *transactional creative writing workshop*—derived from an epistemological view of composing as a process involving writers, texts, and readers in an interactive relationship—I substitute the descriptive terms *instrumental, exploratory,* and *imaginative* for Britton's terms in figures 1 and 2. I present approximate percentages of writing types as I have seen them in classes at institutions where I have taught. My goal in this listing is to show how courses swing the emphasis of discourse types from instrumental to, say, imaginative writing. My goal in the undergraduate writing workshop is to achieve a better balance of discourse exploration.

Also, the lists of activities I provide are ideas for types of writing which teachers might require. The lists are not inclusive, and teachers would not want to try to include, for instance, all the possible types of writing I have listed under my ideal writing workshop description in figure 2.

It is important not to derive any genre rules from the Britton taxonomy. Sharon Crowley (1989) offers one of the most concise discussions of the "genre" problem: "While generic distinctions are useful to readers, since they may (or may not) announce a text's lineage (the texts claimed as progenitors), they apparently do not entirely constrain the writing process as it occurs. When professional writers write, they ordinarily do not begin with generic constraints in mind. Often they do not know what sort of piece will result from their work; sometimes they are unsure even whether it will become prose or poetry" (42; see pp. 41–45 of her book for a fuller discussion of genre). Examples of the genre problem abound in the creative writing workshop. For instance, John McPhee writes exploratory and transactional (and many would claim imaginative) nonfiction narratives. Norman Mailer's novel *The Executioner's Song* confounds most genre distinctions as do women's journals and diaries that are now being used as reading texts in composition and literature classrooms (see Hoffman and Culley 1985).

Contemporary writers are often interested in exploring intergenre forms like the prose poem or short short story and many, these days, move freely between poetry and prose. Ishmael Reed, during an interview, explains: "Well, there's a thin line between fiction and poetry. After all, they're both fictional. A lot of poetry I read appears to be short stories to me . . ." (Bartlett 1987, 169). In other words, these categories are nothing more than categories—useful for making observations and for deriving overviews but not any more valuable than the fluid texts they hold within their confines.

The lists in figures 1 and 2 address the issues of content—discourse types—but not sequencing in a creative writing class. It is my belief that by adding strong components of exploratory and instrumental writing to the undergraduate writing workshop, we better help novice writers understand what it is to become a writer. Additionally, by informing the creative writing classroom with the intuitive knowledge of professional writers, the cognitive research of compositionists, and the theoretical problems of discourse theorists, we introduce students more realistically to the world of writing: writers, texts, and readers.

To do this, I use, particularly, guided journal writing, in-class freewrites, and creative writing about the act of writing to help students explore these issues. For example, early in the semester, I regularly ask students to answer prompts about themselves as writers. Here is a writer telling in some detail about his writer's rituals (see Susan Wyche-Smith's 1987 article, suggesting basic writers should focus directly on such rituals):

> I find that only a quiet environment is conducive to writing. I generally do all of my writing on the 6th floor of the library, as I am now. Noise easily distracts me, so I usually write in the morning or at night when there aren't quite so many people trundling around. Being tired also distracts me, so I generally write when I am rested.

Many process composition textbooks start with questions writers can ask themselves about their writing process, and these can be adapted to the creative writing classroom. My own prompt list, borrowed over the years from various teachers' handouts, can be found in figure 3.

The writer's journal can also help students track the process of composing a single piece of writing or even every piece they write. It is useful for students to report formally on the generation, revision, and final presentation of one piece of creative writing in the final portfolio. Questions developed by Alberta Turner for *Fifty Contemporary Poets* (1977) are useful for this project. Turner sent questions about writing process to well-known poets, and I have turned her poetry prompts into the more general, multigenre prompts found in figure 4. By answering such prompts, the writer performs a self-interview. Having students read a section of Turner's book may encourage them to provide the most thorough answers and set them to thinking about writers' composing habits and rituals.

To enhance students' thinking about writing, I include guided class freewrites about writing early in the semester (to assess students' attitudes) and late in the semester (to help students summarize their learning). To my great interest, most students take these freewrites and turn them into final portfolio pieces that show a great investment of time, energy, and belief. For this writing-about-writing, guided freewrite, I list the following prompts on the board: "Writing is a . . ." and "Recipe for . . ." and "Why write?" and ask students to choose one prompt and write with me, nonstop, for ten minutes.

At the end of ten minutes, I ask them to read to themselves whatever they have just written and then see if they would like to share their writing by reading it aloud to the class. If no one volunteers, I read my own freewrite and then ask again for volunteers. After students have read, I ask them to choose a different prompt, and we write for another ten minutes and then share once again. At this point, the class may spend time discussing ideas raised by the in-class writing, or read aloud writing-about-writing which the teacher can glean from anthologies, or share first journal entries on writing processes to see how each class member views writing.

This chapter ends with samples of each of these types of writing-about-writing—in-class writings that students valued enough to revise, share in workshop, and then submit at the end of the semester (except for the last selection, these pieces appear in Bishop 1990d and are used with permission).

Writing Is a Bear
by June Cook

At its worst, writing is a grizzly: a scavenger who makes ordinary garbage his haute cuisine. The grizzly can attack without warning, nibbling the soft underbelly of your conscience, tearing your heart and devouring your blood. Contrariwise, when you search for him he often flees into camouflage, eluding you, frustrating you for days, months or years.

At its best, however, writing is a teddy bear: a never-failing friend in the process of Finding Yourself. This bear is a soundingboard who keeps all secrets and lives on dreams. He believes in breaking any and all rules and he never criticizes. He is special because he *believes*. It doesn't matter *what* he believes; it's enough for him just to believe.

Above all, writing is the Great Bear, Ursa Major. She is the inspiration of Mankind and a symbol of eternity. She is a nightly wanderer, a mother of the stars seeking her lost children—those that no longer are visible. As words are put to paper, the lost become found.

The Wolf
by Mike de Ruiter

I am a writer.
I am a wolf.
In the beginning, I am a pup, playful and carefree.
I wrestle with ideas, toy with stories and yet,
  I am cautious not to stray far.
As I mature, I must learn the skill of the hunt. The writing.
I see my quarry but being too inexperienced, I cannot
  capture it.
Instead, my prey, the novel, taunts me, staying
  just beyond my stride.
I must follow the alphas, the leaders in the hunt,
  the masters of fiction.
I must learn their styles, methods and tricks.

I must be cunning to capture the beast.
I must work at it night and day, wearing it down,
constantly nipping at its heels.
I must be strong, I must persevere.
Eventually, I will bring it down.
I will become the alphas, the leader in the hunt,
the master of fiction.
I will devour the novel.
I will have my own style, methods and tricks.
I will leave footprints in the snow for others to follow.
I am the writer.
I am the wolf.

Strawberry Shortstory
by Heather Jordan

1 qt. fresh strawberries, nurtured in a fertile
patch of inspiration
2 cups experience, well sifted
2 tbsp. spirit
3 tsp. imagination
1 tsp. humor
1/2 cup plot
2 eyes

Wash berries well, then pick them over. Weed out cliches, short cuts and hackneyed expressions. Add about 1 cup pressure and meditate at room temperature to the taste.

Heat workroom to comfort level—make sure brain is hot. Gather fuzzy socks, security blanket, cool drink and paper. With favorite pen in hand, stir experience, spirit, humor and imagination. Cut in plot, scraping bowl constantly to insure an even mixture. Blend in eyes, stiffly beaten for detail. Spread dough on 2 or more blank sheets, 8 1/2 x 11″. Sprinkle with organization. Bake 20 min. to 1 hr.

Place first draft on final paper after cooling with grammar. For a less crusty shortstory, spread first draft on second (and third, if necessary) blank paper. Add 1/2 cup more grammar and organization each to taste. Sprinkle well-polished berries over all and serve warm with plain or whipped readers. Savor reviews. Unlimited servings.

Excerpt from "Why Write?"
by Michael Welsh

[This is a single paragraph from the central section of a four-page essay.]

If the physicist is concerned with understanding the hardware of the universe, the artist is concerned with the software. Literature

> writers are word artists. We seek to understand and explain through fiction and poetry the dynamics of the human heart and mind. The interactions of human hearts and minds with other human hearts and minds does not occur in a vacuum: the artist is well advised to acquaint himself with the rudiments of the physical world. Fluency in quantum mechanics is not necessary but it doesn't hurt a writer to know why and wherefore rain forests exist or to keep in mind that a dolphin is, after all, an air breathing mammal not altogether unlike your mother-in-law, granted that a dolphin's disposition towards you may be more benign. My point in all this physical world business is merely to encourage a would be word artist to read as much *nonfiction* as possible. Unless one is unusually gifted with an ability to remember in great detail the physical attributes of people, places and things, some effort needs to be made to learn, by rote if necessary, the patterns discerned and explained by natural scientists. Incidentally but not coincidentally, there are some great metaphors lurking about the halls of physical science. Just ask Thomas Pynchon.

The creative writing teacher who has students writing such pieces will learn as much as her students. I was interested, looking at the "The Wolf" and "Strawberry Shortstory" meditations, to see how these writers evoked some of the same writer's metaphors that were noted by Tomlinson (Writing is Hunting and Writing is Cooking). Additionally, Mike Welsh's "Why Write?" essay reminded me that a Vietnam veteran who enrolls in an undergraduate creative writing class has a great wealth of knowledge to share with his classmates and teacher and will often be working through some extremely sophisticated issues. In his writing, Welsh carefully defines the roles of artists in general, word artists in particular, and literature writers as particular subcategories of word artists (not advertising copywriters, journalists, or mystery writers). Additionally, he offers suggestions that are remarkably similar to those offered by poet and teacher Kelley Cherry, who suggests that beginning writers should look outside the narrow confines of literary education. Cherry claims that: "The great danger in a young writer's concentrating exclusively on academic analysis of literature is that he's then likely to spend a very long time in his own work recycling metaphors, but if he's studying geology or biochemistry or mathematics or philosophy or history or French, he is always learning to use his mind and also building up a store of knowledge that can be plundered for metaphor, structural metaphor as well as stylistic metaphor . . ." (Bunge 1985, 26–27).

Cherry and Welsh come to similar conclusions from different backgrounds and premises—Welsh believes we should study other fields to raise political consciousness and to develop more writing accuracy while Cherry believes we become narrow, restricted see-ers if we do not branch out—yet both unite in wishing writers could experience more bountiful metaphorical experiences. From Welsh and Cherry, we learn that the views of the novice and professional writer can and do complement each other.

Introduction to Literature or (many) Writing with Literature (literature-based composition) Classes:

15% *Exploratory*
reader-response journals
position papers
drafts of interpretations

80% *Instrumental*
biographical essays
critical essays
book reviews, etc.

5% *Imaginative*
imitations
creative writing options

Rhetoric- or Language-based Composition Classes:

20% *Exploratory*
process journals
exploratory drafts
in-class freewrites, brainstorming, or invention activities

75% *Instrumental*
essay modes: descriptive, narrative, expository, argumentative
research papers

5% *Imaginative**
imitations
creative writing options
(*Some composition programs require that *no* creative writing be allowed in composition classes.)

Traditional Creative Writer's Workshop:

10% *Exploratory*
suggestion to keep a writer's notebook
reading notes

0% *Instrumental*

90% *Imaginative***
poetry
fiction
drama
formal imitations
(**Often the imaginative writing is limited by class to a single genre.)

Fig. 1. Writing in three types of English classes.

Suggested Introductory Creative Writer's Workshop

30–40% *Exploratory* (personal focus)

- writer's journal or notebook with required and free entries
- frequent in-class writing opportunities that may or may not be developed into portfolio drafts
- exploratory drafts

20–30% *Instrumental* (offers metacognitive [MC] and metalinguistic [ML] analysis opportunities)

- craft presentations
- introductions to writers (class members share reviews of professional writers' work)
- Why I Write essays (MC)
- How I Write essays (MC)
- Writing Is Like essays (MC & ML)
- summary of Personal Beliefs about poetry (poetics) or fiction or writing in general (MC & ML)
- writing process analysis—cover sheet or essay that accompanies a piece of work and discusses the process of making a piece of writing (MC & ML)
- imitations and analysis of imitative process (ML)

30–40% *Imaginative* (includes all categories of "creative" writing)

- poetry
- fiction
- drama
- inter-genre forms like prose poems, sketches, dialogues, etc., which often develop from invention exercises
- (Final writing portfolio develops out of genre and inter-genre explorations.)

Fig. 2. Writing in the transactional workshop.

Prompts

1. What kinds of experiences with writing in general and creative writing in particular did you have as a student before college?
2. What approaches and assignments did you like and dislike?
3. What teacher helped you most with your writing? In what ways? Tell stories.
4. What kinds of things do you write outside of school? Who reads them? Do you like to share?
5. Writing Process:
   (a) How do you get ideas or inspiration for writing? How do you get started? Get down to what your really do (take a walk, avoid, stare into space, make lists, what else?).
   (b) What conditions (time, place, etc.) for writing seem to be best for you?
   (c) How much do you revise *as* you write? *After* a first draft?
   (d) Do you write drafts in longhand, on typewriter, computer?
   (e) Do you need deadlines? Why or why not?
6. What do you think makes writing good? What does one need to be a good, successful writer? Can everyone be a good writer?
7. What is writing *like* for you (compare it to something else)?
8. Who are your favorite writers? What do you like about their writing?
9. What would you like to learn this semester about writing? What would you like to be able to do as a result of this course?

Fig. 3. Prompts for writing about one's own writing process.

Questions

1. How did the piece of writing start?
2. What changes did it go through from start to finish?
3. What principles of technique did you consciously use?
4. Whom do you visualize as your reader?
5. Can the piece of writing be paraphrased? How?
6. How does this piece of writing differ from an earlier piece of your writing in:
   (a) quality (b) theme (c) technique?

Please add any other remarks which you consider pertinent:

Fig. 4. Questions about the "history" of a piece of writing.

3 Options in Design

> So the product is expendable, but the process is precious. This is what I'd like to say. . . . the process is the process of living centrally and paying attention to your own life. Surely that's worth doing. If you don't, who will?
>
> —William Stafford, from *Finding the Words*, edited by Nancy Bunge, 1985

A group of future creative writing teachers helped me explore a difficult question: "What should writing teachers *cover* in a fourteen-week, mixed-genre, college-level creative writing workshop?" We compiled this list as a partial answer:

> Images, metaphors, history of storytelling, rhythm, plot, point of view, closure, tension, detail, structure, cliché, style, characterization, experimentation, effective openings (first sentence/line/paragraph), revision, symbolism, overview of poetic forms, detail, simile, character portrait, narration, impact, development of line, sound, persona, effective repetition, active/vivid versus stale language, place/scene/setting, plot, undirected activities (free time), telling versus showing (exposition/scene), dialogue, review of proofreading/editing marks, stanza/scenes (use of white space or transitions),value of oral reading, flashback, rhyme.

Not unexpectedly, as we built this wish-list, we were mirroring personal writing concerns. Particularly, these graduate students echoed the focus of their own M.F.A. graduate writing program, one that asked them to enroll not only in writing workshops but also in numerous craft classes. Several items on this impossible-to-accomplish list interested me, including history of storytelling, developing closure and tension, experimentation, learning/teaching effective openings, and undirected activities. It is also worth noting that no one listed "being a writer" as a potential topic, for these individuals already felt like, and in fact *were*, writers.

The graduate students were not at fault for neglecting the obvious. In fact, this list meshes well with topics covered by currently available craft textbooks. These books encourage students and teachers to review craft issues—like simile in poetry or point of view in fiction—and to read poems and stories by successful writers who have mastered each technique. However, novice writers need introductions as well as reviews. They need to experience techniques, not just to hear about techniques. Even more, beginning writers need to learn what it feels like to be a writer, someone who generates, drafts, revises, shares, and publishes writing, someone who experiences blocks, anxiety, elation, and success.

Clearly, an introductory creative writing workshop can cover only a limited amount of material. And a workshop could be organized according to one of the currently prevalent models discussed in chapter 1, parts to whole or whole to parts teaching. Writer Jim Heynan (1983) discusses the allure of each model to writing teachers:

> I see that I have espoused an approach to teaching poetry from the outside in. Starting with words and forms and working toward the students' felt experience. Very well. But I can imagine someone achieving similar ends with a totally reverse approach! Indeed, I can recall an argument among teachers of poetry which broke down into two camps: those who would start by encouraging self-expression and those who were more inclined toward emphasizing ways of writing, or technique. . . . Alas, the two camps do in some way represent that old distinction between the poet as maker and the poet as seer, as craftsman or visionary. But I do not believe that distinction has ever been very useful for the making of poems or even for the instruction and inspiration of young poets. (93)

If Heynan is right—that neither the craft (text-oriented) nor the visionary (author-oriented) method is foundational—it is worth considering other possibilities, particularly the transactional model introduced in chapter 1 and discussed taxonomically in chapter 2. Over time, I have learned from my students that they value such a classroom. Figure 5 summarizes their observations by category; students felt they developed audience awareness, an aural appreciation of writing, an ability to draft, an understanding of response and revision, and a sense of self as *writer*. Their remarks are drawn from end-of-semester class evaluations collected over several semesters.

These students also explored craft issues. They learned they had trouble with detail and point of view, for instance. And they shared methods for resolving their craft problems. But overwhelmingly, novice writers described how unusual it felt to be allowed to experience fully the processes that professional writers experience every hour of their writing lives.

I understand that writing teachers at each college or university will have different department requirements and classroom agendas. But those requirements will need to be realized within a carefully designed course which has clearly articulated goals. The teaching goals for the transactional creative writing workshop that my students were responding to included the following:

> Students develop a sense of *being* a writer, by experiencing a full writer's process, including but not limited to invention, drafting, revision, performance, editing, and production. They learn to analyze that process to discover their own strengths, weaknesses, and goals as a writer.
>
> Students contribute to the class through participation in peer response groups and by conferencing regularly with peers, teacher, and writing center tutors.
>
> Students develop the ability to critique their own work and the work of others and develop an understanding of audience concerns.
>
> Students study the basics of craft in their preferred genre(s) and become more sensitive readers of writing.

To create the transactional writing workshop, teachers must first believe in the potential of *all* writing students. This prerequisite is emphasized by William Stafford. During an interview, he explains: "The kind of process we are talking about is native to everyone, kids with their hopscotch and so on. Everyone. Everyone I've ever met, everyone, has what to me is the essential element of what we're talking about. They may not write what they call poems, but they make remarks they like better than other remarks. They have that lipsmacking realization of differences in discourse" (Bunge 1985, 115).

The transactional workshop aims for student understanding of what it means to have a "lipsmacking realization of differences in discourse," for each student's own benefit as a lifelong user of language and writer of meaningful texts. And this workshop includes expanded roles for both student and teacher:

> One important result of this change of emphasis should be the validation of the private voice in that the process of discovery becomes as important, if not more so, than the summarized product of discovery. Revisionist writing theorists also affirm the importance of the inner voice, its forms of discourse, and its language: prewriting, free writing, rough drafts and their revisions, learning logs, reading diaries, journals, and exploratory essays are as valued as the more traditional, linear modes of expression. The teacher, while she must eventually move into the role of evaluator,

> is more of a collaborator with the student in his struggle for "fluency," a term which includes generating ideas and information, selecting, focusing, getting started, composing, communicating, and correcting. When the teacher moves into the role of evaluator, her "ideal texts" are formed by both the experiences of the students and her authority as a more practiced and knowledgeable member of the learning community. (Caywood and Overing 1987, xiii)

Cynthia Caywood and Gillian Overing's extensive definition was drafted for a composition classroom, but it suffices very well for the transactional creative writing workshop. It is not necessary to avoid craft issues or models of excellent writing, but it is necessary to refocus those traditional concerns, inserting them into a curriculum that allows students to immerse themselves in the exciting, complicated, and ongoing flow of composing. Opportunities will exist in this workshop for allowing students a full spectrum of activities that focus on text, author, *and* reader concerns.

The overriding goal of a transactional writing workshop, then, is to release all students into language and in so doing to seek the dramatic results promised by several teacher-writers. Jim Heynan (1983) claims, "This may sound outrageous, but if you can help that mass of students see the relationship between words and power, you may be opening the doors to more personal and committed writing" (91). When we do this, sorting best writers for future graduate work in writing or developing, primarily, a mass readership for literature no longer are functional justifications for our pedagogy. Instead, teachers aim for student empowerment.

During an interview, Clarence Major explains why empowerment is desirable: "Most students in college today aren't going to have an opportunity to be in touch with who they are and where they come from in such an intense way ever again as they will in a workshop. They will go into different kinds of things: business, engineering, the sciences; but hopefully, they will remember how important it was to create a wedding of that voice that was theirs and that history that was theirs" (Bunge 1985, 67).

Members in the transactional workshop support each other's writing development and explore, illuminate, and come to understand the emotional value and the emotional harm of writer's myths, including the myth that only craft can be taught while talent and genius cannot be enhanced or nurtured. Kelley Cherry, for instance, takes exception to such views, asserting that talent and genius *can* be taught. Obviously, she defines these two terms very precisely:

> Talent has to do with learning what the creative process is, and that takes us back to the business of draft, critique, and revision. Once a student grasps that process, he can incorporate it. That's all talent is—learning to have the courage to do something. And you have to learn to have courage. Learning how to have the courage to do something; learning how to see your failures; learning how to tolerate those failures long enough to *do* them and then learning how to tolerate them for an even longer period of time so that you can correct them: this is a process that one can teach oneself, but there's no reason that X cannot teach it to Y.
>
> Beyond that, genius is a state one reaches when one comes to understand the nature of one's understanding. . . . Genius is comprehending not only that process, but also the relation one's own mind bears to that process. Once you learn this and then go on to study and learn the nature of your understanding, the way *your mind* works, you can analyze the way your mind works in relation to that process, and you begin to work with yourself rather than against yourself. (Bunge 1985, 23–24)

Cherry insists that teachers must allow students opportunities to take chances. She suggests that the ability to analyze one's own process (metacognition) provides the backdrop to genius. In the same vein, developments in composition research, like the work reviewed in chapter 2, lead a teacher like Joseph Moxley (1989b) to argue that creativity is "the natural consequence of learning, involvement, and commitment" (28).

The work of these individuals helps me make important assertions about the writing classroom: (1) all writing students have a natural interest in discourse; (2) all writing students benefit from the opportunity to explore their own histories in their own voices; and (3) all writing students benefit from learning more about the general processes of writing and their own processes in particular. Acting on these assertions may require a change in writing teachers' worldviews. Further, in the creative writing classroom, creativity will be considered a *natural consequence* of supportive teaching.

Clearly, an option-filled undergraduate creative writing workshop is required, one which encourages students to work for themselves rather than against themselves (and each other). Yet the day-to-day procedures of this workshop rest on definable modes of teaching and practical activities which may help students take Stafford's lipsmacking realization of the differences in discourse and elevate those understandings to artistic insight and practice. The rest of this chapter reviews traditional and innovative teaching modes.

Class Modes

Traditional class modes are teacher lecture and class discussion. Extended possibilities for the transactional creative writing workshop include:

- teacher lecture *and* student lecture;
- teacher-led discussion *and* student-led discussion;
- in-class writing and sharing of new drafts *and* out-of-class writing;
- full-group critique *and* small-group critique;
- one-to-one conferencing—student to teacher *and* peer to peer;
- performance (writers reading writing) by class members *and* visiting writers; and
- publication through class, department, *and* public media.

The value of mixing traditional and innovative modes can be understood by listening to the creative writing student who wrote a class evaluation for me, saying: "I don't think there was a most valuable aspect [of this creative writing workshop]. When it is all combined together is when I learned the most." Teachers will want to utilize several modes because they understand that each student has a different learning style. For instance, large-group critique is valuable for many students, but small-group critique offers other, shyer students an opportunity to learn by sharing under more comfortable conditions.

There is nothing inherently wrong with a student sometimes experiencing a less-favored class mode. As one student explains, "Some things [in the class] were boring; however, they helped to improve my writing a little." Teachers should expect to *alternate and vary* class modes in order to allow all students to experience some degree of comfort and success and to allow all students to experience useful challenges. Because of this, it is worth reviewing the strengths and weaknesses of each classroom mode (for research in this area, see Cazden 1988).

Teacher Lecture and Student Lecture

Since teacher lecture is a fast, efficient method for "covering" subject-specific information, it has been used extensively for most educational purposes. Basically, when the teacher is considered the most important member of the classroom, she literally tells the student what the student should know. For instance, wishing to review metrical patterns in poetry or symbols in Faulkner's novels or the social forces shaping the work of expatriate writers living in France in the 1920s and 1930s, the teacher reads up on her subject, reviews old notes, studies the critics, reviews articles, writes new notes, and presents this material in an orderly fashion to a classroom of students.

However, such a view of learning assumes that teachers are active and students are passive and that teachers "own" knowledge and transmit it to students who are "blank slates" or "empty vessels." Most unfortunate, working under such assumptions, teachers often learn more than their students learn. Ideally, teacher lecture should add a kinesthetic, aural, visual, and perhaps emotional depth to a topic, for, as we know, good lecturers are fascinating to watch (so are good actors and good television programs). However, lectures that enforce student passivity are less than desirable; they cannot help students acquire writing experience and develop a productive writing process.

Certainly teacher lecture, in moderate doses, can be functional. It can allow teachers to share their past experiences and knowledge. I feel, however, that such sharing should start off slowly to keep students from viewing the teacher as the only expert in class rather than as the truly fallible collaborator, the "senior" learner, that she really is. Lecturing about "writers I have known" works to place the teacher in the pantheon of great writers and is satisfying to the teacher's ego, but a steady diet of these lectures can be detrimental to the new writer's growth.

Teachers can consider augmenting their presentations with outlines or readings that allow students to follow the conversation more clearly, with overhead projection of difficult or key points, or with handouts that include professional *and* student writing. In addition, teachers might plan to stop or interrupt their lectures for a period of freewriting during which students summarize, question, or extend the points they have just heard.

Teacher lecture in a creative writing class may also be saidto encompass the reading of original writing. Many writing students recall with great fondness the class periods when their teachers spontaneously quoted a favorite poem or read a moving passage from a play or story. Equally, these teachers might consider reading their own work (in moderate doses) and student work that they have come to value. These readings may prove more effective for novice writers if teachers circulate samples of writing in an unfinished state or in several versions to illustrate drafting choices.

If teacher lecture allows the teacher to be active and learn, then allowing for student lecture in the creative writing classroom creates the same benefits for students. Lucy Calkins (1986) reminds us that "I need to teach because my ideas are kept alive by being shared. And I am not alone—we are the teaching species. What we sometimes forget is that our students are also part of the teaching species. They, too, need to keep ideas alive by teaching them to others" (272). For instance, there are always too many craft topics that teachers hope to cover in a quarter or semester, as seen in the list that begins this chapter. However, teachers can ask each student to research, write up, and present a craft talk. Students often learn eagerly from each other and just may remain more alert when listening to peers. Additionally, each student becomes intimately involved with one aspect of craft and so becomes an expert at it, like the professional writer or teacher of writers. To make an effective presentation he must read not only craft definitions but also writing in an anthology or collection. He will probably need to conference with a group. He will write up an effective handout or contribution to a class craft book and, through writing, solidify his thinking. He will, naturally, begin to look for and use this technique in his own writing.

By asking students to present craft talks to the whole class, teachers involve them in performance. Hopefully, students will also be "performing" their own, original writing, but some students find it less threatening to prepare and present a craft talk, and this presentation can make a useful bridge to performing original work later in the term. Apprehensive students may be encouraged to explore their feelings about speaking in public when they write in their journals. For these students, it is possible to provide an alternative to full-group presentations; they can move from small group to small group and present their craft talk in a congenial atmosphere. In addition, moving from group to group allows students to present material several times, learning it better.

Craft topics can be taken from the class textbook (if one is used); in this case, students are reading for each other and simplifying craft discussions and illustrating their presentations with samples of personally relevant writing. In other cases, topics can be chosen to focus on basic class issues, and students can be asked to review several craft books and writing encyclopedias. They can also be asked to interview practicing writers so that they develop a broader understanding of the topic which will be shared in class. By shifting some of the research and preparation time from teacher lecture to teacher-guided student lecture, writing classes become more interactive and more egalitarian.

Teacher-led Discussion and Student-led Discussion

Classroom discussion is a natural outgrowth of classroom lecture. In the discussion mode, a topic is introduced or a talk is given; then other participants are asked to interact, pooling, sharing, and extending knowledge. Ideally, everyone would speak and share, and insights would compound exponentially. Unfortunately, class discussion takes many forms and shapes, and all too often it becomes an event not very distinct from teacher lecture. The teacher maintains control of the topic and direction of all discussion, guiding a class to a preordained end result.

In the least productive version of teacher-led discussion, students are "told" they should participate but then are not allowed to do so. Sometimes the teacher cuts off unwanted conversational directions. Sometimes the teacher is too nervous to allow students time to think and respond. A teacher may ask only questions with a set "right" answer or may not allow adequate "wait time," jumping in to answer a question immediately after asking it. In productive teacher-led discussion, the teacher does not have all the answers and, in fact, may elicit questions from the students. As class begins, students can be asked to write down several questions they have about a craft reading or sample poem, play, or story. Those questions are shared with the teacher who uses them to orchestrate a response session where her interests *and* student interests are served.

Many teachers assume they are committed to a discussion classroom when, really, they dominate rather than guide the session. To understand if this is so, teachers will want to ask an outside observer to spend a week tracking their teaching modes, or they may want to video- or audiotape a few class sessions. Writing researchers often enter composition classrooms to do this, and they sometimes find there is a certain amount of teacher self-deception involved, teachers thinking they are engaged in more sharing of the conversational floor than they really are (see Cazden 1988). Equally, a teacher might spend a few hours noting his questions. Does he follow student interests or only his own agenda? Similarly, teachers may find it enlightening to try intentionally to extend their wait time, answering their own questions only after no student responds and moving from a two-second waiting period to an unnervingly long (but productive) ten-second waiting period.

Finally, research into gender and classroom discussion indicates that teachers may not offer female students as many response opportunities as they offer male students. In the classroom, females may ask more questions and provide more supportive remarks, but males often control the choice of topics, and their topics are more thoroughly pursued than the topics raised by females (see Lavine 1987; Frank and Treichler 1989). Teachers studying discussion patterns in their classrooms will also want to keep track of the support they give to female and male students, favorite and problem students, adept and underprepared students.

By allowing for regular student-led discussions, teachers can avoid some of the problems I have just described. When students are asked to lead reading discussions or the writing workshop on a week-by-week basis, they are also being asked to undertake some of the learning that a teacher usually experiences. A student leading a reading discussion is sure to read more thoroughly than usual. A student leading a workshop critique session is sure to spend more time than usual reading and responding to the class worksheet of poems, stories, or scripts. Certainly, the teacher may want to lead discussions early in the term, modeling positive discussion behaviors (which include open-ended questions, significant wait time, equal attention to all class discussants). Ideally, a sequence of teacher modeling followed by student-led discussion produces a workshop where preparation and responsibility are assigned to no one and shared by all.

In-Class Writing and Out-of-Class Writing

Over the last ten years the largest change in my own creative writing workshops has occurred in the amounts of time I provide for in-class writing and sharing of new drafts and for out-of-class writing. Currently, I try to allow for significant in-class writing and sharing time to emphasize writing processes and to illustrate the transactional relationship between writers and readers. When I was a creative writing student, at both the undergraduate and graduate levels, I was never asked to write in class nor did my teachers write in public or show me their drafts. In fact, they did not show me any work in manuscript form. I hope this impoverished learning history was an exception, for I now meet writers and teachers of writers who believe in and use in-class writing, but I am afraid a great many workshops still maintain an exclusive pattern of in-class discussion followed by out-of-class writing.

In-class writing can be developed through invention activities which are, in terms of lineage, integral parts of the rhetorical tradition. Many compositionists teach invention strategies to help writers get started, to help writers continue writing and avoid writing blocks, and to help explore writers' activities and rituals. One of my goals during in-class writing is to assure that not a single student leaves the room that day without a discovery or a surprise that will lead her into productive out-of-class writing (see Murray 1984). This does not mean that she writes exclusively from in-class writing notes; rather, she leaves believing that she can write and that she has a "fall-back" position (notes) or activity (method for generating ideas).

In the text- or author-centered creative writing workshop, students are asked to bring in copies of their work, which has been produced entirely on their own time. They are told to return with "a story" or "three poems" or "a dialogue between two characters who are opposites" or "exercise no. 2, page 116" completed. How they should achieve such products—generate, select, collect, focus, get started again, shape, and so on—is not actively addressed, in spite of the many techniques professional writers know *they* use for getting from nowhere to somewhere (techniques that are discussed in detail in chapters 5 and 6).

For example, Alberta Turner (1977), in asking poets for discussions of how they composed their poems, noted that:

> Aware of the ways that poems take them by surprise, the poets record every surprise that comes in the form of either their own words or another's and that might later become a poem. The commonest method is to keep a notebook of ideas, quotations, and given yet undeveloped fragments. They hope these scraps may fuse or generate or trigger the preconscious workings of felt ideas and present themselves in the form of poems later. Further conscious stimulation or at least facilitation of the preconscious given is provided by Stafford, who deliberately free-associated with no specific expectation; by McPherson, who initiated her poem by means of a class exercise in sensory perception; by Francis, who made a list; by Reiss, who played the first movement of Mahler's Ninth Symphony "over and over again, loud"; by Chester, who played Ravel's *Pavanne pour une infante defunte*, which was "a perfect complement to my melancholy"; and by Klappert, who, intrigued by the character of Dr. O'Connor in Djuna Barnes' *Nightwood*, retired to the MacDowell Colony and then to Yaddo to read relevant historical and psychological material, a process he calls reading reactively—that is, reading with "a pad at hand for anything that might trigger O'Connor's voice. (4)

These are the possibilities that can be explored with in-class writing, by using the very same prompts; students can be asked to write in response to music, in response to reading, in response to guided, association-generating sentences, and so on.

Without attention to such activities, novice creative writers become basic writers; they become blocked or avoid writing. Inattentive teachers, those interested in sorting good from bad, too often assume these students do not write because they cannot, not because they do not yet have the internalized behaviors and habits of practicing writers. Such a teacher, who gives out-of-class assignments with minimal support, will reenact this discouraging scenario:

> This was a young lady—you know, sometimes in the course of a semester, writers develop blocks of one kind or another or simply can't do anything—and we were both reading and writing which is what it's all about, and this lady never could write anything. . . . This young lady was one that I failed with completely, because she finally had written nothing. I said, "All right. If you can't do a story or a poem, we really ought to do something in a writing course. We've been reading some books, along with our writing—how about doing me just a little paper, your impressions of one of them?" She said, "Okay, I'll write a paper on *In Cold Blood*," which was new and which we'd been reading, and I said that sounded fine, and then she came back and couldn't write the paper. So finally we reached a compromise. I said, "Well, do whatever you do best," and waited to see if it would be singing, dancing. . . . What happened was, I got it wrapped up in tissue paper and a little note, this necktie with a label on it, since lost, which said, "This is a Nancy Clutter original." It was worth it. She got an A in the course. (Garrett 1974, 15)

I feel that this student could have written. She could have written about how she could not write and why she wanted to write and what writing meant to her. She could have participated, composing in-class writings about objects or about her family. She could have read muse poems and written a request to her absent muse. Finally, she could have written about doing what she does well—making a handmade tie. And her teacher and peers could have written along with her, discussing what was or was not happening along the way.

I do not deny a writer's need to experience self-initiated, out-of-class writing. I do not assume, either, that all students enjoy in-class writing or perform such writing well. Still, many find it valuable as reflected in the responses of these undergraduate writers: "I especially liked it when we did the in-class writings. They were really interesting" and "I would like more in-class writing activities. I liked those. I really enjoyed the one where we started the story and then passed it on to the next person to add onto." Some students find they participate during in-class writings but continue to prefer the writing they generated from their own sources: "I didn't use any of our in-class writing to generate poems; it just didn't work out." Students' responses to in-class writing will be influenced by the degree to which they feel "safe" in their workshop community. Teachers who write these exercises with their students and who share their own, obviously flawed and informal, work will help produce a congenial atmosphere for experimentation and response.

Beginning students—and sometimes advanced students—need to learn their own best methods for generating ideas and forms and also need to resist the sometimes too dominant "scene of writing" that makes them assume *good* writing only occurs if composing is done in private. Writing teachers who have been raised under the influence of the scene of writing and who never participated in workshops where in-class writing was valued will have to overcome their own hesitations to experiment, share, and appear vulnerable with and among their students. Sandra Alcosser considers her own preferences:

> At the same time as a writer, I know there are some problems with collaborative learning. I know that I will refrain, in group, from certain discourse, unless I am given permission for that discourse. I know that I've withheld or shifted language patterns and thoughts in the presence of others, and I know that as an artist, alone, with no resistance, no fear of grimace or negative feedback, I will order these thoughts, examine them and in this way, put them forward. I know that everything I am offered in a group context, I must take home, digest, become intimate with. (Haake, Alcosser, and Bishop 1989, 4)

Obviously, teachers will need to find their own balance. I often request an equal number of in-class and out-of-class writings in a student's final writing portfolio. Some of either of these types of writing may usefully come from textbook assignments which can help to connect process to craft.

Sometimes, in-class writings help develop a sense of class community early in the term by providing student writing examples for noncompetitive comparison. For instance, in Janet Burroway's text, *Writing Fiction* (1987), there is an exercise that asks for an original description of blue eyes. In one of my classes, we each wrote a description, much like this one by Regina: "His eyes are the ocean. Deep and blue they fill my lungs. I start to go under, but not without a fight. I grasp for solid land, but find none. My body relaxes, and the struggle is over. His blue eyes drown me." We each wrote our version of the exercise on the chalkboard and examined them for variations. Our discussion, along the way, touched on cliché, detail, vividness, outrageousness, and extended conceit. Most important, we quickly connected to each other, to the text, and to our invention abilities. We were primed to write.

For those who prefer to generate their work outside of class and alone, lists of invention techniques or textbook assignments can still provide a much needed and much valued composing safety net. Chapters 4, 5, and 6 discuss generation, invention, and imitation in detail.

Full-Group Critique and Small-Group Critique

The traditional format for creative writing workshops is the full-group response or critique session, led by the teacher who is an experienced writer. Students submit copies of their original work to other class members before the workshop and then share oral and/or written comments during class as the teacher orchestrates and directs responses. On the positive side, the workshop allows writers "to have [their] work read by all the members of the workshop, and publicly criticized and praised by your instructors in the weekly meetings; [it] represents a helpful and at the same time less hazardous form of publication" (Engle 1961, xxxvi).

For graduate writing students, workshops have also proven tobe extremely stressful. Here is a journalist's view of a competitive, graduate writing workshop: "In most programs, weekly seminars tear through students' works line by line, giving criticism that may or may not be constructive. 'You're generally naked here,' said Professor Barth, 'and if you've botched it, it's there for all to see. It was fiercely competitive,' said Miss Robison of her year at Johns Hopkins, 'though now those students are like family. But it took pounds off me'" (Churchman 1984, 43).

Understandably, undergraduates will find it difficult to participate in public sharing of their work, especially if it is done in the competitive atmosphere often found in the graduate workshop. Instead, undergraduates need to be carefully trained to share and respond to writing, and it is possible that a movement from dyadic critique (peer sharing with a single peer) to small-group critique (sharing early drafts in groups of three to six students) to full-class critique may help students who are new to the workshop format acquire stronger response skills (see Elbow and Belanoff 1986).

Teachers can also teach response skills by modeling them in a variety of ways. Any remarks a teacher writes on student work begin to transmit useful vocabulary. Additionally, she can hold a mock critique session during which she illustrates group rules (who reads and when, who responds and when) and then the class can critique samples of student writing from previous semesters. A mock critique can take place with the teacher displaying short works on an overhead projector and writing down class-negotiated responses. Teachers can set up "fishbowl" modeling exercises. In the fishbowl exercise, a group of three or four students acts out the roles of a peer group. They nominate a "writer" and share copies of a sample student paper. The "writer" reads the paper and the group members respond to his writing. The rest of the class members observe these "fish in the fishbowl" and take notes. At the end of the fishbowl activity, the class discusses what happened in the model group's interactions and what could have been done to make the critique even more effective. Then, the entire class "practices" by performing a simulated critique. Finally, the class moves on to a critique session using class members' own writing.

Currently, in the composition studies literature, there are a variety of useful sources for setting up critique groups (see, especially, Beaven 1977; Bishop 1988a, 1987a; Bruffee 1984; Elbow 1981, 1977; Gere 1987; Hawkins 1976; Johnson and Johnson 1984, 1975; Weiner 1986). The role of groups in responding to and evaluating writing is covered more extensively in chapters 6 and 7.

Traditional writing workshops, it must be remembered, rely almost exclusively on the large-group format. However, small groups help to train writers to critique more ably and help them to develop these skills in a nonthreatening format. Small groups allow each student—even the shyest—to learn by publicly sharing ideas and impressions. At the same time, students realize they learn a lot by listening to a multitude of views about a piece of writing. Sharing work in a large-group format allows them to gather and evaluate divergent opinions. The large group gives novice writers a sense of the larger discourse community of professional writers.

Responses from my undergraduate students indicate that a *mixture* of large- and small-group critique can be valuable for novice writers. Here is John talking at mid-semester about group critique:

> My participation in group work is, I admit, a problem. I do well in small-group critiques. I contribute comments, and I think I do fairly well in critiquing others and receive criticism well. . . . I don't say a whole lot in large-group critiques, though, and I'm not sure why. It's really no excuse, but I don't do very well in large groups (as far as participation goes), even in an open,

> nonjudgemental atmosphere as in our class. . . . I do well in critiquing others' work (in small-group sessions, at least.) I think I've done well in keeping comments nonpersonal (not confusing the author with the person in a poem) and keep my comments as helpful as possible.

And here is John reflecting on group work, again, at the end of the semester:

> Now, for my albatross. I know that my class participation leaves a lot to be desired. It's really no excuse . . . but I really never feel comfortable talking in a large group. Blame it on shyness, some weird hang-up of mine or whatever, but I really do not do well in large groups, in ANY of my classes. I do think I do well in small-group workshops, though, or working with one other person. . . . I think the most valuable aspect of class, for me, at least, is (paradoxically) the full-class critiques. Even though I keep fairly quiet in them, all of the different views and opinions that I get about my poetry helps me a lot. The suggestions about things that could be better are just as helpful as the ones that affirm what I have written. I always hope to get a few comments that agree with, or understand, what I'm saying, but if I got only agreeing opinions, that wouldn't help all that much. And I always get different opinions. Full-class critique has helped me a lot.

Without exception, undergraduate writers feel critiquing the work of peers is difficult but, ultimately, rewarding, with the full-group activity being the hardest to manage. "It felt like when everyone was waiting for someone else to start the critique, I was always the one to open her big mouth. I could only think of how awful I'd feel if it was my story and no one had anything to say," said one writer to explain why she made herself break the ice and start to respond. Another observed, "I like the whole-class workshops because getting other readers' opinions helps me to understand the poems I read in the critique sessions. It also helps to hear how poets read their own poems instead of just reading them myself. Sometimes critiquing can be hard, though, because I know that I would do the same thing [make the same mistakes]."

Students realize they need to develop and *are* developing as critics: "I have improved on my critiquing methods in this class since the beginning of the semester. I find it easier to critique in small groups than big groups. You can talk more freely and really get into the story with the writer." And, for a few, the small groups remain the preferred method: "The most help I got all semester was probably the day that we broke into smaller groups and talked about the piece on the experience as a kid. It was a lot more open in such a small group."

My students' responses made clear to me the continuing value of the traditional writers' workshop format where twelve to twenty writers sit in a circle and respond to the writing of a given individual. This model strongly influenced composition classes in the late 1960s and early 1970s, encouraging teachers to allow for student response to essays. At the same time, more recent pedagogical developments in composition studies—a strong commitment to more personalized instruction, small-group response, and conferencing—have started to influence creative writing classes. More drafts in progress are brought to these classrooms, and alternatives to response are more fully explored, with a gain that students themselves can point out. Here is Paul summarizing his feelings about group work:

> I still don't speak out in group critique—the whole class, that is. The small groups are fun. I attend every time. I like to show my poetry around, I offer what I know, which isn't always on the same level or proportion as the other people—and rightfully so. I think that's great that in workshop [full group] for example you get sixteen pages back of comments on your poem. Where else but class would you get that amount of feedback, and unbiased, by other poets? It's very enlightening.

Paul's end-of-semester comments show how a mixture of small and large groups achieves several goals of the transactional creative writing workshop. Small groups help students to enjoy sharing and responding and to support their fluency, while large-group critique helps introduce them to academic conventions and the variability of judgment and response.

One-to-One Conferencing

One-to-one conferencing has long been a part of the traditional writing workshop. Some students feel they learn as much outside of class, in private consultation with the professional writer, as they do inside of class, when they share with their peers. For graduate students, this seems to be particularly true since graduate students are hoping to learn everything possible about the life cycle of a professional writer. For graduate student writers, the mentoring teacher can help in the ways that mentors always have helped—by introducing young writers to editors and famous authors, by guiding their reading, by explaining the hidden conventions of the field, and so on. At the undergraduate level, however, there is a larger distance between the professional life of the writer-teacher and the life of the student writer.

It may be that the conferencing model at the undergraduate level should be broadened and include less reliance on the teacher as primary conferee. Just as they do for composition students, well-trained creative writing tutors may act as *translators* between the students' and the teacher's worlds, for they participate in both (see Hawkins 1980).

While responding in his journal to a writing center visit, John explains the value of such tutor support:

> My first poem for class was "The Whales." The way I ended up is sort of weird. To shorten the story, I was absolutely nowhere as to getting the poem done, so I took it to the W.C. [writing center] where Ken & John helped me. The problem was that I knew what I wanted to write about, but simply didn't know how; it was my first one, and I guess I had "poem fright." What we ended up doing was to make a list of fifteen words pertaining to the ocean (my topic), each of us contributing five; this was the "Safety List." We started to write our own poems, and whenever we got stuck, we'd pick a word from the list, which usually helped.

In this instance, the writing center tutors provided an audience and aid that the teacher could not have provided.

Peer and writing center conferences provide students with valuable alternative learning situations and support a teacher's classroom without overloading his already busy schedule. Additionally, while small groups are working together in the classroom, it is possible for the teacher to conduct several short conferences. This variation is especially useful for the part-time teacher who may commute to a campus and who may not have adequate office space or energy for extensive out-of-class conferencing.

The single most useful book on the one-to-one conference is Muriel Harris's *Teaching One-to-One* (1986). Harris examines the benefits of this type of instruction: it encourages student exploration; it allows for a direct discussion of a writer's composing process; it stimulates independent learning; it helps the writer focus on specific strategies; it provides instant feedback. The one-to-one conference also provides a time to focus on editing concerns, many of which cannot be covered during the more freewheeling full-class workshops.

Performance by Class Members and Visiting Writers

In the writing workshop, it is easy to begrudge the time for oral presentation of student work or to forget the performance tradition upon which writing is based, storytelling and poetry in particular.

Teachers of writing and literature are comfortable reading examples of moving prose and poetry to their classes (what I classified above as a form of teacher-led lecture). It is equally important to allow students opportunities to hear *their* original work read aloud.

These readings can help writers revise and edit their work. If they do not enjoy reading their own work over or *cannot* read their own work, due to technical impediments, they will quickly realize that an audience will not be able to negotiate the material they are presenting either. The student's peer group offers a good place to begin when emphasizing the benefits of oral performance. Hearing and then responding to work in progress that the writer has just read aloud, the group focuses on meaning first and shares and enjoys a good story, a revealing dialog, or a rhythmic poem. Also, students who gain practice by reading in small groups will experience less stage fright and tension when they do present their writing in larger groups. Small-group sharing offers a safe practice step before students move to full-class reading.

Sharing can also occur in the form of reading class freewrites aloud. To facilitate this sharing, the teacher writes with her class and volunteers to share her own, imperfect thoughts and musings. Eventually, almost every student writer in class will want to share writings. I should note, though, that it is not that easy for teachers to share their spontaneous writing. Here are the thoughts of a graduate student who was trying invention activities for the first time and reading his efforts aloud to teacher and peers: "It was interesting to share work that was really spontaneous, when prior to this course the material I would turn in to a workshop was stuff I thought was polished. I felt much more exposed in this class." This writer's experience shows why it can be worthwhile for teachers to try any and all classroom modes to better understand what they are like for students (see Schwartz 1989).

I often ask campus writers to come and read to my classes. This proves to be a memorable experience for students, especially since many undergraduate students do not make time to go to campus readings given by famous authors. Here is a student reflecting on an in-class reading:

> I really enjoyed having them [visiting M.F.A. TAs] read their poems, and realized that it's one thing to read others' poetry, but a completely different matter to have them *read* it. . . . I learned a lot just from hearing the poems being read, as well as the insights that each of them gave before or after their poems. I definitely suggest that this "poetry reading" be used in future classes—maybe even more than once per semester, if possible.

Novice writers should experience performance. They should also be initiated into the world of publication.

Publication through Class, Department, or Public Media

Class publication of student work can be one of the easiest and most satisfying ways of letting students undertake the full range of writers' activities from process to product. Two-thirds of the way through the term, I ask students to select their three favorite pieces from their own class writing and to bring four copies of each selection to our next class meeting. In peer groups, students read another group's submitted pieces, and then each group acts to "edit" another group's writing by voting on a favorite from the three selections provided by each of that group's members. These writings will be included in our end-of-semester anthology. Additionally, the "editing" group chooses a "critics' choice" piece: their favorite out of the twelve (three pieces each by the other four group members) that were submitted. The anthology, then, is composed of a selected sample of each student's writing and, from the remaining work, one "best" piece of writing, balancing sharing and competition. Finally, each editing group suggests changes a writer might want to consider before publication.

Here is one class member talking about the class book publication process:

> Today in class we got in our mini editorial groups and chose the poems our classmates will be represented by in the class anthology.
>
> I found it was not easy. For instance, my favorite all-around (critics' choice) was not the same as Karina and Lance's favorite, but by the system of democratic majority, I was over-ridden. (It's true, I didn't argue much—maybe I should have. . . . It would have meant the difference of having two of Donna's poems in the anthology instead of two of John's). Our group spent a lot of time critiquing the four poems we chose—although they were our favorites, we felt they could be even stronger.
>
> When we were informed which of our poems had been chosen by the other group, both Karina and I were disappointed with their decision. But that's life, eh? Your particular favorite poem may not be everyone else's favorite poem. All in all, today was "enlightening." We all gained insight.

As we compile a class anthology, we turn from issues of revision and development to editorial concerns, checking punctuation and spelling, considering a new title or an alternative format, and so on. Additionally, I use this week to introduce students to literary magazines. I show them the campus magazine and other local or regional publications. I also ask students to write contributors' notes for our anthology, and they come up with statements that are both concise and revealing (of themselves and their attitudes toward writing):

> Rob Roys: I try to paint a picture for the reader. The pictures are events in my life that had meaning for me, and, hopefully, the readers will take new meaning from the pictures I paint for them.
>
> Tamara L. Holm: Form Forever/Archaic Voice/Cliches & Rhymes/ The Poet's Choice.
>
> Nick Goult once won a turkey in a Christmas raffle and has recently introduced a third finger to speed up his typing process.
>
> Tamara Mills: A dreamer, and to her, her poems are written dreams she's had during both the night and day.
>
> Jim Foley has never lived in a town without another man named Jim Foley. His favorite hobbies include sensing, worrying, and existing.

To produce an anthology, students bring enough copies of their contribution for everyone in class, and books are assembled on the spot. I provide a title page, table of contents, and contributors' notes. If funds are available, anthologies can be bound. If local, professional writers are available, one can often be recruited to write an introduction. The book-making sequence lets students experience the intricate issues of selection, arrangement, and presentation that concern regularly publishing writers. Additionally, the anthology can be shared with department members, students' families, and future classes. To connect with the class goal of exploring oral presentation and celebration, my class final usually consists of students reading their contributions to the anthology. Often, I contribute to the anthology and participate in the submission and revision process with one of the class groups.

Book publication, then, can be built into the creative writing class structure. Many other forms of publication can also be explored—developing campus posters; producing a special issue of the campus newspaper; supporting student entries to English department-sponsored contests or department publications; and encouraging submissions to local journals, newspapers, and literary magazines. With an advanced undergraduate class, I often have a publication session where I bring sample copies of literary magazines and all my reference books, like the *International Directory of Small Presses and Magazines* or *Writers Market,* and *my* submission files—including my own acceptance and rejection notes. In essence, I use my own experiences to describe the business of publishing original work in America. While an occasional teacher requires a "real" submission as part of the class credit system,

I find coercion unnecessary since students spontaneously submit work to publications they read and may even have writing accepted during the same term. When that happens, with the writer's permission I copy the writing and the acceptance letter and we share it in class, celebrating the final product at the end of our long learning process.

The creative writing workshop, then, should offer students a rich set of classroom modes. The next several chapters discuss specific classroom activities that can be used within those modes. These will help students learn the ways of professional writers and challenge them to produce their best original writing. To rephrase Clarence Major slightly, writing students will be creating "a wedding of the voice that is theirs and the history that is theirs" as they look at, listen to, play with, and enter into discourse that matters.

Workshops Fostered:

Audience Awareness

"The different interpretations show me how a poem 'looks to someone else.' "

"I think I've changed it [sketch] enough so the reader isn't mystified."

An Aural Appreciation of Writing

"The reading of poetry out loud in the class and hearing people's interpretations has been helping."

"[I] realized that it's one thing to read others' poetry, but a completely different matter to have them *read* it."

An Ability to Draft

"My writing outside of class is flourishing. I have little scraps of paper all around with ideas and thoughts."

"One of my biggest problems was just trying to write. something. . . . All my writing I had done had always had a guideline to it. . . . Now I can write about just about anything that comes to mind."

An Understanding of Response and Revision

"Showing someone else what's good or bad and how I would improve anything helps me see what's wrong with my writing."

"I only wish that we could have had the time to review the same stories through more versions. . . . After the class critique, I was able to do a more thorough revision. Now I wish it could be reviewed again."

A Sense of Self as "Writer"

"I feel that every time I write I am able to see the problems more clearly."

"I'm very surprised that my stories were good enough to be of interest to the other students of the class."

"I'm learning mostly all I need to know, or rather, as much as I can 'afford' to absorb with my time schedule. I'm developing more as a writer of poetry."

"Before [intro to creative writing—poetry], I can also honestly say that I had never truly been creative."

Fig. 5. Students' observations about transactional creative writing workshops.

4 Generating Writing

> Most of us don't like to write at all; we like to have written.
>
> —Janet Burroway, *Writing Fiction*, 2nd ed., 1987

> The teacher's job is to keep them writing, keep them enthusiastic about what they're doing, and keep them believing in what they're doing. When someone has no proof that he *can* write, it's easy for him to feel that this is not the way to spend his life.
>
> —Wallace Stegner, *On the Teaching of Creative Writing*, 1988

Student writers expect to receive some help learning how to discover alternative ways of seeing. At a writer's conference I attended, Marvin Bell claimed that the primary task of the writer is to get in motion. And my writing students make it very clear that they enroll in a workshop for that reason, for the structure and prompting and prodding, for the demands and deadlines and activities that will help them generate new work. Clearly, then, generation is the first requirement of a writing process. Everything that happens to a writer until pen touches paper or finger taps keyboard could be considered prewriting. The marking of letters on paper can more accurately be labeled transcription. After transcription, the balance of writing activity *may* shift to drafting and evaluation and editing, although most writers continue to generate new material at all points in their writing until it is published, put aside, or abandoned.

Before helping students with methods for generating material—invention techniques and guided imitation—it may be worth giving them insights into writing processes based on the research and the professional writers' self-reports reviewed in chapter 2. This can happen, as I mentioned, when teachers ask students to write journal entries on their own writing processes. By pooling those responses in

Portions of this chapter appeared in somewhat different form in Wendy Bishop. 1990d. "Learning about Invention by Calling on the Muse." *Arizona English Bulletin* 32 (2): 7–10. Used with permission.

groups, students can also discover class commonalities about process (for example, we like to write in the morning, to loud music, after taking a walk, etc.). It may be worthwhile, at that point, to share models of the writing process, from the elaborate schematic model still being explored by researchers Flower and Hayes and first presented in "A Cognitive Process Theory of Writing" (1981), to the dynamic sketches of writing and reading interrelatedness in Donald Murray's "Writing As Process: How Writing Finds Its Own Meaning" (1980), to a written description included in Thomas Reigstad and Donald McAndrew's *Training Tutors for Writing Conferences* (1984).

Teachers can use written, sketched, or diagrammed writing process models to instigate class discussion and to raise intriguing questions: How do the models vary? Are there any steps in the idealized process that class writers do not utilize and why? How does a creative writer's process vary from these descriptions or does it? To augment researchers' models, it is possible to ask students to develop metaphors for writing during a brief in-class activity. When responding to the prompts "For me, writing is like . . ." and "For me, revision is like . . . ," students in one of my writing classes came up with the images of writing and revising found in figures 6 and 7 (see Ronald and Volkmer 1989; Tobin 1989).

Sometimes, to help students synthesize models, I bring large sheets of paper and marking pens to class and ask them to draw a model of their own writing process like the two versions found in figures 8 and 9. Next, I ask students to share their individual models in small groups, in order to *negotiate* a group model that will encompass their differing individual processes; samples of group models are found in figure 10. Finally, I ask the groups to compare their models to the researchers' process models that we have looked at.

Students' individual process models often provide insights into a writer's composing habits and attitudes toward writing; for some writers, composing occurs in bursts of energy, a big bang version of inspiration (figure 8), or writing is as difficult as leaping over a high wall (figure 9). As students negotiate composing models, idiosyncratic behaviors are subsumed and commonalities surface. For instance, in figure 10, students agree on a volcanic representation for their processes (bubbling, eruption, solidification). A second group of students relies on the hydrological cycle, introducing a metaphor for writing that is new to my experience; in this case, students present their writing as a fluent, organic cycle of accumulation, drafting, and refining of ideas into forms.

In addition to eliciting student and group models of writing and comparing them to researchers' models, teachers may wish to explore the metaphors for writing process discussed by Tomlinson and mentioned in chapter 2, drafting pictures of "writing is cooking," and so on, to discover what each of those models includes and omits. In any event, after discussing the entire writing process, through professional or student models, students are sure to understand the reason for, and focus of, generation activities. I move on, then, to a discussion of invention.

Invention for Getting in Motion

Invention is one of the five parts of classical rhetoric; George Kennedy (1980) reminds us that " 'Invent' (from Latin *invenire*) literally means 'to discover or find out,' and only secondarily comes to mean 'create'" (8). Invention techniques are intended to help writers discover and find out what they mean to say, rather than to create entirely new insights, forms, or written products. In a writing workshop, I explore invention as both a *topic* for writers and an *activity* by having students draft a muse poem or muse sketch. Writing a muse poem or sketch helps students understand the sources of their own writing. Since students often have little or no idea of the variety of methods professional writers use to generate text and then to keep writing, discussing the concept of writer's muse and writer's inspiration can fruitfully lead into all subsequent classroom invention exercises. Additionally, since writers often seem to want to write about the act of writing (or nonwriting, being blocked), muse poems and sketches provide a guided alternative to the generally predictable "blank white page" piece. Further, discussing the writing process through this activity helps students access their tacit knowledge about writers' rituals; they call on the muse to better understand themselves as writers.

The Muse Activity

I ask students to help me list sources for writing—where they find inspiration. I do this by telling them I get writing ideas when I go running, go shopping, read other writers, and so on. I ask them to brainstorm individually or in groups to discover where they (or writers they have been reading) get their writing ideas. One class came up with this composite list:

> dreams; the past; books; people I catch glimpses of; clothes; photos; staring at maps; listening to language; eavesdropping;

> traveling and eating strange meals; watching people—friends, relatives, family; newspaper articles; postcards; family objects; powerful moments considered later; the muse; wanting to send a message; being upset but not knowing why; to show off; from being hungry; from things I'm dying to say.

Sharing such a list and asking students, in groups, to add to it allows for a discussion of inspiration. After one or several of these warm-ups, I share sample writing with students as well as a definition of the muse. I use the "Muse" entry from the *Princeton Encyclopedia of Poetry and Poetics* which begins: "MUSE. One of the nine Gr. goddesses who preside over poetry, song, and the arts, traditionally invoked by poets to grant them inspiration" (533). I also share sample poems by published writers, such as James Laughlin's "My Muse," and Ted Kooser's "Selecting a Reader" (these may be found in Wallace 1987).

Finally, I share student work, including "A-Musing" by Tamara Mills; "Muse" by Jo'al Hill; "Confessions of a Male Muse" by Jennifer Wasileski; "Unamused" by Steve Bailey; and my own poem, "Groveling," generated through this activity; these works are included below.

We take turns reading the samples aloud. Usually we read them several times and just listen to the humor and pathos of these writers' interactions with the writing process. A sharing of sample poems and prose is followed by a writing activity. First, I conduct a directed, class freewrite, asking students to respond to the prompts, "To my muse . . . ," or to a sample first line that I have borrowed or derived from other muse writings. Sometimes we spend ten minutes writing about one prompt and stop and share; sometimes we write a few minutes on several prompts to generate a greater number of possibilities. Next, I ask students to complete the project at home, drafting a muse poem or sketch for our next writer's workshop. It is possible to ask writers to follow-up on this activity by having them discuss their writing process again in their journals. To avoid writer's block about inspiration—the last thing this activity is designed to have happen—I try to include significant freewriting and sharing time in the classroom to assure that no writer leaves without a beginning.

Through this activity, student writers continue to discover revealing metaphors for the act of writing (when a muse is transformed into a cat, or a man, or a vampire-like opponent), and they explore their own beliefs and disbelief and their reasons for writing. Sometimes I share my muse poems and sketches, written over several semesters, because, through them, I can trace and talk about a writer's changing complex of writing frustration, exaltation, and interests. Students can track the same type of growth if teachers ask them to write letters to their "muse" at the beginning of the term and then again at the end of the term, perhaps as a final project. The following muse pieces were all generated from this in-class writing exercise (except for my poem they are adapted from Bishop 1990d; used with permission).

A-MUSING
by Tamara Mills

Before born
   I asked to be a Muse.
Now I am,
   a mangy cat.
Alley hunter,
   visiting a poet.
Bring ideas, inspiration,
   padding on four paws.
Does she know "precious"
   is her Muse?
Not a fabrication,
   a handsome human,
But her tough tom
   eating at her feet.
She is the dream poet.
   I, not the imagined one.
Wanted human form
   got fur.
Tender Vittles
   in a plastic bowl,
Not a steak
   and candle lit table for two.
She gets her words,
   her fame, from me.
I get a litter box
   and scratching post.
At night I yowl;
   cat voiced songs of sorrow.
Life is cruel.
   but I'll live—
      Poet loves me.

MUSE
by Jo'al Hill

I'm the part of you,
you refuse to
believe exist.

When you try to sleep
I begin to creep,

like blood flowing
threw your veins
I send thoughts,
images to your brain.

I have been called
many humanly things
but you cant see me
you can only feel me.

You called last night
I refused to come,
I want you to remember
I'm running this pencil
you aren't the one.

I think you like it
when I control your
mind, night after
night, time after time.

Why don't you just relax
and allow me to help you
write. Let's stop fighting
so we can both rest tonight.

CONFESSIONS OF A MALE MUSE
by Jennifer Wasileski

I am late,
I see
her pen is poised.
An eager erection,
of sorts.

Face twisted in ignorance.
She's not hearing me,
I'm not there.
Or am I?

"Bastard!"
She's thinking.
"Sunning himself somewhere!"

"I am fashionably late
my dear;"
I announce
throwing open our door.

"Well look what the cat
dragged in."
Says she.
"I almost started without you."

UNAMUSED
by Steve Bailey

I have never claimed to have a "muse." To me, the term has always seemed to romanticize writing in a way that seems false and elitist. Writers, and poets in particular, like to personify their "muse," and create this pretend being who brings inspiration and creativity. This is fine, I guess, but it is also just a game played by writers who would be better served by approaching their writing process with more pragmatism and stating "I write because. . . ."

I do not write because a "muse" drives me. I write for a million different reasons—not all of which have to do with creativity or inspiration. And inspiration, the basis of the whole "muse" idea, is another false writing term, like writer's block. Writing has very little to do with inspiration and "muses." If I waited around to be "inspired," in the romantic sense, I'd produce very little work per semester.

If I had to personify my writing process, I would say that for me, writing is like alcoholism or drug addiction. I am always thinking about writing, always wanting to write, always trying to get high on a new piece of writing, and always hung-over or strung-out when I am not writing. I am a writer—I have no other skills.

Nothing romantic about that—writing is work, and for true writers, it is also an obsession. Is obsession the same as inspiration? Maybe, but for now, consider me "unamused."

GROVELING
by Wendy Bishop

for the MUSE

Please let me sleep nights
Not waking dark AMs to write imaginary pencil
On elusive scrolls of dreams, determined
To *get it right* this time.

Please let the editor be unbusy
When stiff paper and these inky traces
Shriek out their individuality
From a much elbowed stack by the *TV Guide*.

Please let the word processor
Scramble its symboled languages
On other writers' time. Let all
Electrical circuits await me, benign.

Please let small children grow into
Their lines, hold books right side up,
An endlessly restocked readership
Called to the examined life, and reading mine.

Look. I'll pay—squash dreams, dredge with
Coffee cup, salute masters, submit in ASCII,

Disappoint my kids, read *Curious George*
Aloud tomorrow night, never tonight.

Please. Please. Dress my small thoughts
In your furious and durable print.

The muse activity is only one of a nearly infinite set of in-class and out-of-class invention activities that creative writing teachers will want to explore (see chapters 5 and 6).

Finding, Designing, and Using Invention Activities

Invention activities give student writers insights into the ways writers actually write. In essence, all writers apprentice themselves to other (often more adept) writers by reading and imitating the more successful writer's work and then by giving themselves assignments that challenge their own skills and abilities. A writer reading a Yeats poem may decide to write a modern poem to his daughter using Yeats's tone or forms. A writer reading Anne Beattie may decide to write a short, bleak, ultramodern, present-tense, first-person story to capture her experience: winter in the Arctic (a rather un-Beattie-like environment).

Generally, writers prefer to talk about craft or inspiration and to ignore the issue of writing to a task. Most, however, do admit to giving themselves assignments to get the writing in motion on those mornings or evenings when it just isn't flowing. Additionally, writers also write by commission: an award-winning novelist might be asked to write a screenplay or a poet might write verse to be set to music. Many writers are asked to (and do) contribute to themed anthologies, and many writers choose to write the same assignments they give their students to optimize their teaching time and make it count for their own personal development. In fact, writing teachers often develop a set of semester-long assignments around *their* ongoing professional interests. I have taken courses where I was asked to write a sequence of connected poems, for instance, by a master poet who was then, himself, studying sequences and writing a sequenced book. As long as the teacher's interests do not overwhelm the students' needs, class assignments that enhance the teacher's class involvement seem reasonable. The best classes, though, result when the teacher's and students' self-assignments merge in interest and usefulness.

I visualize invention on a continuum from writer's apprentice work and, often experimental, self-assignments to more conventional, commissioned work. Some writers dislike commissioned work, viewing it, at worst, in the same category as "occasional verse," Hallmark-card-like rhyming stuff or prose eulogies meant to please relatives and the overly sentimental. However, a significant amount of well-regarded writing through the centuries has centered on ritual occasions—marriages, the death of children or statespersons or celebrities, memorials to wars and uprisings, and so on, and this type of social writing should not be dismissed too summarily.

My understanding of the demands of invention is illustrated in figure 11. I place the creative workshop centrally along this continuum because the workshop seeks to show students how the private assignments of writers develop as well as to describe the requirements and functions of more accessible, public, commissioned work. The traditional creative writing workshop relies on out-of-class assignment making, while the transactional workshop uses frequent in-class assignments to illuminate the process of self-assignment and to offer a first step for students who will, later, need to work alone.

Over time, my own sequence of class assignments has developed as I learned to construct invention activities that allowed students to imitate work I liked or to imitate after I had imitated. That is to say, I often look back through my own apprentice work and ask myself, what exercises worked best? How did my teachers teach me or how did I go about writing when I was at home? Can I stimulate similar writing in class?

Other very important sources for teachers who teach by invention are the assignment lists that can be found in craft textbooks. Often, I have to adapt and explore those assignments before I tailor them to my class. I have used, particularly, the work cited at the end of this book by Janet Burroway, John Gardner, Florence Grossman, David Kirby, Kenneth Koch, Joseph Tsujimoto, Alberta Turner, and Alan Ziegler, as well as activities designed by graduate writing students with whom I have worked.

In my own teaching experience, *before* I started using regular, weekly, in-class writing activities, I would offer students lists of such activities through class handouts like the ones in figures 12 and 13 which, again, were influenced by or adapted from some of the writers I have mentioned. My students liked these lists since the lists condensed the advice of several writers' textbooks and my own invention explorations. However, students could not use the lists productively since many of the directions for writing assume extensive prior knowledge on the student's part. Telling a student to write a sonnet or a story with authorial intrusion will usually result in a bad sonnet or an ugly intrusion rather than an illuminating language exploration. Also, I now believe that these writing tasks separate genres in an unproductive manner. I produced lists like these because I was expected by English departments to teach genres separately and to focus exclusively on craft. Currently, I think invention self-assignments can function best if they encourage a writer to experiment and to cross genre boundaries.

In particular, I have come to be less interested in genre-specific exercises at the introductory level and for the novice writer. I think an activity that encourages metaphorical description, or one that is written in response to sound stimuli, or writing that explores the uses and abuses of cliché or dialect can all work from a common exploratory base in language and be shaped by the writer to that writer's own genre purposes. Therefore, I use invention exercises to get writers in motion, realizing that later in their drafting process, and their own writing lives, they will want to give more and more attention to issues of craft and convention.

No one I know of has categorized invention activities; some do seem to lead to sound and rhythm explorations (list poems), others lead to language exploration (writing intentionally clichéd prose and poetry, metaphorical description, or character sketches), and others help students look for resonant details (writing about family artifacts or actual objects). But, writers do not write sound-filled, rhythmic list poems without using evocative detail. And they do not develop a strong character without using metaphor and avoiding cliché.

Adapting and Tailoring Invention Exercises

There is no single, best, in-class invention technique that will get all writers drafting productively. Rather, in-class invention activities can be used to provide novice writers with insights into professional writers' self-challenges. I have discovered no preferable sequencing system. That is, there is nothing that says a list poem should precede or follow a metaphorical description since these activities are not genre-specific but, rather, utilize the language-making potential of all students, who then shape meaning from their explorations. Composition textbooks these days give a great deal of attention to "invention heuristics," and sometimes teachers run students through all these techniques as if the techniques will elicit writing appropriate for preconceived forms like the personal essay or persuasive essay. However, the in-class invention activity does not provide a set of inflexible rules to be followed rigidly.

Rather, invention activities should provide students with exploratory moments and drafting options that develop flexibility and fluidity in a writer.

Many of the invention techniques found in composition textbooks are thoroughly adaptable to creative writing classrooms. For instance, a well-known composition text, Elizabeth Cowan Neeld's *Writing*, third edition (1990), includes a chapter entitled "The Creating Stage." She covers brainstorming, reporter's formula, list making, chaining, and looping. In other chapters Neeld introduces cubing, track switching, and classical invention. It is likely that, over time,these heuristics were derived, in part, from the written products of professional writers. Certainly, brainstorming, list making, chaining, and even track switching are variations of list/repetition prose and poetry. The reporter's formula—asking who, what, where, when, why, and how—is used by fiction writers and playwrights somewhere in the plotting and drafting process. Cubing offers writers six perspectives for viewing an issue or object (describe it, compare it, associate it, analyze it, apply it, argue for or against it), but the perspectives are nothing more than one person's suggestions for experimenting with alternatives and could be adapted for point of view or used with variations in imaginative situations.

Think of Wallace Stevens's "Thirteen Ways of Looking at a Blackbird" as, in the broadest sense, the result of poetic cubing. One of my own apprentice poems came as a response to a similar exercise. My teacher asked us—students in a first-quarter introduction to poetry writing workshop—to go home, sit down, and imitate Stevens's poem; by doing so, she was really asking us to perform a surrealistic exercise in cubing. Here is my poem, saved for fifteen years. Even though the poem was never published and remains "just an exercise," it teaches me something about Stevens's vision (and about my own).

Six Ways of Looking at Ghosts
by Wendy Bishop

She closed the door softly,
but stepped back into the ghost.

Safely out of the house,
the ghost raced after the crowd,
disappearing from sight.

The rescued man
had the look
of one who spends long nights
searching for ghosts.

The gun exploded,
a ghostly scream,
then silence.

The ghost signaled me to a stop,
thrust his head in the window
and asked for a lift.

Confident it was over,
the men went home
to their soft ghosts.
They hardly knew
they had been gone.

In her text, Elizabeth Neeld uses a technique developed by Peter Elbow: Center of Gravity writing (described fully in Elbow 1981). A writer freewrites for ten minutes, stops, rereads, and circles the most important sentence. Next, he begins with that circled sentence, writes ten minutes more, stops, rereads, again circles the most important sentence, starts there and writes again, etc., completing three or more loops and finding several center of gravity sentences. Carolyn Kremers used a variation on this technique in her multimedia cross-cultural writing activity that I describe in chapter 5. Carolyn directed the looping and center of gravity freewrite by providing writers with rich audio and visual stimuli. She then asked them to write and center on important discoveries made through writing about those stimuli, and so on. Center of gravity writing can also be a useful technique for a writer who has trouble choosing a title; by writing about the work afterward, she may be able to focus on an important aspect of the work. Similarly, by performing center of gravity freewriting before starting a longer work, writers may generate a memorable first line in the guise of a center of gravity sentence.

Peter Elbow's metaphorical description exercise (also discussed in chapter 5) seems to echo tagmemic invention techniques; in tagmemic invention, writers are asked to consider an object or situation as a particle, wave, and/or field. In his exercise, Elbow asks writers to consider an individual as a food, a weather, an ecology, and so on (1986a).

Essentially, in creating class invention activities, teachers move freely from product to process and back. They will need to experience this type of writing themselves and to study their own self-assignments and self-challenges to help students produce better written products. Composition theorists C. H. Knoblauch and Lil Brannon (1984) suggest many benefits accrue from such teacher involvement:

> We all need time, thought, and second chances, teachers not less than students. The process of making assertions about difficult, substantial questions takes effort and energy, requires an investment of personal resources and a search for outside sources as well. Teachers who write often themselves know this, but they also need to show it to students, who sometimes think that skilled writers can generate consistently publishable writing on first tries, with no anxieties and no mistakes, in isolation from critical readers, with help from no one but the Muses. Teachers who acknowledge the perspective of modern rhetoric, who understand the heuristic value of composing and its progressive, endlessly renovative character, resist the fiction that writing is formulaic, that ideas spring readily to mind and organize themselves like magic, given a prescribed structure in which to locate them, that tidy end-products matter more than the on-going effort to make sense of the world. . . . Their own writing in workshop is a constant reminder, to themselves and to their students, of how writing actually happens and what makes it worth all the trouble. (112)

Before presenting ten invention activities and their variations in chapter 5, I would like to provide an example of how I develop an invention activity and how I might organize a whole semester around a set of such activities. To begin, when looking back through my own writing, I was struck by the number of times I used odd epigraphs. I collect quotes from other writers or wry statements from a newspaper or magazine and use these to head a poem. Obviously, for me, epigraphs have generative power. Writers also use such epigraphs to set the tone for a larger work, a book of poems or a novel. Here are several epigraphs that led to published poems for me.

> In only one of Daguerre's pictures does a man appear; by chance a pedestrian on the boulevard had stopped to have his shoes shined, and had held still during most of the image.
>
> —Newhall, *History of Photography*

> Justice Marshall McComb, 82, did not contest his wife's petition to be named conservator of his estate after she told the court her husband is "obsessed with the moon. He gets quite excited about it. . . . He enjoys it but it's not a normal enjoyment of the moon."
>
> —UPI

Intrigued by these "stories," I proceeded to write a poem about an invisible shoeshiner and a poem about a man who entertains an unnatural enjoyment for the moon. These odd facts are the types of material I collect in my writer's notebook or clippings file, and they also illustrate the reading process I go through as a writer.

To develop an epigraph activity, I started collecting samples of epigraphs from my own poems that I thought students would enjoy. I also began looking through my collection of poetry anthologies to learn how other writers used epigraphs. I noted that the epigraphs chosen by writers of the 1920s to 1950s were highly erudite (often appearing in an untranslated Latin, Italian, German and so on); writers in the 1970s and 1980s more often chose to respond to media—newspapers, movies, songs—and to quote in English. For the invention activity, I decided to bring in a selection of provocative quotes, like those I have listed above, *without poems*; I would glean these quotes from the work of other writers.

Next, students would choose a quote that engaged their interest and freewrite on it and then take that freewriting home and see if they could shape this material into a poem or prose piece. In a future class, I would show students the pieces of writing that originally followed the epigraphs, and we could see upon what varied journeys these same, provocative quotes took writers (novices and professionals). Finally, I wanted to ask writers to consider the relationship of the epigraph to the writing: Did the need for the prompt disappear? Was it possible to remove the epigraph and still have a strong piece? These questions would lead to considerations of revision and closure.

From my verb tenses ("I would ask") it should be obvious that this is a class invention technique in the process of development. I have not yet used it, although I am pretty sure it will work. But, I do not know for which writers it will work and in what ways. As a teacher of writing, designing these activities is productive and exciting for the questions they raise. Using these activities, I am forced to carefully observe myself and other writers at work. After each activity, I must ask students if the activity worked for them, and how.

In short, invention activities can be developed by working from texts back to process (i.e., "Some writers use epigraphs; how do they use them and how could other writers use them?") My muse poem activity was generated in exactly this manner.

Inventions can also be developed by setting constraints on the process, resulting in directed texts (i.e., "Most poems rely on rhythm—what if we make every line have ____ beats and ____ syllables? Write a complete short story in 100 lines [500 lines, three pages]").

Equally, invention self-challenges can come from combining many constraints (i.e., "What if you take a list-poem activity and write about objects in your room and also require a reversal to achieve closure?" "Borrow from the parts of a failed poem—one you like but didn't pursue—and use those parts to help set the scene for the opening of a short story.").

As I have mentioned, in many cases, I borrow and adapt invention activities from other writers who have already explored the effectiveness of writing about objects, writing color poems, writing prose dialogues with no tags and no characters' names, or writing from the point of view of an animal or an object. In the next chapter, I illustrate a selection of what have proved to be predictably successful invention activities, even as I acknowledge that I am indebted to many writing teachers for the *kernel* inventions or composing insights upon which the activities are based. It is from this rich set that I have generated my own variations.

Images of Writing

Writing is power, having control, a release of energy, and draining (yet satisfying) at the end.

Writing is like painting a picture with words and lots of detail.

Writing is like catharsis, expressing whether I am happy, sad, or indifferent.

Writing is like giving birth, conception of an idea, delivery of the idea onto paper (strain, stress, pain, and anxiety) and completion (relief and joy), leaving one empty and exhausted yet elated with the product and anxious for its future.

Writing is like extending personality onto paper with the ability to take out stutters, use perfect word choice, and eliminate "uh's" and "ya' knows."

Writing is like talking; it should be entertaining.

Writing is like a test; I test my skills, imagination, and creativity, and my ability to meet the expectations.

Writing is like therapy; I sort things out in my brain; it makes me feel organized and a better person, in a happier mood, satisfied with what I've done.

Writing is like relieving stress and tension that builds up inside; sometimes it makes a situation seem less hopeless and often makes the good times even more enjoyable.

Writing is like expressing an opinion or viewpoint about life. The story—whether fact or fiction—is told as only I can tell it.

Writing is like having a special person to share my ideas, feel my feelings and be myself.

Writing is like freedom; I can give voice to any kind of strange bizarre thought that enters my head. It doesn't matter because I don't have to show it to anyone, unless I choose to.

Fig. 6 Students' images of writing.

Images of Revising

Revising is a pain—finding a better way to say something.

Revising is a chore because I like to think the way I wrote the first time was perfect.

Revising is like making the already interesting ideas attractive to read.

Revising is like improving what I have, putting on the finishing touches.

Revising is like diluting an original brew, working on an assembling line for twenty years, going through labor again to bear the same child.

Revising is like dwelling on past mistakes with a chance to set things right; I would rather, however, continue to surge forward in life, leaving imperfection and chalking them up as character builders.

Revising is like a secret; I hide all the stupid things I wrote (when I was obviously not myself) the first time.

Revising is like a medieval form of torture.

Revising is like a challenge—to sort things in a logical order and make it a pleasure to read.

Revising is like cleaning the house; everything is there in front of you just not in an order you're satisfied with. It takes valuable time and effort to get just like you want it.

Revising is like a never-ending story; it's hard for me to leave my work alone. I always find some sort of problem or something I want to change.

Revising is like rethinking that opinion or viewpoint to make certain it is clear and understandable.

Revising is like putting a fine-honed edge on a blade.

Revising for me is like a kind of control that I don't get anywhere else. I can change the words, erase them, create others. It's a chance to polish and perfect ideas before someone else sees them.

Fig. 7. Students' images of revising.

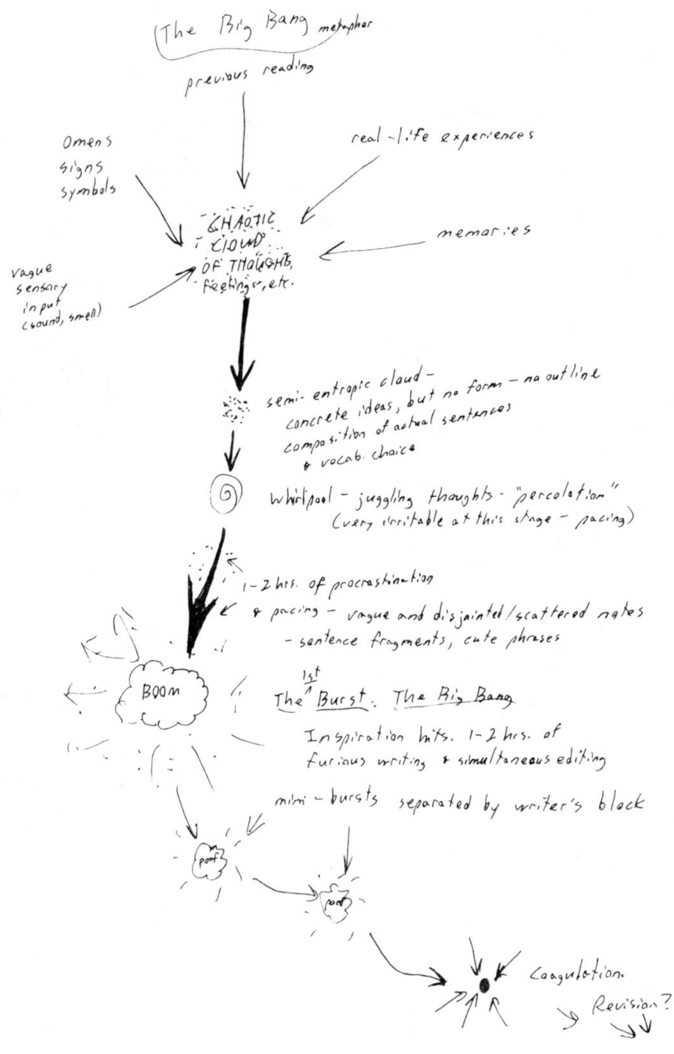

Fig. 8. Individual models of writing process—writing as explosion, the Big Bang.

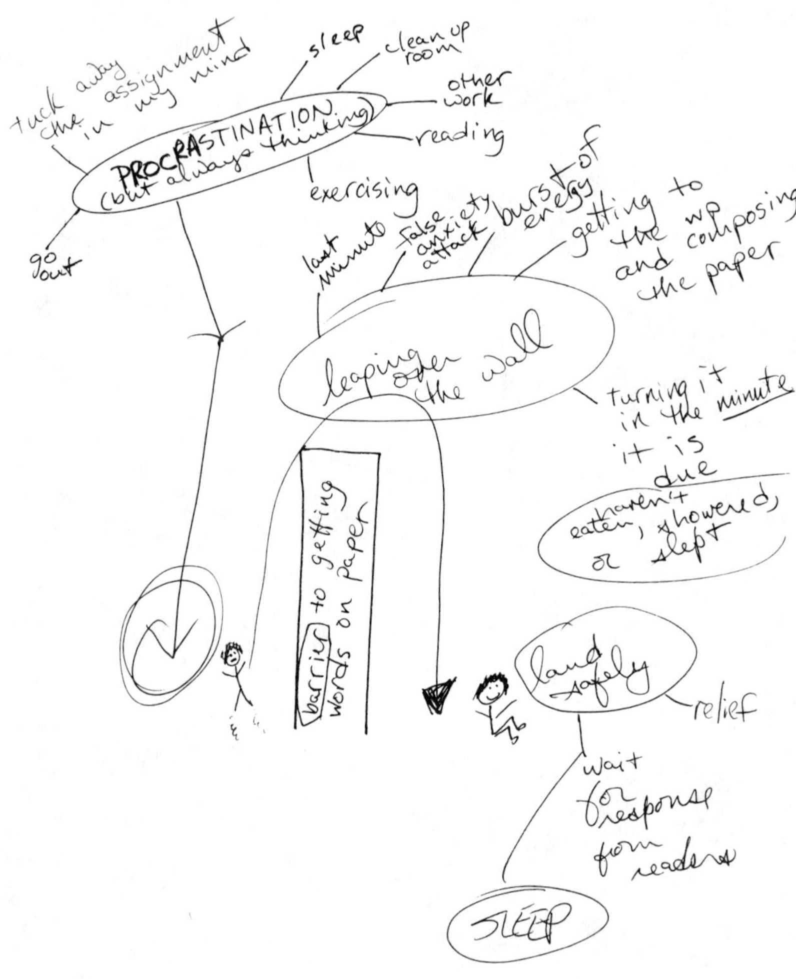

Fig. 9. Individual models of writing process—writing as leaping a wall.

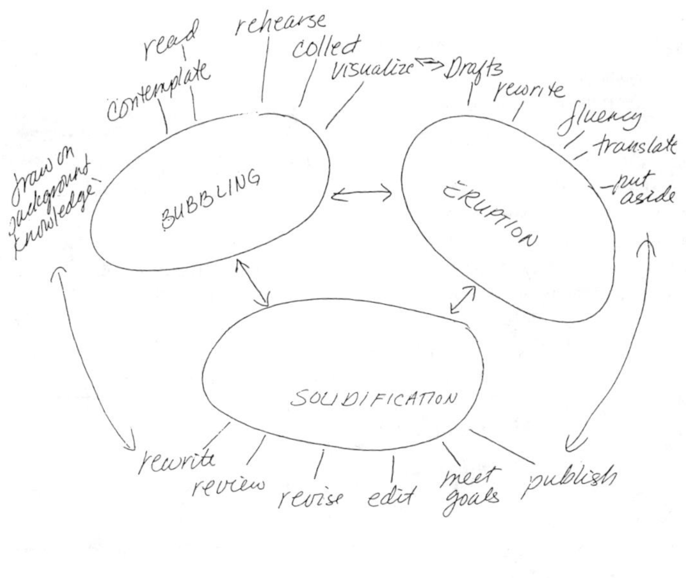

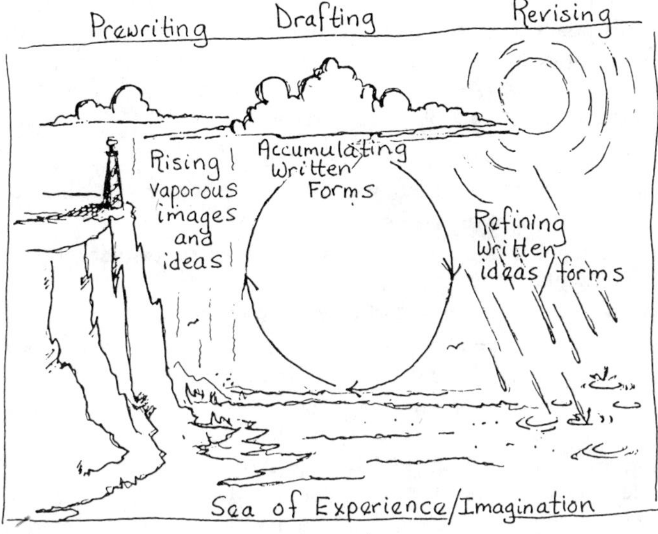

Fig. 10. Group models of writing process—writing as volcanic action or writing as a hydrological cycle.

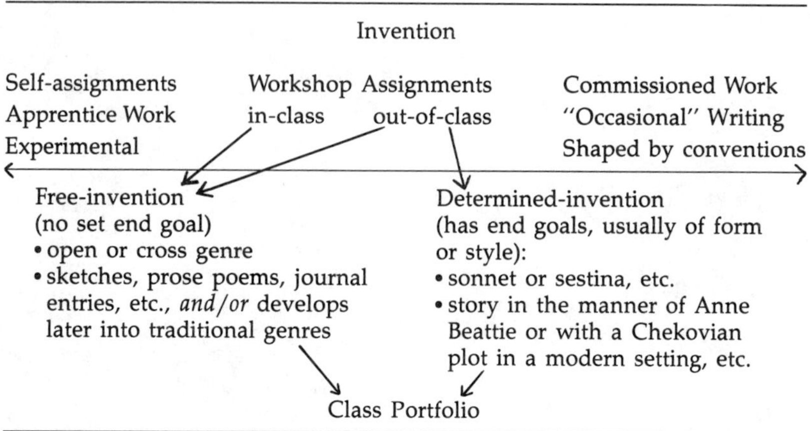

Fig. 11. The invention continuum.

Poem Topics/Techniques

1. Write a poem based on a historical incident or a myth.
2. Write a poem that uses colors repetitively.
3. Write a series of poems or write a poem in parts.
4. Write a prose poem.
5. Write a sonnet.
6. Write a poem that is highly alliterative.
7. Write a poem based on a newspaper article or any verifiable fact.
8. Write a poem that uses an epigraph.
9. Write a poem which mourns a lost time, person, or place, but try not to be sentimental about loss.
10. Write a poem with very short or very long lines.
11. Create a person (persona) and write a poem in that person's voice.
12. Use refrains or regular repetition in a poem.
13. Write about a location you remember; try to capture the essence of that location in words.
14. Imagine you are an animal (or an object, or a person from another culture or planet), write a poem from that point of view.
15. In your poem, tell a story from your past or predict a story into the future.
16. Write a self-portrait.

Fig. 12. Sample writing topics handout: poetry.

Fiction

1. Write a story occurring in the present tense.
2. Write a story with a frame.
3. Write a story relying primarily on dialogue.
4. Write a very short descriptive story which shuns dialogue.
5. Write a story from a child's point of view.
6. Write an outlandish plot and stick to it when telling your story *or* write a predictable plot but make it come alive due to your unusual writing style.
7. Write a story with authorial digression and/or intrusion.
8. Fictionalize a real event that occurred to you. Improve it; increase the dramatic tension; change the outcome.

Nonfiction

1. Write the first chapter of your autobiography. Read several other authors for models.
2. Report a local campus/town occurrence in the manner of modern new journalism (see Joan Didion, Hunter Thompson, Tom Wolfe, Norman Mailer). Your audience: readers of *Rolling Stone, Esquire, Vanity Fair.*
3. Write an article about an unusual subject, making it suitable for publication in the *Wall Street Journal.*
4. Write an essay on a concept such as love, honor, and so on. Make us want to read it.
5. Write a diary for a week (real or imagined) in the manner of Thoreau.
6. Write an essay about writers/writing or literature. Tie your ideas to examples from "real life" and from literature. See Robert Hass: *Twentieth Century Pleasures.*
7. Interview someone and write a chapter for his or her biography.

Fig. 13. Sample writing topics handout: fiction, nonfiction.

5 Ten Inventions and Variations

I start off but I don't know where I'm going; I try this avenue and that avenue, that turns out to be a dead end, this is a dead end, and so on. The search takes a long time and I have to backtrack often.

—Galway Kinnell, quoted in *Learning by Teaching* by Donald Murray, 1982

We tried all kinds of experiments—cut-ups, working with music (Satie, Mozart, jazz), visual imagery (a random collection of postcards). I also suggested at one point that students work with the seven [sic] most used words in the language (*the, of, and, to, in, that*) in terms of musical rhythms. We worked with sensory idea—five words related to touch, five related to smell, etc., working with twenty-five words in five-line clusters. So in a way one can invent one's own forms. All these possibilities overlap anyway.

—Anne Waldman, from *Finding the Words,* edited by Nancy Bunge, 1985

By presenting the following inventions and variations, I hope to encourage creative writing teachers to develop and discover their own, best, in-class writing options. Of course, these activities should not be applied piecemeal. They should be inserted into a carefully planned and coherent writing workshop. Additionally, I would urge teachers to write during invention activities themselves to gauge how useful each activity will be for their classes and to explore language with their students. To illustrate these inventions, I include examples from my own writing, from the writing of undergraduates, and from that of graduate students who were preparing to become creative writing teachers.

Portions of this chapter appeared in somewhat different form in the following publications: Bishop, Wendy. 1990b. "The 15 Sentence Portrait." *Exercise Exchange* 35 (2): 5–8, and 1989b. "Using Postcards for Invention." *Exercise Exchange* 35 (5): 27–31; Kremers, Carolyn. 1989. "Through the Eyes and Ears of Another Culture: Invention Activities and a Writer's Workshop." *Exercise Exchange* 35 (5): 3–11; Robinson, Jill. 1989. "Clichés: Finding Fresh Language." *Exercise Exchange* 2: 16–20. Used with permission.

Cliché Writing

Creative writing teachers who try to eliminate all the clichés in student writing meet with a familiar result: everyone becomes hyperconscious of clichés. I like to explore the functional use of cliché by writing intentionally clichéd pieces; this helps me discover how clichés actually help or hinder writers. Jill Robinson's article, "Clichés: Finding Fresh Language" (1989), can provide teachers with a set of ideas for starting discussions about clichéd language, as can most craft textbooks.

I start this activity a week in advance by asking students to collect short lists of clichés to share at the next class meeting. At that meeting, we add to a list of clichés that I have put on the board, such as the following

- dark as a dungeon
- hot to trot
- cold as ice
- crazy as a loon
- high as a kite
- as fast as greased lightning
- blind as a bat
- the apple of my eye

Next, we read samples, collected over several semesters, of intentionally clichéd prose and poetry written in response to this invention activity. Following are some examples:

> That's the Way the Ball Bounces
> by Karina Possenti
>
> That referee was cool, cool as a cat, cold as ice, and tough as nails. He stood alone without batting an eye and called the shots as loud as thunder. Blind as bats, the players lunged forward making waves in the sea of drowned rats. They slowly but surely looked high and mighty, then quick as a wink and fast as lightning took the ref by storm. The world was at their feet, they became crazy as loons that are as high as a kite. The goalie looked fierce as a lion. The crowd went hog-wild, yelled loud as can be and got madder than a wet hen. All of a sudden, out of the blue, the room was as quiet as a graveyard. Slow as molasses in January, the ref turned red as a beet. His goose was cooked—they had caught him red-handed trying to beat the system—so he turned in his badge and killed the lights.

> One of These Days
> by Tonie Bonilla
>
> You just wait and see
> Sooner or later you'll have some of your own.
> Crumb snatchers, rug rats, curtain climbers, house apes

Soft as velvet and tough as nails
Bright as a button picking up bad habits
Dumb as a box of rocks learning manners
Good as gold at Gramma's house
Then screaming mimis in the mall.
They'll be fast as greased lightning at bath time
fighting you tooth and nail all the way to the tub
Because they're all hands—into everything in sight
and happy as a pig in mud when they're up to
their armpits in dirt and filth
Smooth as silk or stubborn as a mule
It won't make a speck of difference if
they're pretty as a picture or plain as a mud fence
They'll be your little darlings
the light of your life and apple of your eye
Just running you around in circles
till you're crazy as a loon and
more than three sheets to the wind.
Then you'll come crawling here to me
Begging me to watch your little monsters
and I'll look you straight in the eye
and say, "See there, I told you so," because
what goes around comes around
You just wait and see.

Trite

by Ken Waldman

It was Saturday night. She was standing there pretty as a picture and I was drunk as a skunk and hot to trot. Yessirree, Peter Van and the Econolines were playing the rockin' rhythm and blues—you had to see them to believe them. The drummer pounded away nuttier than a fruitcake. The bass player looked crazy as a loon. The guy playing lead guitar, Peter Van, well, his fingers moved fast as lightning and the sounds coming out of that thing hit you where it hurts. All in all, though the harmonica player was the one who really turned me on—the guy knew his business. You could really tell he had a rock and roll heart.

Anyway, she was standing by the bar cute as a button, and by the way she was moving it was plain as day she wanted to dance. Like I say I was higher than a kite, so, sharp as a knife I made my way across the room. Quick as a wink I said, "Hey baby, you wanna dance?" Light as a a feather she took my hand. Then we looked into each other's eyes.

She was gentler than a lamb, I thought.

It was Christmas come early, I thought.

I must be in heaven, I thought.

I felt like I was floating on cloud nine while we danced. I looked around and for a split second I saw everything as clear as a bell. I'll never forget that moment for as long as I live. Everyone else looked stiff as boards while me and my partner moved smooth as silk. I felt as happy as a lark. If anybody I knew had seen me, they'd have said, "Mac, what's with Mac? He looks like a million dollars out on the dance floor, hey."

The fast song ended and another began. It was a slow, gut bucket blues. I held her tight like I'd never let her go. I was prouder than a peacock, feeling her leaning against me—all warm as toast. For a minute we danced like that. I began to whisper sweet nothings into her ear.

But then—from warm as toast, to cool as a cucumber, to cold as ice. What? What?? Had the bubble burst??? A guy bigger than a house was running across the dance floor.

"Elmo!" she shrieked.

I knew it! Her boyfriend!! I knew I had smelled trouble. The guy looked madder than a hornet and strong as an ox.

The band stopped playing, and the bar grew as quiet as a grave. You could have heard a pin drop.

I could see what was about to happen as clear as glass.

His right fist met my left temple like a ton of bricks.

The room went dark as dungeon, then black as night, then I saw stars.

I woke up with a crowd surrounding me. "Is there a doctor in the house?"

I heard someone shout.

"Doctor, my ass," I said. "Get me a beer and I'll be good as new." I got up and wiped the blood from my lip. I felt fit as a fiddle and free as a bird. "Get me a beer," I repeated. "I'm as dry as a bone."

I drank the beer and ordered one more. Inside me I knew that something special had happened and this was the first day of the rest of my life.

Byrd In Love

by Wendy Bishop

Summer

It was hot as hell,
Hot as the day is long. I turned
As brown as a bean,
Making hay while the sun shines,
Keeping fit as a fiddle
Before I fell.

Autumn

First dry as a bone
Then raining pitchforks
And devils. Smiling on the outside,
I was crying on the inside,
For she was hard as nails

And dressed to kill:
A demon of delight.

Winter

Cold as a dead man's bones
And dark as night. I was stubborn
As a mule, crazy as a loon,
For being willing to kiss her boot.
Plain as the nose
On my face, I who had been
As tough as a nut was lost
In the funhouse
Of love.

Spring

Bright as a penny
And good as gold,
I broke into blossom,
Drank dews of delight
And danced until dawn—
Went dark as a dungeon
to high as a kite
When she called my name.

Reader, I felt drunk as a skunk
on love.

(Source: Robinson 1989, 17. Used with permission)

After reading these selections aloud and talking about what the authors did with, relatively, the same set of clichés, I ask students to freewrite their own beginnings to intentionally clichéd pieces. The resulting in-class writing can be shared immediately, or it can be taken home, revised, and returned. Class writers can share this work in groups or as a whole class and even have a "worst" piece contest which turns competition upside down; for, of course, the worst piece is the best intentionally clichéd piece of work. Best of all, in future classes, I do not need to explain why "this was the first day of the rest of my life" is an overused phrase. A cliché writing session can show the variety of options writers can follow with even the most predictable and constrained of forms. It can be followed up by asking students to analyze the language of their other writings for clichéd words or phrases. By writing into clichés instead of listening to lectures against their use, students develop a vivid sense of the problems writers experience with this type of language.

Writing from Objects

My version of this exercise stems from a variety of sources. I was originally introduced to an activity called Hats and Shoes. In Hats and Shoes, the teacher brings a bag full of odd assorted hats and a bag full of the same number of shoes to class. First, she places the hats onto the table and asks everyone to choose one. Then students freewrite for ten minutes, creating a character to suit the hat. Second, she places the shoes on the table and asks students to freewrite to create a second character, now based on the shoe. Third, the teacher asks students to freewrite for ten minutes more, creating a scene in which these two characters meet and talk. Freewrites can be shared at each stage (after hats, after shoes) or at the end of the entire activity. This is an exercise for early in the semester since it is active and triggers some fine, fantastic writing. Students enjoy sharing after each writing phase, and it is worth having a few students read their complete set of consecutive inventions so peers can hear how one character develops and then the other and, finally, how the characters come together and *live* in the scene.

Since I do not always have access to twenty well-worn shoes and twenty extraordinary hats (although thrift stores are useful for determined collectors), I bring in twenty to forty evocative objects, large and small. I wander around my house collecting silver teaspoons I have inherited from my grandmother, carved African masks, a Peruvian knitted hat, and so on. In class, we perform the same type of character building (using two objects to create two characters) and scene building (placing the owners of those objects in a scene) as we would for a Hats and Shoes in-class writing exercise.

Here is one prose sketch that started to develop as our in-class contemplation of a heavy white coffee mug and a carved Japanese fan:

> Trapper and Oriental Fan
> by Carolyn Kremers
>
> A fair-haired trapper with big, rough hands walked quietly out of a frigid night into the roadhouse bar at Mile 96 and ordered a mug-up of straight black coffee. Two acquaintances motioned him over to a table by the piano. He sat down, unzipping his black snow-machine suit and doffing his beaver hat. Later, when they got up to leave, he stayed. He kept looking at the brass lamp on top of the piano. He wanted someone to come over and turn it on, then spread music under the soft yellow glow and begin

> playing. But no one came. Finally, he rose to turn on the lamp himself. Then he noticed the fan.
>
> He picked it up off the worn walnut piano top, not dusty at all. He rubbed the stack of slick black enameled sticks between his thumb and forefinger, let the faded pink tassels dangle down. Gently, with big, rough hands that smelled now of soap and green shampoo, but belonged with deep raw cold, axe and chain-saw, case-hardened steel traps, and the smooth handle of a razor-sharp Buck knife, he let the fan fall open. A rush of pink blossoms with yellow pistils and stamens fluttered over the slender bamboo sticks, revealing snatches of gnarled brown trunk on an orange field. A silver border hugged the edge of the crinkled paper. Small circles and hearts had been carved out of each flat stick. And there were buds.
>
> Sideways, with one hand, he let the fan open and close, in rhythm, music, and flight. He put it down. Without thinking, he turned on the lamp and sat on the piano bench. Then he picked up the fan again, opened it firmly like a clipped ptarmigan wing, and gazed through the circles and hearts at the soft yellow glow; fanning, remembering cherries, and the brush of dark eyelashes, like butterflies.

Often during revisions of this type of writing, one of the original objects or characters can disappear as the invention turns into a piece of writing that the writer values. Object writings work because humans invest their possessions with so much meaning—the way an object is cared for and shaped by wear often provides insight into the life of the owner. Additionally, juxtaposing two objects that are not normally related to each other lets writers explore a writing type that David Kirby (1989) calls a marriage. For Kirby, marriages occur when the writer chooses "two objects or ideas that are normally unrelated and the poet's job is to unite them in a way that seems natural. . . . The trick is to treat two contrary themes or suppositions or whatchamacallits in such a way that the reader can never again think of one without automatically thinking of the other" (48). In the trapper and fan sketch, Carolyn united a woodsman with a delicately carved fan, a mysterious object we would not expect him to have in hand.

Anne Waldman (Bunge 1985) describes another object exercise: "Another thing I've done is ask students to bring in objects that are relevant to them and have some history that they can relate. Everyone else takes notes and can ask questions about the objects and many stories come up that transcend the personal . . ." (150–152). On those days when a teacher has not had the time or energy to request the objects required for Waldman's activity, she can ask students to provide objects on the spot. To do this, I ask students to delve into book bags or purses for *talismanic* objects: items they have carried around for a long time. These sometimes trivial looking coins, combs, tickets, or toys often have layers of imbedded value for the owners.

Writers can freewrite about their own or about someone else's object, and this in-class contemplation can be continued and worked on out of class, as in the following poem by an undergraduate writer:

Alaskan Clan Friendship Bracelet
by Kelly Sheets

Its silver age craves brightening.
Shaped like a "C", on either side of the opening
to fit your wrist through is the squarish,
bold head of an eagle on the left and
the angular, shrewd head of a raven on the right.
Their eyes lock on each other eternally
from across the small space.
Their bodies share the rest of the circlet,
tailfeathers meeting at the middle of the underside.
So thin around you can barely make out
the detailed etchings patiently enscribed
by the crafting hand of a Southeast native
whose life and whose father's life and
whose grandfather's life is worked into
the tiny symbols.

Wavy lines like river waves
crossed by canoes and flown over by the birds
harvesting the wealth of fish.
Zig-zag lines like their
feathered bodies or the mountains
they have ascended.
Straight lines like totem poles.
Small circles like pebbles
or moons of time past.
Cross-hatched lines portraying both the
Interrelationship between the birds
and the clans they represent
and
the friendship shared between
the Eagle and Raven tribes

Simple lines form intricate patterns
The beauty of this bracelet understates
the beauty of its origin.

Or, as in Anne Waldman's exercise, we could have heard Kelly's oral story about the Alaskan Clan Friendship Bracelet, passed it around the class, and anyone who was so moved could have also written about the object—an intricately carved silver bracelet—or about Kelly's story.

Pictures for Description

Postcard Invention I: Literal Description

I begin this exercise by gathering together a set of postcards that show a scene or a landscape rather than an individual or a static object like a painting. I shuffle together a deck of unusual scenes, more than the number of students in the class, and walk past each student, asking each to draw a card from the deck, which is presented with the pictures turned down. Each student draws a postcard he or she has never before seen and is asked not to show it to other students.

I ask the students to write a careful description of the scene in their postcards but *not* to add to it, *not* to tell a story. They should describe the postcard so carefully that another student could choose their card from a mixed stack of postcards after having read the writer's description. I suggest they use a painter's eye to explain proportions and relationships, to detail patterns and textures and shapes and sizes. Students usually take anywhere from ten to thirty minutes to describe their postcards. During this time, I write a postcard description too.

When the written descriptions are completed, I ask for one volunteer who would be willing to read his description aloud to the class. I also ask for another volunteer who will go to the front of the classroom and draw the scene that is being read aloud. We use this method to check the accuracy of the written description. The writer reads his entire description as we listen. Then he begins to read again, sentence by sentence, as the class tells the student at the chalkboard just what should be drawn. We have only one ground rule: we cannot embellish the written description. We must try to draw only those details that have been included in the written description. Inevitably, we begin to argue about perspective or missing details as we try to interpret the written document in a coherent manner. We talk about generalities, vague directions, imprecise or overly detailed description. A picture, often quite amusing, grows on the chalkboard.

When the drawing is done—and sometimes we listen to the original description several times before it is—the writer passes around the postcard he wrote about so that each class member can see how well the written description, the postcard, and our chalkboard drawing match. Generally, there are large areas of agreement and also difficult portions of the postcard which we may have misdrawn. Our final discussion details ways we, as readers of the written postcard description, could have been helped: through an organizational pattern, such as describing the postcard from top to bottom or right to left, through clearer, descriptive details, by providing the relative proportions of one object to another, and so on.

Finally, each author exchanges his own written description with another author and begins to draw the postcard scene. At this point, I insert my description into the pile so that every writer has a paper to work from. While this is occurring, I collect all the postcards and line them up together on an empty table. When each student is done with the drawing, she is free to come to the table and find the postcard she just drew from a written description. Then, she returns to her paper one last time to write a note to the original author, telling the author what details would have made the drawing more successful (see figure 14).

Postcard Invention II: Figurative Description

In this exercise, students are encouraged not only to use what they see in the postcard, but also to use the postcard to trigger their imaginative prose or poetry. Again, I gather up a set of postcards. I try, this time, to find the most evocative set that I can: old postcards, hand-tinted postcards, foreign and regional postcards, cards that have been sent and contain enigmatic messages, and so on. I bring *at least* twice as many cards as students, and I separate the cards into two stacks, circulating them through the class. Each student is asked to choose one card for use during in-class writing.

I give a few suggestions. After finding a postcard that "talks" to him, the writer should write for about ten minutes and describe the scene. It may be the scene he sees in the card, or it may be a scene *evoked* by the card, the message on the card, and so on. He should use all his senses and feel free to add to what he finds in the postcard. By describing colors, tastes, textures, smells, sounds, and so on, he should place the reader of his description right there—let the reader *feel* this scene.

When students finish writing, I encourage them to read their descriptions. After each reading, the postcard is passed around class so we can all see just how close or how far the description is from the actual card. If time is available to build on this exercise over several class periods, this piece of writing can be extended. In the next phase, students develop a character to fit the scene and continue to develop it. At this point, the postcard constraint is abandoned to allow for the growth of a sketch or a story (adapted from Bishop 1989b).

Writing about objects—fans or bracelets or hats or shoes—helps students develop tactile and visual precision. Writing about scenes found in prompts like postcards (paintings or photographs or a visit to a museum can be substituted) also helps a writer to develop visual accuracy and the ability to re-situate an experience-based character or autobiographical incident. The postcard can provide a new landscape—which in turn can help the writer achieve distance from the character or autobiographical incident. However, as most writing teachers know, students' visual sense is constantly stimulated, and they may need activities that help to develop other senses—sound, for instance.

Sound Activity

This in-class audio activity was developed by Terry Wike. Terry made a tape of environmental sounds (jungle birds and rain) and music (Gregorian chants) and "canned" noises (doors slamming) that he found in his own and library record collections.

To use this activity, a teacher compiles a similar tape and brings it to class to play for writers. Teachers may be able to dim the lights to allow students to concentrate. After each sound, the teacher stops the tape and lets the students write. After the entire session, students may share their sound impressions and see how differently each interpreted the audio prompts. At the end of the activity, students are asked to develop a piece of writing from any aspect of their notes.

This set of responses follows one writer, Scott Herzer, through the entire in-class exercise (sound by sound). It is also possible to compare several students' responses to one sound. Both ways of looking at this sound activity are enlightening.

> Notes to the Audio Exercise
> by Scott Herzer
>
> 1. From what is interpreted as a tinkling of silverware and someone humming.
>
> The scene: a man preparing a set of lightweight sculpting tools in a sunlit room. The air is cool, the room a little drafty but still comfortable. The walls, originally white, are splattered with paint and clay.
>
> The man: He's fifty-three, tall, thin, with a large Adam's apple. He wears dirty coveralls and black hightop Converse tennis shoes. No shirt. He has a lot of hair and a face that is wide and mobile.

2. Jungle sounds and "space music."

In the heart of the Amazon, buried in dense jungle brush amidst the cacophony of monkeys, pumas, and parrots an alien spacecraft lands. It is rectangular, painted like a Reeboks shoe box, sky blue with the Union Jack painted on it. Elvis Presley, smaller, at least thinner than we remember him, struts out of one of the red doors in the spacecraft. He stops about ten feet into the jungle. He carries an electric guitar with a portable amplifier strapped to his back. He looks to his left, then to his right, starts to hum "O When the Saints go Marching In." The jungle sounds stop. Reverence is in the air. Piranhas leave the nearby streams and rivers, walking on their tails to a jive beat. Elvis takes his sunglasses off, looks around, puts them in his shirt pocket and says, "Thank you very much."

3. Gregorian Chants.

Kneeling on a velvet-covered bench in St. Mark's Cathedral, Brett Davidson listens to Gregorian chants, sung by twelve white-robed men, echo off the rock walls towering above him. He leans forward, watching a little black, bald soprano with rimless glasses. The singer seems to be peering over his music right at Brett, but of course, he isn't. He's too busy trying to hit the high notes.

The sanctuary is cool, damp. It feels like you should hear the sound of dripping water.

Connect with me, thinks Brett. Someone connect with me.

Suddenly, it is time for communion. Brett rises from his knees, joins the line that moves toward the communion table. Shoes scuff and grate on the concrete floor. The line moves slowly. Brett looks steadily at the back of the collar of the shirt the man in front of him is wearing. The collar looks expensive; it has a vertical seam right down the middle of it.

Brett moves forward in the line, swayed by the music cascading around him. He anticipates the crumble of bread and the tangy bite of wine in his mouth, wonders about eating and drinking Jesus. He has never felt so completely alone.

4. Water sounds, oar locks (?), walking on a dock.

It's a black and white movie. Night time. Steam rising from a dingy harbor somewhere. Fishing boats. Stray cats. A rat runs up an anchor line. The sound of heavy, purposeful footsteps. A sense of pending doom. The footsteps stop.

Boats creak at their moorings. Someone stands in a shadow, lights a cigarette, flicks the match into the oily water. Clouds pass in front of a sliver of moon. A foghorn blows, far away.

The footsteps begin again. The camera zooms in on the shoes, men's shoes, expensive Italian oxfords, showing each step taken on the weather beaten dock. They stop once more, met by someone in deck shoes. A quick-paced conversation in a foreign tongue. Voices raise in anger. A shot rings out. It became a dark and stormy night.

Looking at Scott's audio responses, it is clear that he moved in and out of the sound experience, sometimes narrating what he heard—trying to figure out what the sounds were—and sometimes slipping right into the scene with a fully formed character who moved through the atmosphere. Teachers can ask students, intentionally, to write either or both types of responses.

Multimedia Cross-Cultural Activity

Carolyn Kremers (1989) has developed a culture-based activity that relies on multiple sensory stimuli. To share this activity with a class, Carolyn brought in slides of an Eskimo village where she once lived and taught, and showed them to class members, asking students to write after the display and her introductory talk. She also brought an audiotape of a village elder telling a story in Yupik, with a reproduction in English by an interpreter. Students wrote in response to that stimulus also. Next, Carolyn passed around photo books, Eskimo language ABC books, and other artifacts, and gave students a list of cultural stereotypes—what one culture thinks about another culture (the stereotypes she included flowed in both directions). She asked students to write dialogue from the point of view of a character from the presented (new) culture.

Finally, Carolyn asked students to write out-of-class pieces, generated by any portion of their extensive freewriting. It would be possible to add other sensory stimuli to such a cultural display by bringing artifacts (clothing, carvings, and so on) and food (moose stew, Eskimo ice cream) from that culture to further stimulate the class writers; each sharing should be followed by an opportunity for immediate freewriting. My own writing from this activity resulted in a prose poem that utilized many of Carolyn's prompts, so I will include it here to illustrate.

> Cross-Cultural Genres
> by Wendy Bishop
>
> Here is an Eskimo ABC book. Here is Tununak graveyard, filled with snow, blown in shapes of animals moving just beneath the cold skin. Picket fence pierces like spearheads, herds life toward an orthodox cross.
>
> Houses in a white on white landscape sit as square ships, antennae pointed toward outer space which doesn't exist in a land where "they deny planning." The universe exists, yet an elder's narrative seems, unfairly, a mouthful of glottal stops, remolding

my conception of story—plot, tension, dramatic moment—I drift and slip into another meaning system with Adam Fisher, nasal laugh and nasal laugh and nasal laugh.

We have no real patience for stories. We who "always talk about what's going to happen later" never stop to examine what is. She's young—just started having periods. Shimmys skinny slim hips, squeezes them into comfortable straight Wranglers, walks different but like her older brother, calls electricity to the ends of crackling black hair that she smooths in hanks.

Silence is built into the land, pale off-tan grass, gathered Sundays after the traveling priest moves out of thevillage on a snow machine. Machine sputters and shrives silence then engulfs the Bering Sea while Adam Fisher tells a story, nasal laugh and nasal laugh and nasal laugh.

Things with hair stand out: musk ox, seal, men, women. Perspective is plotted by color of bronze skin and enlivened faces against muted palate of weathered buildings, steam of sweat houses, undergreen of tundra, far grey of airplane shadow. "They are too indirect, too inexplicit. They don't make sense. They just leave without saying anything." In the Tununak graveyard, snow shifts shapes, graves fill, grass bows down, As Bs Cs tussle with sea wind. They leave, they leave without saying anything.

(Source: *The Midnight Lamp* 2 (Fall 1990); Kremers 1989, 8–9. Used with permission)

Another class member, Trecie Melnick, wrote a humorous piece that is also a reversal poem (as defined by David Kirby), an invention type that I will explore briefly in another section. Obviously, reversals are useful ways to look at cultural stereotypes. Here is Trecie's poem, which looks at Eskimo seal hunting from the seals' perspective.

Seal Party
by Trecie Melnick

One slides and winds,
a skater on the underside
of the ice sheet. He takes
air from one hole then another,
brown spotted nose pointing
to the next—a spike thrusts down
but misses the jet seal flank rolling
in victory.

Seals, an avalanche of fur,
slide belly up, twist down
several at a time drinking air
at the gaps, dark

glass eyes watching for the stiff-legged
men with lances.

At the head of the pack
the brown spotted one
sees boots on the other side
his cold eyes
see the trap and five
seals seize the spear,
the hands, the shoulders, hauling
the body in, till the shaking and jerking stills.

Seals with grey mottled
snouts are passed choice parts, liver, heart.
Younger ones get bearded
cheeks to pull on. Some get flank
shoulder, hand—everything
is shared—until the last boot
is tossed away.
(Source: Kremers 1989, 7–8. Used with permission)

Trecie, in analyzing her composing process called this a "Farside kind of idea . . . seals having a people party," but the idea was triggered by the slides shown by Carolyn, for they included several post-seal-hunt celebrations in the Eskimo village of Tununak where hunters shared seal meat with the community.

Guided Portraits

The Fifteen-Sentence Portrait

This exercise helps writers build a descriptive paragraph, a portrait of someone they know or knew and have strong feelings about. While writing a portrait about a person they are familiar with, under the influence of guided directions, writers may discover new aspects of this individual since they are following sentence-level prompts even as they develop their own content. Following these prompts keeps writers from directing their observations in familiar, perhaps predictable, ways. First, I ask class writers to:

1. Picture in your mind a person you have strong feelings for. The subject may not be someone you like, but should be someone you feel strongly about nonetheless. The person can be living or dead but should be someone you know or knew rather than a famous character. (Generally, it is more useful to write about people rather than animals although one student did write a successful portrait, once, of her dog.)

2. For a title, choose an emotion or a color that represents this person to you. You will not mention the individual's name in the writing.
3. For a first-line starter, choose one of the following:
   a. You stand there . . .
   b. No one is here . . .
   c. In this (memory, photograph, dream, etc.), you are . . .
   d. I think sometimes . . .
   e. The face is . . .
   f. We had been . . .

   Complete this sentence.
4. Following your first sentence, build a portrait of this individual, writing the sentences according to my directions:
   Sentence 2: Write a sentence with a color in it.
   Sentence 3: Write a sentence with a part of the body in it.
   Sentence 4: Write a sentence with a simile (a comparison using *like* or *as*).
   Sentence 5: Write a sentence of over 25 words.
   Sentence 6: Write a sentence under 8 words.
   Sentence 7: Write a sentence with a piece of clothing in it.
   Sentence 8: Write a sentence with a wish in it.
   Sentence 9: Write a sentence with an animal in it.
   Sentence 10: Write a sentence in which three or more words alliterate; that is, they begin with the same initial consonant: she has been *l*eft, *l*ately, with *l*ess and *l*ess time to think . . . .
   Sentence 11: Write a sentence with two commas.
   Sentence 12: Write a sentence with a smell and a color in it.
   Sentence 13: Write a sentence with a simile (a comparison using *like* or *as*).
   Sentence 14: Write a sentence that could carry an exclamation point (but do not use the exclamation point).
   Sentence 15: Write a sentence to end this portrait that uses the word or words you chose for a title.
5. Now, read this freewrite to yourself. Underline sentences in which you discovered new things about this individual or your feelings and attitudes toward him or her.
6. Volunteers may read portraits aloud and discover the variation possible within the guided sentence format.
7. Use this freewrite as a starting point for a poem or prose portrait

or simply revise what you have. Do anything you need to make this a piece of writing that you like. Choose a new title, use the person's real name, and so on.

Teachers can try one of several follow-up activities or variations for this exercise. They can use these prompts but ask students to write a self-portrait or a portrait of a famous person. They can use these prompts but alter the directions so the activity teaches punctuation or technique more obviously. They can turn this into a full-class round-robin, prose writing activity by having each writer start a paragraph using a narrative (storytelling) prompt line such as: "Listen Jim . . ." or "During those years, Sheila . . ." Or, first lines from famous novels or stories can be used. Each student, obeying the sentence directions given by the teacher, writes a line and then passes the paper clockwise, adding to the story, line by line. The round-robin challenges writers' abilities to maintain a story line and provides a good warm-up for the Fifteen Sentence Portrait. In another variation, teachers ask all writers to begin with the same prompt line to see the variations that are possible when students add personal context to a predictable beginning, under the constraints of similar format directions (see chapter 6 for more ideas on collaborative invention). Portions from two student drafts for a fifteen-sentence portrait follow:

Student 1: Prose poem
Peach Brandy

Peaches bloom hot in the hill country. The face is round but with a square jaw, she always worried about her jaw being too square. Fat toes dangled in a cool cement pool water green. She talked, still does, like a beach bird running, talking, running.

Student 2: Poem
Christmas: Portrait of a Couple

He repacks the nativity displayed on the table,
rolls the Three Wise Men into a sheet
of newsprint and imagines her anger
at his late decision. Along the stair's railing,
he pauses at each scenic cannister—
can he live with these? Nelsons, he thinks, driven
people. . . .

Writing fifteen-sentence portraits, student writers find new ways to look at individuals for whom they feel powerful emotions. Prompts allow students to experiment with content *and* structure while writing pieces they care about (adapted from Bishop 1990b). Several other writing teachers suggest using in-class description exercises, particularly metaphorical description. I use the activities that follow since they encourage both poetry and prose writers to explore metaphor.

Metaphorical Description

Theorists Lakoff and Johnson (1980) claim that metaphor deeply affects how we perceive our world and that "new metaphors have the power to create a new reality" (145). Alberta Turner's text, *To Make a Poem* (1982), includes metaphorical exercises, and Peter Elbow, in several of his books, explores metaphor in ways that push writers to explore very unusual connections about a character the writer is imagining (see Elbow 1981, chapter 9, and 1986a). Samples of Elbow's prompts include the following: "Imagine _____ as an animal. What animal? In this form, _____ falls in love with a different animal. What animal? What do they have for children?" Other examples include "Think of _____ as an ecological system: tell as many things as you can that go into _____ . What is his input? What, in every sense of the word, does _____ eat?" (Elbow 1986a, 36–37). I read these prompts aloud in class (since there are nineteen of them, teachers may want to pick and choose from, and adapt, the prompts). I ask students to write in response to each prompt and then, after we write, to share some of these responses aloud. Each writer is asked to develop these metaphorical character sketches into more developed pieces of prose or poetry for a future workshop.

Because I am usually the one to read the prompts, I tried this exercise on my own, typing fast at the word processor to limit my self-censoring. I found they also worked well in an out-of-class situation. Here is a draft of my prose-poem sequence:

GILLIAN ALONE

"I am not depressed by my depression
if you know what I mean."

—Rebecca West

Gillian at Home

Gillian at the moment she really understands. The reclining chair where he rests, mountain of male, white T-shirt stretched thin, like a screen door across a shaded front porch. Children, playing outside, breed static, entering into and underlining the argument.

Gillian's TV

I look gray, factual, unwise. But I watch near their dinner table; they gnaw at manners, hold pungent arguments, smile like meatloaf and canned peas, casseroles with yellow cheese. When the children finish and go outside, the parents shift size, equalize. His bulk in commerce with her fury, they're paired like shadow and shadow-maker, like salt and pepper shaker. Distinct, indispensable, is the tension they save for each other.

Gillian's Changes

Gillian as a fragrant, appalling, husky dairy cow, high bony back shanks, folds of skin falling groundward. Her once lovely pelt sports black and white Holstein spots, splotched Rorschachs of her times.

Gillian as a darkened room in which the ungirdled flesh of women feels comfortable.

She's a patio at night with water making worried noises.

She's the stars clicking outward, under remote control.

Her galaxy turns audibly.

Into and Out of Gillian

Soap and German goblets and Japanese brocades, self-help books and trashy scenic paintings—heavy with green heavy with yellow—and sweetly sour red wine on Sunday, late, and seersucker bathing suits and empty lipstick tubes, go into Gillian.

Wishes and cheese casseroles, some 1950s acceptable behavior for unknown neighbors, some late night terror—blankets that smell pink and leaden at the same time—and a way of reading any print—signs, contracts, cereal boxes, menus, church bulletins, inoculation and report cards, billboards, and TV evangelists' phone numbers repeated twice—and a way of sitting very very still, disallowing sharp hand movements, before the opinions of doctors, come out of Gillian.

Post Gillian

She sees the stars as street lamps. She sees the earth's bulk as a householder's joke. She stretches up on tiptoes to see her children, her children's children, her children's children's children. She surprises.

Portrait of Gillian

There is no picture. There is no picture. The set is blank. The moment is edited by memory, rigid, unyielding, rigid, unyielding, and unwise.

Since metaphor allows writers to systematically view one thing in terms of another, often different but resonant, thing (or concept), teachers can build their own metaphorical description prompts by borrowing from Turner or Elbow or the following activity:

Directions: Close your eyes and visualize a person you know about whom you have strong feelings. Open your eyes and write the name of or a code name for that person on the top of a sheet of paper. Then quickly write responses to the following prompts:

1. Think of this person as a landscape. What landscape would he or she be?
2. Describe this person as a kind of fruit, a metal, a wood, a time of day, a time period in history, a piece of clothing, etc. (person reading prompts can add to or change the order of any of the prompts—classes like to add to the prompt list after the writing activity).
3. Think of this person in his/her favorite location. Describe it. Have him/her speak? Bring someone else into the scene and let them talk together.
4. What would this person like to say but never says? What does this person dream about? Tell some lies for this person.

For teachers who want to add analysis and readings to metaphorical invention, an innovative discussion of metaphor and writing can be found in Robert Scholes, Nancy R. Comley, and Gregory L. Ulmer's *Textbook: An Introduction to Literary Language* (1985).

Autobiography—Past, Present, Future

Each of the description exercises I have already discussed can be used for self-description. Students can use the prompts to see themselves in new ways. Additionally, one simple exercise, adapted from an activity designed by Natalie Kusz, can help writers look at their own lives (or characters' lives) over time. Natalie's exercise originally asked writers to respond to prompts that progressed specifically through time: "When I was born . . . , when I was six, when I was sixteen, but now I am (multiple age)," ending with "when I'm in charge [of the world]." I found the specific ages in this sequence could constrain my student writers, so I simplified the prompts, after explaining the activity by using sample ages (6, 16, 36, 86). I suggested that, as I prompted them, they would want to choose time periods that were important (going to kindergarten, graduating from high school, having a first child—we list samples like these on the chalkboard) and use their own time frame, including ages in the future, that they thought would matter to them (65/retirement, 85/wisdom, etc.).

The primary focus of this exercise remained to move the self (as a character) *through* time. The work of these three undergraduate students developed in fairly different directions.

Miller
by Pam Miller

When I was first born, my parents brought me home in a bright red Ford convertible. Their apartment was in the upstairs of a carriage house which had been built by my great-grandmother Duffy. At that time her estate was separated from downtown Cleveland by miles of farms and well-kept residential neighborhoods. The houses had been lost from the family's holdings along with everything else when her will was torn up. But the building had special meaning for my father; it was still family.

For my mother, once I arrived the modest apartment was merely inadequately heated and cramped. The stucco and brick-house, crowded between apartment buildings, faced a narrow street paved with wooden bricks. A wooden street! From the time my father first pointed it out during one of his innumerable Miller family history tours of the city, I always found it fascinating. During junior high I roller skated over its uneven surface. My friend Roberta lived around the corner on Hessler Street where I went to my first street fair during my freshman year of college.

By two, we moved to Buttternut Lane in Warrensville Heights. While my mother breast fed my brother Paul and dressed my father's mother Ahben, I stuck a barrette in the electrical outlet under the stairs, and still remember the surprise of having the scalloped edges of the blue bow melt around the metal clasp. My father fondly recalls tucking me into bed at that house and my insistence on reading the book about mammals. He quizzed me about which was an opposum, a cougar, a marten. Though I don't remember those early lessons, he believes it was the beginning of my interest in biology.

By the time I hit six, I lived in a three story house on Derbyshire Road in Cleveland Heights, and my youngest brother Peter was already one. My father had lived across the street in a white house smaller than ours during his elementary school years, and partly for his sentimental memories had chosen our new house.

But only one year since we had moved, my father no longer lived with us. I have a hazy memory of his first moving from my mother's room to the back bedroom. I've been told that Paul helped my father load up the convertible, three different times in all, but I likely disappeared to my room, closed the door, and tried to act as though this was just what happened to everyone. I decorated and rearranged my seven foot long, three story dollhouse constructed of wallpapered cardboard boxes. I talked with my 6-inch tall dolls about the new furniture I would make them, though I didn't play with the dolls as much as I moved things around the house. I never wanted a Barbie doll like my friend Susan had; her sexy shape was too embarrassing and unreal. I read voraciously in the evenings while my mother watched old movies with Paul, and often finished three "Snip, Snap, and Snur" books during lunchtime. We went to my father's apartment on the west side of town once. It felt strange, even though he tried to make us comfortable by having games there for us to play. I preferred to read.

At 16, I fit in for the first time in my life, and had my first love, in the Wind River mountains of Wyoming during a five week summer mountaineering course. Waiting for our break to bake nestled in the coals, watching the constellations, I lay with "Q" as he sang ". . . If I were a miller, at a mill wheel grinding, would you still love me? . . ." I was still skinny, wore two long braids, and was terribly self-conscious. Yet as I learned the names of the peaks and the alpine flowers, to use an ice-axe and glissade through ass-deep snow in July, I found my own voice. Many years afterward, my brothers agreed that it was the best thing that ever happened to me, and to them, since I stopped harassing them with the shrill voice of a mother they didn't need. As one of only two women in the group of ten, I found myself in a minority, a pattern often repeated since then.

For most of high school I immersed myself in playing flute: practicing over an hour a day in my room so that I could maintain my second chair in the orchestra; dreading marching band practice in the early fall mornings (I wanted to put peace symbols in the tubas for parades). While I still often found myself curled up in my big white easy chair on Saturday nights, reading the diaries of Anais Nin, I didn't spend as much time reading. Roberta called "Hey Miller" down the school hallways to include me in things. I drank hot cocoa while my friends drank coffee and smoked cigarettes after concerts. I went with Roberta on a bus to a protest rally in Washington D.C., one of the massive ones against the war. Everytime I saw a TV camera I backed away, sure that my father would see me in the evening news.

Right now, I'm typing in the small log cabin in the woods where I live alone. The rest of my family lives far away and does not understand why I choose this northern life. Peter struggles in Hollywood editing other people's lousy movies and realizing that he'd rather be a writer. The others are still in Cleveland where I could never live again having known the wildness of the west. My mother lives alone, only four blocks from my brother Paul who has two children. A whole new family fills my father's expansive brick house.

Everybody thinks I will never get married. Both of my brothers married when they were below the average national age. My father has been married four times. But my mother never remarried, though she was wilder when I was still at home than I realized then. Perhaps I am overly skeptical of marriage because all I have really known was divorce.

When I'm 36, perhaps I will be married. But somehow I can't envision myself at 76 looking over to my husband in a rocking chair. Instead I hear my good friend Sally, or my niece Kristen cooking dinner in the kitchen.

When I'm in charge, fathers will cook more than french toast and no one will eat peanut butter sandwiches for lunch after the age of ten. Third graders will love apples more than McDonalds. Unborn children will meet snow leopards and condors won't live in cages. My family will all live in the same part of the world, but in the places we all want to be. Biologists will spend all year walking the rivers, tundra, and hills and still have their reports and papers get written. Congressmen won't be bought and sold like drugs, and the people who actually do the work will make the decisions. And Fairbanks would have 12 hours of daylight on the winter solstice.

When I Was Black

by Jo'al Hill

When I was black

the clothing I wore was
clean, the language I
spoke was acceptable
the color of my eyes
were pretty, the naps in
my hair were unique,
the stutter in my voice
was natural, the
charcoal color of
my skin was a symbol
of pride.

Cornbread was good
Chitterlings were
tasty
Ham hocks were
deepfried
Southern Fried was
not KFC or Churches
Chickens, but it
was Mother's.
Pig ears were
considered desert.

I thought of black things,
like stealing or cheating
or lying, or beatings
and even killing.

Now I'm okay;

From Me
by Lance Nutter

When I was a kid;

Nixon was a good president,
there were no personal computers, or microwave ovens,
man had not quite reached the moon,
clerks still rang in the price through digital dexterity.

When my mother was a kid;

The second Roosevelt had just become president,
there were no t.v.'s, or the 'Atomic age',
men hadn't gotten into space yet,
clothes were washed by a wringer washer.

When my grandmother was a kid;

The first Roosevelt was president,
there were no radios, no worldwar one,
man was flying on very shaky wings,
going forty miles to visit was an all day trip.

When my greatgrandmother was a kid;

Themptander was Prime Minister of Sweden,
there were no telephones, no moving pictures,
men had only looked to the sky and stars; dreaming,
books were read by candlelight.

Onehundred and two years, and we all live.
This one's for you, greatgrandma.

As these samples show, family stories are powerful writing prompts in and of themselves. Many successful writing assignments can be developed around family artifacts (letters or antiques, for instance) and stories. Writer-teacher Katharine Haake asks students to write a family story. The stories themselves are worth exploring, but she also asks class members to exchange stories andwrite in response to another writer's story. These second-stage writings, she finds, are very promising and unexpected.

To begin a writing class, I sometimes ask students to tell a story about their name on the back of an eight-inch-by-five-inch card:

> My given name sounds French, but there is no French blood in my family. My parents' names happen to be Pierre and Sherrie, so they decided to give their children French names. My younger sister's name is Nicole Suzanne and I am Michelle Rene.
>
> My father named me Sarah when I was born—after an old girl friend, I understand. He was like that, with women. Mom always called me Sally—in retaliation, just as my little sister was called

> Buzzy instead of her birth name, Marjorie. There must have been a Marge in Dad's background, too.

Class members exchange these cards to learn about the other writer and how he or she received a name, and then the class members introduce each other to the class.

Family stories evoke powerful feelings and wonderful detail. We could all respond to these two naming stories or to Pam Miller's personal essay, "Miller." Most of us would find some connection—writing about what it means to grow up as a female, what it means to grow up as a child of divorced parents, or what it means to study one's own relationships in light of one's parents' relationship—topics worth any writer's time.

Letter Forms

Equally, letter poems present a powerful writing prompt. Lance's poem, above, took the form of a letter from him to his 102-year-old great-grandmother. Here is a letter poem that was turned in by a student before I started to use formal exercises in letter writing in a creative writing class:

> Post Script
> by Mark Winford
>
> Dear Sam:
>
> There are some things
> you need to know
> and get used to
> there are also a few things
> you need to do.
> Scratch her back when
> she wants you to—
> she likes that.
> Fix her oatmeal lumpy,
> her toast light,
> keep the eggs a bit
> runny—but not to runny,
> if they hold form their just
> right. She likes to listen
> to the yodel and twang of country music—
> the same Dwight Yoakam record
> all day—over and over,
> it seems like sonic
> torture at first
> but you get used to it.

When you sleep with her
pull the covers up tight
to her chin. Then roll over
away from her, she kicks
like a mule once she falls asleep.
When she cries
just leave her alone,
anything else just makes it worse.
Late at night when she
whispers those catchy
three words in your ear
ask her just what she means
and she has a spot on her
left breast and when you touch it—
you probably know about that already.

Sincerely,

Jack

In creating this persona of Jack, writing to an ex-friend Sam about an ex-wife or girlfriend, Mark used the letter form to build a full and vivid story about a love affair, reversing our usual expectations about who would be writing to whom and why.

Peg Peoples developed a letter exercise that uses the following prompts which a teacher can read to students to help them explore the letter forms (for more ideas on letter assignments, see Kirby):

1. Choose a person you know fairly well, someone you've shared several experiences with or have known for a few years and would like to write a letter to.
2. Address this person on paper as you would in a letter: "Dear Tessie," "Hey George—" or "My Dear Friend . . ." Use a fictive name if it would help you feel more comfortable.
3. Write for three or four minutes on the following prompts:
   a. Describe today's weather to this person.
   b. Describe to this person where you imagine he/she is.
   c. Remind this person of an event or experience that you shared.
   d. Describe your relationship in a metaphor—do not explain the metaphor to the person.
   e. Ask the person two questions.
   f. Describe some aspect of your living situation to this person that you wish they could see.
   g. Say something to this person you wanted to say to him or her the last time you were together but didn't have the courage to, or were too nervous, shy, or afraid to say.

h. Remind this person of the best advice he or she has given you—quote them.
i. Tell this person something that really didn't happen to you but that you're going to say happened to you anyway.
j. Tell this person how you have physically changed since he or she last saw you.
k. Tell this person you have to go but that you'll finish this letter when you get home because you have to tell them about _____ . Fill in the blank.

4. Take a minute and jot down the strongest feelings you have about this person.
5. Use this creating material to write a letter poem, letter essay, or letter short-short fiction. You may break out of the letter form if you feel you need to.

Here are three beginnings of early, workshop drafts, created during this letter writing activity:

> The Sparrow Hawk Watercolor
>
> The last time I wrote you it was
> minus forty-six degrees with no birds flying,
> Old yeller's tires were square
> and people were tossing cupfuls
> of hissing hot coffee up into the air
> to see them not come down.
> This week the thermometer soared to
> negative twenty and the trees are so frosted and still
> that I savor their skeletons every morning,
> the ice fog burned up,
> my tires again round.

> Letter to K from Alaska
>
> Dear K:
>
> Today was a new start. Fog flying
> south and the degrees climbing toward zero,
> Mountains out in going light
> on the drive home: Heart's ease, cold, bright.
>
> Say you're sitting at a table. The beer
> has been set down or is on its way.
> Where I would be sitting is probably full.
> You push up your glasses and grin, it's slow.

Dear George

It is a warm day here in Fairbanks, Alaska. Despite all the hype that's been in the media lately, Alaska isn't a bad place to live.

I imagine you are out there somewhere working as an electrical engineer. I remember that was what you told me you were studying at Wisconsin, but I saw you at an Anti-Apartheid demonstration on campus once, and somehow I can't picture you as a money hungry yuppie. I still wonder why you chose to study engineering.

Reversals

In *Writing Poems* (1989), David Kirby describes reversals as those "in which a stereotype or received truth is simply turned on its head" (47). I have found that students particularly enjoy such turnings and perform them naturally as in the "Confessions of a Male Muse" found in chapter 4 and "Seal Hunt" in this chapter. Those poems were written in classes where reversals were not being taught as a form. Here are two other reversals, developed by using Kirby's text and discussion for illustration, and then by beginning the pieces in class (each student brainstormed a list of absurd connections and shared those connections with her writing group).

Doin' Da Funky Chicken
by John Pelz

Late at night
when the farmer's bedside lamp
finally goes out,
his chickens release themselves
and gather in the yard
under the full moon.

Three
then four
then five
strut to one side.
One pulls a trumpet
from under his wing,
fingers the valves.
One pulls out a sax—
another a harmonica.
One rolls a piano
into view
as the other sets up
the skins.

Cacophony,
dizzying glissandos

they warm up.
The cock on trumpet
claws the dust four times,
leads the others in.

They play "Lullaby of Birdland"—
they're doin' da funky chicken.
Sax solo starts
builds
swirls
drives the others
into a fowl ecstasy.

The farmer's bedside lamp
flicks on.
He sticks his head out the window,
listens.
Hears nothing.
Scratches his head
as the chickens quietly file
back into their coops.

Another Silly Love Poem

by Lance Nutter

Holding the flowers stem up,
I forcefully cram them down the
sinks garbage grinding unit.
I flip the switch and the room
is instantly filled with a cupboard
shaking incessant roaring;
which slowly oscillates toward
a high pitched squeal
as the blades begin moving freely.
Still feeling less than vindicated,
I leave the grinder running,
slowly walk out of the kitchen,
and snap off the light.
After all, it is her house. . . .

An entirely different type of reversal was brought to my attention by Dave Stark. In his classes, he asks students to "rewrite" a famous poem but to reverse the meanings of words. That is, *hot* becomes *cold* and *mothers* become *daughters* and *night* becomes *day* and *moons* become *suns*. Word-for-word reversals result in surreal, exotic collaborative parodies involving antonym swapping, as in my own foolish sample, included for illustration with apologies to William Stafford.

[*original*]
Traveling Through the Dark
by William Stafford

Traveling through the dark I found a deer
dead on the edge of the Wilson River road.
It is usually best to roll them into the canyon:
that road is narrow; to swerve might make more dead.

[*reversal*]
Returning Through the Light

Returning through the light I found a fish
alive in the center of the Wilson Canyon bridge.
It is not good to toss them into the river:
that bridge is narrow; to resist might make more live.

Of course the reversal soon breaks down, but reversal wordplay helps writers discover the effect of oxymorons and intentionally weird juxtaposition.

The inventions and variations that I have presented here prove that teachers did not discover invention activities—writers did. My students wrote letter poems, object sketches, and sound pieces, shaped reversals, and shared "challenges" long before I specifically taught such activities through in-class freewriting and sharing. However, students enjoy performing teacher-organized freewriting, and they learn a great deal from seeing how others in class respond to similar prompts or constraints. Even the student who is resistant to exploring and sharing spontaneous writing seems to learn something about writing and writers through such exercises. Here is the view from the other side—a poem about writing poetry in class by a student who had mixed feelings about sharing anything in a rough draft state. Her peers chose the poem for inclusion in our class anthology, partly, I believe, because it was the first piece this writer composed that did not rely on heavy, predictable rhyme. In the poem she addresses real frustrations and gains insight about herself as a class writer.

In Class Writing
by Tamara Holm

A film screen hangs
above a word infested chalkboard.

Four walls trap the air (in or out?)
Embeded in the asbestos roof
glow and artificial lights.

Before me sits my muse
judging pupils
forced inspirations.

There I sit,
in a chair
a cat could not find cozy.

Naked pages
confront me.
I stare.
They stare back.

I draw my weapon
and attack
with ink poisoned tip.

Blank empty eyes
fill with emotion

I giggle
with satisfaction.

I win.

Then again,
I always win.

And Tamara's view will need to be balanced with Regina's view: "I especially liked the in-class writing assignments such as the postcards, and writing a character with the hat and shoes. I developed the characters in 'Partings' from the hat and shoes we worked with. They have undergone some major changes, but the assignment helped me to get started."

Teachers will want to design, modify, evaluate, integrate, and adapt invention techniques to their class design and to their students' needs. Inventions are waiting to be discovered. There are mundane objects to explore (paper clips and Scotch tape). There are imaginary trips to take (the teacher can talk students halfway into a dramatic scene and ask them to complete the scene in writing). There are unsaid things (withheld effects that can include talking about families without mentioning family members; describing a color without using colors). And there are exercises to be built around exploring the senses, around impersonations and personas, around change (seasons, series, permutations). Inventions are self-assignments waiting to be completed.

Literal Description. Student 1.

Nice summer day on the beach. There's a couple people sitting on chairs under a grass shade. Next to them is a lady laying on a green air mattress wearing a blue swim-suit. To the right away from the crowd is lady standing with striped bikini on and straw hat, (like a small sombrero) taking a picture of the man parachuting on the crowd of people standing in a distance to her left. The crowd of people are standing watching the parachutes coming down. The water on the other side of the crowd is royal blue with a few people in it. To the left of the crowd is a small island or a large rock w/some grass on it toward the left. Across the bay looks like a city with rolling hills in the background. The sky is blue with light clouds and the parachutes rising a white parachute w/a little red on the backside.

Student 2 draws a picture from Student 1's description:

Student 2 comments: It would have helped to know what was in the center of the card and where the seated couple were on the card, since I started with them. I never knew where they were.

Fig. 14. Sample literal description for postcard invention. (Source: Bishop, Wendy. 1989b. "Using Postcards for Invention." *Exercise Exchange* 35 (5): 29. Used with permission.)

6 Collaborative Composing and Imitations

> What is much more difficult is to expand one's capabilities, to push the limits, to begin to discover how form can be molded to reflect a personal worldview. Such expansion of vision often requires that a student experiment and, invariably, produce awkward work on the way to a broader understanding and polishing of forms.
>
> —Eve Shelnutt, from *Creative Writing in America,* edited by Joseph Moxley, 1989

> Then, after Christmas break, Kesey introduced a new plan of attack. "Forget this going home and writing," he told the class. "You get too convoluted. We're going to learn how to write under pressure, just like a newspaper with a deadline." From now on, they would write in class together and would finish a chapter during each three-hour session. The students would each be assigned a chapter to edit. They would outline their chapter into fourteen separate beats of action. At the beginning of each class session, the fourteen scenes would be written down on pieces of paper, tossed in a hat and passed around the table. Everyone, including Kesey, would draw a slip at random, and when he said, "Go," they would begin writing. At the end of an hour—presto!—they would have a completed chapter.
>
> —David Weddle, *Rolling Stone,* October 8, 1989

Students often turn in-class invention exercises into pieces of personal writing that they revise and retain. But this is not the only goal of invention activities. There is a place for language experiments in the creative writing workshop, occasions when the owner of the final product is not clear (collaborative composing) or where the experiment does not necessarily lead to a form or a revision or even a final product. The exercise on ways to describe blue eyes (chapter 3) is a sample of the latter. The former, collaborative composing, can occur at many

Portions of this chapter appeared in somewhat different form in Bishop, Wendy. 1990f. "Poetry Parodies: Explorations and Imitations." *Teaching English in the Two-Year College* 17: 40–44; Herzer, Scott, and Jill Robinson. 1989. "Your Ideas Are Unique." *Exercise Exchange* 35 (5): 43–45. Used with permission.

points in the creative writing workshop or may even become the goal of an advanced workshop like the one conducted by Ken Kesey; members of that experimental workshop recently published a collaborative novel, *Caverns* (see Weddle 1989; McMillen 1990).

For instance, on the first day of a poetry class, I have students participate in the writing of a group poem while I am taking roll. I invent and write down a rhythmic first line or write down another poet's line that is chiming in my head. The writer next to me is asked to add a second line and then fold back my line so only his line remains visible. The next writer adds a line, folds back a line, and so on. Eventually, everyone contributes a line to the class poem, without seeing more than one earlier line, and I read the completed poem aloud. Sometimes I write the piece on the chalkboard, and we collaborate on a title before discussing the coherence that is there (did the next writer link ideas by either sound or sense) and what we feel is missing. We have written a poem together, and this event introduces us to our semester's work.

To write collaborative prose, I use an activity developed by Ken Waldman. After providing a list of twenty or thirty opening lines (invented or taken from published fiction), I ask each class writer to choose a different opening line. The writer writes that line at the top of a blank sheet of paper and starts to develop a narrative, writing for two or three minutes. At that point, I ask each writer to stop and hand her sheet to the student at her left, to read the story so far, and to keep writing; the papers are passed on every three to five minutes (it is possible to play "mood music" while orchestrating such an exercise). At the end of the twenty or thirty minutes, I ask the writer who is currently in possession of each story to "end" his story, to try to give it a sense of closure. When the exercise is finished, we read aloud as many of these as we can. They offer entertainment but also provide a reason to talk about plot, melodrama, and closure (see Smelcer 1989 for a round-robin writing exercise that uses opening and closing lines of a well-known writer's prose). Although most of us will not write complete collaborative novels, we might consider starting a semester of fiction writing by composing stories in groups.

Two other activities are particularly useful for allowing students to look together at topic generation and a writer's individuality. Normally, I try to reduce competition in class, but I have noticed students like to give each other assignments or *challenges* and share the results of challenge writing. Teachers can suggest that students participate in challenge writing in groups or as a full class. Here are poems written by two undergraduate creative writing students, John and Rob, when they went together to the writing center to work with tutor Ken Waldman. For an ever-to-remain-secret reason, the topic these three writers picked to compete over when writing a challenge poem was fast-food restaurants. Ken's poem has not survived, but John's and Paul's were included by popular class demand in our class anthology. Class members enjoyed seeing how different these two *reversal* challenge poems were.

McDonald's Aliens
by John Pelz

Their heads
  pock-marked sesame buns.
Their faces
  sliced ribbons of tomatoes.
Their hair
  outgrowths of lettuce.
Their eyes
  snot-green pickles.
Their torsos
  limp hamburger patties.
Their arms
  tentacles of onion.
Their blood
  steams of grease.
Their trunks
  soggy mates of the heads.

Over sixty billion aliens
are taking over.
Just watch.
You'll see.

The Secret of Meat
by Rob Roys

Crackling fat,
Grease sizzling.
Senses devour
The screaming
Cow.

Standing; head
Pierces the blue
Haze ceiling.
Walking:
Ears, nostrils
Pulling.

Red marble
Scorched brown.

Kernals of grease
Dancing in a black
Pan.

A cow dressed up.
Bread overcoat, mustard
Underwear stained
By ketchup. Lettuce
T-shirt, mayonnaise
Socks, pickled
Trousers.

Grabbing the over
Coat.
Cow recoiling
From the gaping
Maw.

I bite.
Green grass,
Morning
Dew.
A thousand
Glowing sunrises,
Sunsets.
I eat.

I have also discovered that class writers will write responses to a classmate's work they admire (or dislike) and sometimes dedicate particular pieces of writing to each other.

Finally, in terms of group writing, the teacher needs to be aware that many writers are extremely possessive about their work. They worry that other writers will steal their ideas, lines, plots. In a way, English teachers have contributed to this idea of spontaneous, pure, and original generation through their lectures on great writers, creative geniuses, and seemingly inviolate genre distinctions, and even through their talks on research paper plagiarism. Students need to learn how few absolutely original new ideas there are in the world and how productive borrowing and imitation can be; they need to understand that:

> Writers are always borrowing. . . . This is a basic element of textuality. Texts are produced through a combination of the writer's experiences as a human being and the writer's knowledge of earlier texts. Sometimes, however, the intertextual relationship is very much in the foreground: this is true in translation, interpretation, adaptation, and parody. (Scholes, Comley, and Ulmer 1988, 129)

Of course, and in addition, students do need to learn to understand what plagiarism is and how writers can work to know and acknowledge their own influences. It is a compliment to imitate another writer's work, but writers are wise to track their own learning and borrowing in a journal or in notes to their work. I think in-class group writing practice is particularly useful for bringing up these issues, allowing students to explore their own feelings about originality and borrowing.

This exploration can also be orchestrated by the teacher. In an effort to show the many directions a piece of writing can take, even when generated by the same image, Scott Herzer and Jill Robinson (1989) have devised an exercise that asks students to compose poems or prose pieces from the same basic images in order to compare the results. Herzer and Robinson divide a writing class into groups of three or four. Each member of the group is given a 3″ X 5″ notecard and asked to write down four "original" images. Here are the images contributed by one student:

1. I shake hands with a handless man
2. A filmstrip on cell division
3. green, glowing sheets of ice
4. the child cheers the snow shoveler with sharp barks

Next, group members read their images to each other, and then the group lists the best image from each member on another 3″ X 5″ card. Here are the images compiled from one group (one image per group member):

Group A

1. Cassette tape of Albert King . . . "I been lookin' you over, but I see that your bread ain't done."
2. The blood had hardened like pavement.
3. The lawn sprawled out like a dog.
4. A filmstrip on cell division.

After compiling images, groups exchange cards of *best* images with each other (Group A with Group C, Group D with Group B, etc.). Students in each group choose the single most interesting image from the card they have received and freewrite about that image for ten minutes; in essence, the group accepts the challenge of writing from the same image. Last, each student takes the freewrite home and writes a piece, in any genre, that in some manner retains the reference to the image used in the freewrite.

When these pieces are compared during the next workshop, students see vastly different pieces of writing develop from the same image prompt. Here are some samples of writing developed through this activity:

Original Image of "a shaved pink poodle"

Student 1

[center portion of short prose passage]

. . . I . . . am hungry enough to eat a hot dog—my first in fifteen years. We pry four from the rock-hard package cached outside on a spruce branch, tuck them into boiling macaroni water. When they swell like shaved pink poodles, I chase them around and around, dicing up buttons that wiggle in cheese sauce. Sitting on milk crates, we savor the peppery, nitrate dogs.

Student 2

[start of a short story]

We had to shave one of the poodles. Mom held her and I got out the razor and clippers; Daffel whined and shook all through her bones. I moved the razor up and down her back, the grey curls sliding over Mom's hands closed around Daffel's legs. It reminded me of shearing time—the piled wool floating off the sheep. But Daffel lay there more frightened and bewildered than any sheep.

Student 3

[central section of a short story]

A thick column of army ants swarmed across the road. The Kenworth ground two swaths through the column. Ron waved at the driver. The driver, in mirrored sunglasses, and wearing a leather bombardier's hat waved back. A toy stuffed poodle dangled from the side-view mirror. The road dust kicked up by the big Kenworth caught in Ron's throat.

Original Image of "the lawn sprawled out like a dog"

Student 1

[end of poem]

With concurrent greenness,
green of a new body, body fat, wiry,
he is ready, like a dog sprawled out
on a lawn, but alive, partly quivering,
waiting for anything,
for how anything always happens.

Student 2
[beginning of poem]

The lawn sprawled out like a dog.
A lazy dog in the midday sun.
A dead dog.
Bones gray and splitting into fibers.

Imitation as Guided Invention

Because imitation has been used extensively in creative writing workshops, I focus on in-class free invention in my classes. At the same time, I do not ignore the great deal of learning that can take place when a novice writer studies professional writing and seeks to imitate it in form or in content or both. As students develop as writers, imitation offers them challenges and insight. Imitation is also gaining ground as a legitimate writing activity in introductory literature courses. The student who has to write an imitation or a parody of Robert Frost will need to engage fully with that writer as she learns for herself how Frost achieved his effects and chose his directions. Parody can be a productive first step toward more sophisticated forms of imitation (see Bishop 1990f).

Additionally, when I ask students to imitate, I ask them, really, to *impersonate* the writer by trying to understand the process the writer went through (decisions the writer made) as well as to work toward the end product—the imitation. I do this by asking for a narrative of the imitation, and I evaluate that narrative of the impersonation/ imitation journey as well as give credit for the product of the journey—the poem or story.

Students parody best when they have strong feelings about a piece of writing, so the authors they choose to parody should be self-selected. Strong negative feelings will sometimes lead to heavy-handed or simplistic satire. Making fun of an author in lieu of understanding him does not seem to lead a parodist to greater understanding of a writer's concerns and techniques. To develop an understanding of the work being imitated, a parodist needs to read more than a single work by the author in order to arrive at an implicit and then an explicit understanding of the writer's work—this means reading an entire anthology section or a writer's book-length collection.

Parodists can focus in on one piece of writing (a poem or story or novel) in particular for imitation, what I call focused parody. Focused parody requires close technical analysis. Or, the parodist can decide to write an overall parody of the writer, what I call general parody.

General parody works to capture the original writer's representative tone and themes and, possibly, an often-used form. First-time writers of parody often choose focused imitation, while advanced parodists often choose general imitation. For prose writers, I suggest the alternatives of following an author's plot and modernizing the writing (as in *West Side Story*, which updates *Romeo and Juliet*) or the reverse, providing a plot but imitating the style of Margaret Atwood or Toby Olson (or any other prose writer). Here is part of a poem by e.e. cummings and part of a poetry parody of the same piece:

> [original]
>
> Buffalo Bill's
>
> Buffalo Bill's
> defunct
>   who used to
>   ride a watersmooth-silver
>   stallion
> and break   onetwothreefourfive pigeonsjust like that

> [student version]
>
> Jimmy Carter's
> speech
>   he used to talk with a silversmooth
>   tongue
> and convince   onetwothreefourfive congressmenjustlike that

The author of this imitation was, of course, completing a focused imitation. The author of the following short story was completing a general imitation—his plot, in what he hoped was Hemingway's style:

> Hunt for Manhood
>
> [from several pages into the narrative of a young boy's first deer hunt]
>
> This was the most beautiful country Dan had ever seen. Two thousand foot mountains jutted directly up from the beach, covered with nothing but tall grass and here or there a Sitka Spruce or a patch of alder brush. After climbing for about an hour, Dan glanced back over his shoulder. This was the mountain country that he had dreamed about. He could see for miles in all directions. The Zodiac on the beach looked like a child's toy from where he stood. He took out his binoculars and scanned the valley below. The air was crisp and cool and carried the faint autumn odor of decaying vegetation. Dan was beginning to feel the fatigue of the

> day's labor. He decided to take a short nap. Sitting down in a particularly soft tuft of dry grass, he fell asleep.

Parody does not result in great work—usually. And the first time a student writer tries one, he is likely to stick very closely to the original or to create a repetitive or uninspired approximation. But careful attention to other writers' techniques helps all writers improve—and in writing parodies, students sometimes overcome writer's block or fear of not writing well enough because they can call this work practice—parody or imitation—rather than their own. Parody writing, like imitation in general, works to free a writer to study and to take risks.

Suggestions for other imitation exercises can be found in an article by John Clark and Ann Motto (1986), who also discuss the usefulness of parody writing. Michael Segedy (1986) explores a method that puts literature "on trial"; students experience controversial pieces of literature as simulated court cases. Richard Gebhardt (1988) offers several interesting activities for fiction which place writers and readers in the (literature) writer's place: writing new endings, making characters' lives explicit, rewriting fiction from first- to third-person voice, putting characters in dialogue, rewriting openings, and imitating writers' styles using student writers' own content. An exercise in *Textbook* (Scholes et al. 1988) asks students to create a one-act play around dialogue taken from a short story.

Many of these ideas ask students not just to imitate the work of art, the writing, but to extend writers' ideas, themes, conceits, through original written response of their own. One of my students chose to dramatize Robert Frost's poem "Mending Wall" in her own way. She sets her monologue in an old folks home, where wordy Mr. Gebur retells the story found in "Mending Wall" to a wheelchair-bound, nonresponding fellow pensioner. By doing this she creates her own fictional exploration (scene setting, dramatic monologue) that also explicates her understanding of the original poem. Here is a section in which the monologist, Mr. Gebur, begins to speak:

> "But I'm not badmouthing fences. I always said good fences make good neighbors. Built one around my house and garden. Did I ever show you my pictures? This here is the front of my house; that's the corn field; this was my rose garden. . . . Used to grow prize-winning tea roses in it—or try anyway. It wasn't easy with the fella I lived next to always trying to be some kind of modern-day poet.
>
> "Boy, that fella was something. Let his whole place run wild like a jungle. His blue bells were always getting bombed by falling

> apples and his blackberry bushes strangled his apple trees. Pandemoniums's what it was. All untrimmed and shapeless and growing wild to the sky. I always had order in my garden—harmony. Each species in a neat, straight row. But in his, you couldn't see the shrubs through the weeds. They were all twisted together into fat coils. Those weeds'd spread their sneaky roots into my garden like snakes crawling under the ground. . . .
>
> "I used to ask that poet fella if he wouldn't take some of my weed killer or use my help in pruning. I leave it alone, he says; nature will take care of itself, he says. . . ."

This parodist took on the persona in the poem *and* Robert Frost. Writing students will find parodies, re-creations, imitations, and extensions all useful methods for becoming better readers and more analytic writers. Since these exercises do not as often lead to highly valued writing, I mix them into a class schedule slowly, allowing more time for the free-invention exercises discussed above.

Writing in forms has long been the most widely used imitation activity for poetry writers. Most craft textbooks ask students to write sonnets, sometimes by first providing end rhymes. Classes can develop their own end rhymes together or brainstorm metaphorical webs—for metered or syllabic verse, useful for sestinas—that assure that the poem's end words chime the same concept, for example, oceans—kelp, shell, sandpiper, foam, storm-grey—and so on. I find syllabic verse and, surprisingly, sestinas to be particularly successful forms for writers who are exploring formal imitation, even though the sestina constraints are awesome. We often move to sestinas after experiments with list poems. List poems ask students to use repetition freely. Here is a student list and repetition poem:

> Mug Shot: Richard
> by Karina Possenti
>
> He is 14 years old.
> He has dishwater hair and blue-gray eyes.
> He wears hairspray to make his hair stand up.
> He loves cookies and spaghetti.
> His clothes are Levi's and T-shirts.
> He races on downhill skis.
> Late at night, he can talk for hours.
> In the morning, he can sleep just as long.
> He says "I know that" when he doesn't.
> He gets a stupid grin on his face when he's in trouble.
> He would hunt ptarmigan forever.
> He would save the wings and feet.
> He collects dead batteries.
> He has 8 used hockey pucks on the shelf over his bed.

He's never played hockey.
His drawer is filled with empty ammo boxes.
He covers his walls with shot-at targets.
If he went to Rome, he would get the Pope to join NRA.
He leaves the newspaper spread on the table before dinner.
He feeds my dog if I ask.
He holds Macy even if she's crying.
He has a mother who saves "to do" notes.
He says "Toogalook" and tries to talk like an Eskimo.
He annoys me.
He drools on his sheets and makes spots.
He tries to make me smile when I'm mad.
He is my friend.

Karina wrote this list poem, praising her fourteen-year-old brother, in response to a list poem exercise in David Kirby's *Writing Poems* (1989). In the first version, she followed samples that Kirby included, Christopher Smart's *Jubilate Agno,* and an imitation of that poem entitled "My Cat Jack," by Hunt Hawkins. Both models begin each line with "For . . ." Karina used the prompt "*For* he is 14 years old," but decided to leave off the word "for" in her next versions to modernize the language in this portrait of a tough young brother.

It is easy to understand the power of the list/repetition poem. Kirby traces them to Old Testament psalms, and lists are found in New Testament writing like the Sermon on the Mount. Listwriting was used by Shei Shonagan in ninth-century Japan. Florence Grossman's (1982) text provides a discussion of Shonagan's pillow-book writing that students usually respond to with strong imitations. Student Elaine Collett wrote a "Things That Are Unpleasant" list poem using Shonagan's title but using Elaine's own Alaskan imagery: "[Things that are unpleasant] finding that the squirrels have shredded your entire winter supply of toilet paper / waking on a minus fifty-degree morning with the fire gone out in the stove." She later matched it with a "Things That Are Pleasant" poem: "a big, bull moose in the yard when you thought you'd be eating fish casseroles all winter / the black expanse of night ablaze with the Milky Way as you stand small and alone on the frozen lake." Both of Elaine's Alaskan poems were published in the local newspaper. List/repetition poems (and list/repetition prose—see Robert Coover's fiction) allow writers to explore imagistic links, rhythm, line length, alliteration, and assonance.

Similar issues are explored when students write sestinas. I like using sestinas as an early form (see Wallace 1987 for definition and humorous examples, and Dacy and Jauss 1986 for instances of contemporary poets writing in this and other forms) because they utilize repetition, teach stanza and line exploration, even syllabics. Sestinas appear to allow for more narrative development than a villanelle, for example, and do all this without involving students in intricate rhyme schemes, although the repetition schemes certainly *are* complex. In an interview, Diane Wakoski observes:

> Sestinas are fun. If you break the rule for iambic pentameter, which I insist is an English rule and not a French rule, it's a fun-organizing form, because you keep coming back and back and back like a refrain. If you make yourself very conscious of making very long lines and very short lines then there are really interesting musical sounds to the language. I'm not sure that I could write an iambic pentameter sestina. (Packard 1987, 209)

During a writer's craft talk, Jim Heynan (1983) suggested that writers learn most by writing *six* sestinas rather than just one sestina. Writers, Heynan implies, will have fun playing with a form once, but they will learn most about their own writing if they submit to the constraints of the sestina, or possibly any form, several times. For those writers who are interested, most craft textbooks will take student writers through a range of forms, and advanced writing classes often teach a set of forms (sonnet, villanelle, sestina, blank verse, etc.).

The following sestinas were first-time efforts with formal verse for these undergraduate writers.

Happy Hour Sestina
by Jennifer Jo Wasileski

Strut
into bar
turn heads,
with high heels.
Order drink
with a smile.

A big smile.
Study the strut
of ice on the rim of your drink
or the shifty eyes of the bar.
That cruise your way on hot heels
that want to Twist and Shout and Turn,

Turn, turn
and smile
never heel
to your obedient strut
toward the bar.
They follow your lead and drink,

with tongues of fire they drink
and each has a turn
at chaining you to the bar.
With a smile
they strut
away, clicking their heels.

Slinking away polishing their heels.
Drink
another, watch the icy strut
of tricks that turn
into a teasing smile
bought by the bar.

Watch the owner of the bar
kick out the heels,
who cannot pay with more than a smile
for a drink.
Watch them turn
away, watch them strut

past women in the bar, who drink
with high heels. Who turn,
to trade a smile for a strut.

Ring for Ring
by Tamara Mills

Few steps separate the streetlamp's ring
of brilliance from the dusk,
and the subtle change of gray
to black promises, in the whispered
movement of dead leaves,
to renew images of the past.

But, so many small things are now past
recollection, like flower chains, rings
of grass, and the leaves
from the trees under which we whispered
to each other in the dusk.
They're edges of memory, grey

dusty things, like photo albums in grey
jackets, and pictures that are fading past
perception. Turning pages have whispered
of still moments in time: ring after racing ring
expands from pebbles tossed in dusk
dark liquid, mountains of leaves

in which we burrowed until leaves
were in our clothes, everywhere. Grey
turns black, and the sound of dusk
change into the silence of night, hours past

the curfew of childhood. The ring
of phones searching for us whispered,

telling us, that soft whispered
excuses, as quiet as the wind through leaves,
would not stop the ring
of parental voices in our ears. Grey
company we were then, as we walked past
house after hours, our spirits in a dusk

deeper than the electrically lit dusk
of the streets. We whispered
then, in a time now past,
and pulled handfuls of leaves
from each other's hair. We traded one ring
for another and walked head high from the grey

street's dusk. No more am I a child covered with leaves,
I have whispered over and over. My hair is grey
like memories lost to the past, but I remember our trade, ring for
ring.

Putting Invention and Imitation to Work in the Writing Workshop

When inserting invention activities into the curriculum, my general preference remains to keep offering student writers a series of challenges, beginning with the discussions of themselves as writers (inspiration/muse poems, how I write, etc.), and then by setting up a number of in-class (teacher designed) and out-of-class (self-chosen) requirements. It is possible to sequence a class around the twin foci of developing writers' metacognition and exploring a particular theme. Take the theme of family relationships. I can ask students to write short, in-class, self-introductions the first day, telling how they were named or what their nickname is and means to them. We then write about some of my family objects (teaspoons and old postcards) and brainstorm about those things that move us to write about families. Students write family stories and, then, as in the exercise developed by Katharine Haake, are asked to write about someone else's family story.

Students can bring in their own family objects or talismanic pieces and tell the stories they generate (oral sharing). Students write about their own or other students' objects. At some point, it may be productive to follow the family saga through time, writing "when I was," "now I am," "in ____ years I will be" pieces, like the autobiographical essay "Miller" included in chapter 5.

Later, when developing characters for a story which *cannot* be about our own family, we can move around the room, offering associations with particular names—why does the name Fred never occur to me for a character (i.e., because I used to work with a boy named Fred in high school who . . .). In class and out of class, we share spontaneous and planned writing on this theme and still experience great latitude in genres (some students writing poetry and some fiction and some drama) and in developing our ability to talk about our writing—metacognition (discussing associations with names does this especially; what preconceptions and schemas do we bring to our writing choices?). Other themes could as easily be designed (Growing Up in America; Travel; Friendship; Rites of Passage; Conflict; and so on), although introductory classes can work just as well with each student developing, exploring, and learning from his or her own self-chosen themes. Most important, the teacher and workshop function to help each writer to generate, to get in motion.

7 Responding and Revising

> But many writers who have earned their reputations through hard work agree that one writes at first just to have something to rewrite.
>
> —David Madden, *Revising Fiction*, 1988

> Every literary work—and, more generally, artwork—is thus the product of a complex evaluative feedback loop that embraces not only the ever-shifting economy of the artist's own interests and resources as they evolve during and in reaction to the process of composition, but also the all shifting economies of her assumed and imagined audiences, variable conditions of encounter, and rival sources of gratification she will attempt to predict—or will intuitively surmise—and to which, among other things, her own sense of the fittingness of each decision will be responsive.
>
> —Barbara Herrnstein Smith, *Contingencies of Value*, 1988

All writing situations implicate writers in revision. The writer, as he writes, constantly makes choices, deciding when to use this word construction and when to avoid that topical direction. Barbara Herrnstein Smith talks about revision in terms of a "complex evaluative feedback loop." And her words underline the highly interconnected nature of generation and revision, of author and audience.

In "Teaching Two Kinds of Thinking," Peter Elbow (1986b) discusses revision in terms of alternative ways of thinking about writing. Elbow distinguishes between what he calls first-order thinking—exploratory and inventive open-ended writing like that generated by the in-class writing activities described in the last two chapters—and second-order thinking. Second-order thinking is more conscious and controlled, directed to evaluation, revision, and improvement of material already generated. Elbow realizes that writers need, and use, both types of

---

Portions of this chapter appeared in somewhat different form in Bishop, Wendy. 1990a. "Designing a Writing Portfolio Evaluation System." *The English Record* 40 (2): 21–25 and 1988a. "Helping Peer Writing Groups Succeed." *Teaching English in the Two-Year College* 15 (2): 120–25. Used with permission.

thinking. He suggests, however, that writers should be aware that using second-order thinking when they want to generate can be counterproductive, since, as David Madden observes, writers need something to revise. For instance, some composition researchers have found that basic writers too often edit themselves out of text by stopping constantly to worry about word choice or spelling; that is, often basic writers do not produce enough words at all when composing under time constraints.

However, composing involves conscious arrangement. And writing students need to learn to become adept, too, at second-order thinking. They do this when they learn to respond and to evaluate and to revise. Ultimately, a balance in thinking is required: "If we hold off criticism or revising for a while, we can build a safe place for generative thinking or writing. Similarly, if we devote certain times to wholehearted critical thinking or revising, we can be more acute and powerful in our critical assessment" (Elbow 1986b, 61).

In the transactional writing workshop, second-order thinking ability grows through metacognitive exploration. Students self-evaluate and revise when they analyze their own growth in journals and draft folders, participate in large- and small-group critique sessions, participate in student-teacher conferences, complete written self-evaluations, and compile writing portfolios. Teachers do not have to use all these methods, but all these methods allow students to monitor their cognitive growth. For me, evaluation and revision are highly interconnected. Rather than just evaluate students' class products (their poems, stories, dramatic scripts), I am as interested in learning what they have learned and in admitting writer's self-knowledge as a primary class goal. In this case, revision—the practice of self-analysis and self-criticism—is a cornerstone of the writing workshop. Revision is highlighted because revision improves student work. Also, revision improves students, allowing them more insight into what it means to be a writer (see Bishop 1990g and Brooke 1988 for views that writing classes change individuals). In this workshop, evaluation primarily provides feedback and only secondarily provides a final class grade.

Journals: The Dialogue with Self

> When young it's normal to fear losing a good line or phrase and never finding anything comparable again. Carry a small pocket-size notebook and jot down lines and phrases as they occur. This

> may or may not help you write good poems, but it can help reduce your anxiety.
>
> —Richard Hugo, *The Triggering Town*, 1979

As Richard Hugo observes wryly, students who write every "good" line or phrase into a small journal can gain a somewhat deceptive sense of control of their creative expression; perhaps they will reduce their performance anxiety. But journals are more than a receptacle for thoughts that would otherwise be lost, implying a scarcity of good thoughts. Journals provide a focal point for safe first-order thinking and writing exploration; journals also create a place where discovery can be tempered by observations *about* writing. Journals are so important for writers that they could be considered an additional class mode, like teacher lecture or small-group work. For many writers, much of the learning that can consciously be traced will occur in the journal and draft folder—a pile of rough drafts from two to fifty-six that make up the thought-journey of a piece of creative writing, from inception to production or abandonment.

Journals can be a formal or informal element of a writing workshop. Some teachers simply mention them. Other teachers offer sample entries, in-class writing time, guided writing topics (see Stock 1985 for ideas), and a required number of pages. In workshops, I share model entries or pass around my own old journals. One of my former students, writing teacher Alys Culhane, asks students to keep *two* journals, small observation journals that they carry with them everywhere and large collage journals into which they paste drafts, flowers, drawings, comic strips, and so on.

Toby Fulwiler's *The Journal Book* (1987) provides excellent information on journal keeping. Fulwiler defines the function and purposes of journal keeping:

> When people write about something they learn it better. That, in a nutshell, is the idea behind asking students to keep journals. While some of us who assign these personal notebooks might argue about what they should be called—logs, learning logs, daybooks, thinkbooks, dialectical notebooks, field notebooks, diaries, whatever—we would not disagree about their purpose and value: writing helps our students learn things better and these notebooks provide a place in which to write informally yet systematically in order to seek, discover, speculate, and figure things out. (9)

Fulwiler offers a list of attributes of successful journal writing (colloquial diction, first-person pronouns, rhythms of everyday speech, and so on) which can be developed into class handouts. Additionally, he discusses cognitive processes that students access when making entries—observing, questioning, synthesizing, revising, etc. Regarding evaluation, Fulwiler notes that quality journals include frequent entries, long entries, self-sponsored entries, and a clear chronology.

Three other useful sources for learning about journal options are Sharyn Lowenstein's "A Brief History of Journal Keeping" in the Fulwiler volume, and Tristine Rainer's *The New Diary* (1978), which includes invention activities specifically geared to increasing diary writing; these include list making, guided imagery, unsent letters, dream work, etc. Also, Ira Progoff's (1978) journal system requires separate sections for writing about dreams, the body, society, dialogues with people, and so on.

Developing a journal *system* is less important than experiencing journals as a way of thinking and learning; students who write about their creative explorations and the development of their poems and story drafts are increasingly more able to evaluate their own writing accurately. They develop insights into their own writing process. They learn critical vocabulary as they apply the comments of teacher and peers to their own writing in their own way. They do what Ann Berthoff (1981) suggests students do in dialectical notebooks—they look and look again. By saving drafts and by stopping at times and reviewing the changes recorded there, students learn to monitor their own growth.

Student self-monitoring through a journal is illustrated in the following sequence taken from John's semester-long poetry writing journal. Not every student comes to the same realizations as John, but the fact that some attain a large amount of self-knowledge means that teachers should consider journals as a component of a writing workshop. Additionally, collecting a few journals (with the writer's permission) and sharing them with the class can provide an effective introduction to class journal keeping. Although studying professional writers' revisions is a time-honored way of teaching revision, having students study and analyze their own or their peers' revisions in the writing journal seems an equally productive (and possibly more engaging) practice at the introductory level. Here is a sequence, then, from John's poem-by-poem account of his growth as a writer:

> John's journal: 1/22/88
> [First poem]
>
> My first poem for class was "The Whales." The way I ended up is sort of weird. To shorten the story, I was absolutely nowhere

as to getting the poem done, so I took it to the W.C. [writing center] where Ken & John helped me. The problem was that I knew what I wanted to write about, but simply didn't know how; it was my first one, and I guess I had "poem fright."

John's journal: 1/25/88

[Second poem]

My out of class poem is called "Herman Gets His Dinner". . . . I've been working on it a lot, and am satisfied with its present incarnation (for now, at least) . . . I learned quite a lot about poetry from this poem alone. Let's see, what did I learn? The most important thing I learned was condensing the poem and deciding what stuff I don't need. As I look at earlier drafts, I can see quite a big difference. What originally took me 25 words to say took 10 in my most recent version, without eliminating any pertinent ideas.

John's journal

[Between poem musings]

Up to this point, my poems have been rather sparse; I haven't really thought about writing in phrases. I'll have to pay more attention to writing in phrases, because I think I'm sort of in a rut with my sparseness of writing. Oh, well, it's all "food for thought." (Why am I putting quotes around cliches? Because I've become very aware of them and want to cut down my use of them.)

John's journal: 2/5/88

[After class workshop of his second poem]

One idea that came up during the [class group] critique was that the way I read the poem did not correspond with the line breaks. Now that I think about it, this is quite true; the most change will take place in the third stanza. I think this stanza should be changed to:

"you slowly
pass it
with a flick
of your gilded tail."

I also think that the first line of the fourth stanza should be broken up so that it reads:

"I pity you,
waiting for death."

I'm not sure why but I think these changes in the line breaks make more sense than the way the poem is now.

John's journal: 2/13/88

["Round Midnight" poem]

When I originally came up with the poem, I intended it simply to be a little poem about Thelonious Monk. I then took it to Ken at the Writing Center for him to critique. Ken read it and liked it, but said it wasn't "monkish" enough, which I immediately realized. As it was, I don't think the poem did or said much—in view of the eccentric, hardly conventional person that the poem was about, it was an open invitation to be creative in the Monk sort of way. . . . When I returned to the WC, Ken said that the second draft was better, but he also suggested that it still really didn't capture the Monk spirit, so I went & did another draft. I came up with, eventually, the portfolio draft, which I was pleased with. This draft, I feel, was more Monkish without going *completely* overboard in terms of artistic license.

The one problem with my problem is that it will most likely throw the reader off. Thelonious Monk is probably not well-known to the average person, so all my Monk puns (Blue Monkeys, Epistrophizes) and references to him (his Thelonious life) will most likely confuse the reader. I thought about this before I wrote the poem, and intended it to cater to those who do know who Thelonious Monk was. Of course, that leaves everyone else out in the cold, but I think to have done this poem properly, that's all right.

John's journal: 2/20/88

["Death and Cheerios" poem]

[in workshop] I didn't get any comments on whether it needed improvement or not, but it seems in general that the people in my group liked it, and liked the details in it.

As far as I was concerned, I thought that the poem could use a lot of help. I like the idea for the poem, but don't think I expressed it in the best way. . . . I went to the Writing Center with my class-critique and worked with Ken on it. After using and not using some of his suggestions, I came up with the version that can be found in the portfolio section.

John's journal: 2/26/88

["Doin' Da Funky Chicken" poem]

It took about 30 minutes from scratch to the typed version I handed in to be looked at, which makes it the fastest poem I've written. Since the draft I handed in, I changed a few little things around, such as changing "crazy glissandos" to "dizzying" and "slowly file" to "quietly," but it's essentially the same poem.

Although the poem is humorous, it is not without planning and thought. Some of the line breaks gave me trouble.

I wrote the poem as a reaction to a lot of the poems I've read lately, which are usually gushy love poems, or death or other things that the good sensitive poet should write about. Call me unsentimental, insensitive or whatever, but I haven't seen much humor at all in the poetry I've read lately. I guess I don't take a whole lot seriously, but "Doin' Da Funky Chicken" is my answer to all the spurned lovers, suicides, etc., that are popular subjects with poets. Not only that, but I hope it was an enlightening description of what chickens *really* do at night. . . .

John's journal: 3/2/88

[Midsemester self-evaluation]

Before 272, I can also honestly say that I had never truly been creative. All my writing I had done had always had a guideline to it; write about what I did over summer vacation, etc. Going from there to writing about *whatever I wanted to* was really difficult for me at first. It was almost crippling. . . . Now I can write about just about anything that comes to mind. For example, take "Doin' Da Funky Chicken." I never could have written something like that at the beginning of the semester, but I can now. . . . As I leaf through the portfolio, I can see my confidence as a writer grow. I'm not too sure if I'd write or would be able to write something like "The Bow of the Whale" or "Herman Gets His Dinner" [early poems] at this point. To me, those poems don't say anything or don't "live" the way, say, " 'Round Midnight" or "Doin' Da Funky Chicken" do. Granted, these later poems are pretty weird, but I feel that they are closer to "me" than the others, because they relate the askew, bizarre (but humorous) slant of life I have. I think that where I am now, I would not be afraid to write anything, no matter how weird it may be, as long as it was "me."

John's journal: 3/29/88

[Between poem musings]

Form poems have been hell so far for me, sort of like having teeth pulled. What I have written has been with exact rhymes, which, in my case, at least, means that I end up with annoying, nursery rhyme-like schlock . . . As I think about it, I guess that my problem is maybe that I am starting my poems the wrong way; instead of put an idea within the restrictions of a given form, I try to derive an idea *from* the restrictions.

John's journal: 4/15/88

["The Lonely Man" renamed "Solitude"]

I noticed that the class was really divided during critique about my poem. . . .

The first problem with this poem was its title. The title gave the content away and made it too predictable. . . .

The second problem with the poem is that it was too ordinary—the events were too expected. From the feedback I got, "Solitude" was *very* predictable, which sort of surprised me. I know that loneliness is a "poetic" topic—depressing, sad, etc.—just right for the "sensitive" poet." Although I try to avoid these poetic topics, I thought I'd give loneliness a go, because I could identify with the guy in the poem; I've written letters to about 4 friends of mine back East and haven't got a reply in almost 2 months. . . .

Some of the written comments that I really like (and I got several that were similar) are ones that said that "Solitude" reminded the reader of "Fool On the Hill," or "Eleanor Rigby" by the Beatles. As I think about it, the sort of loneliness that those songs so effectively evoked is the sort of thing I was trying to get at. So, since *some* people seemed to see what I was getting at, I think my poem *did* work to some extent.

John's journal: 4/20/88

[Between poem musings]

I've been having trouble with my poetry lately. Even though I've been putting just as much, if not more, work into my poetry since mid-semester, I'm not all that pleased with what I've come up with. If it wasn't so late in the semester, I'd probably scratch my poems and begin anew. Perhaps I'm developing a "poetic sense," or whatever, but I seem to be turning out a lot of schlock. . . . Why am I having this trouble? I'm not sure, but something that just came to mind, may be part of the reason: Since mid-semester, I've been working with various forms, line-lengths, line breaks, more serious ideas, etc. I think I'm more comfortable when I'm writing in my notorious minimalist style, and that these new "angles" to writing that I've been trying simply are not as comfortable. If this is the case, then I'm not worried about the schlock that I am turning out—I admit that one has to put out "bad" (or stuff that the writer is not completely pleased with) writing before one can write "good" stuff. . . . Now that I think about it, I'm not worried about this phase of my poetry. If I weren't interested or just didn't care, I probably wouldn't realize that I wasn't completely pleased with my poetry in the first place, so I guess the only thing to do is keep working at it, reading others' work and keep an open mind. Maybe then I will be more pleased with my poetry, although I don't think I'll ever be completely happy with *all* that I write. (I'm not being a pessimist—I just think that one is never completely pleased; little things, words, line breaks, etc., may annoy the writer.)

John's journal: 4/88

[Final Self-Evaluation]

I sort of see this semester divided into two parts, the division just happening to be about mid-semester. In the first period, I

> was just learning about how to write poetry, the different types and forms, the kinds of poems that there were, and so forth. Since I had never written poetry before that point, I was pleased with the poems that I managed to wrestle onto paper. Just getting ideas and putting them down was enough for me to do. Then, roughly at mid-semester, I became fairly confident with my poetic ability; my writing wasn't anything spectacular or particularly original, but I knew that if I had an idea, I would be able to write it down without leaving the reader out in left field. Once I reached this point, I thought that it was about time that I learned what good, effective poetry should be, so I started reading others' poetry and trying different forms, subjects, tones, etc. in my own poetry. That's where my problem began. You see, I had ideas of what makes poetry work, and some of the pitfalls to avoid; I employed these observations as much as I could, yet wasn't especially pleased with what I ended up with. I'd write something, knew that it could be better, but didn't know just how. I'm still in this "phase," if you will. As I noted in my learning log, I think that simply being aware that my poetry can be better is half of the battle. I sort of see it as getting all the "bad" poetry out before I can write "good" poetry. (I'm not saying my poetry is necessarily bad—I use "bad" as a general term.)

John's journal is a strong one but not an unusual one. In other students' journals, I see similar self-analysis that clearly signals writing development. Note how John divides his writing into early and later work. He sees phases and problems. He analyzes writer's blocks and writer's gains. John clearly views himself as a writer; he talks about his writing seriously in his journal. The journal also offers many insights into the sometimes mysterious revision process of writers. John details where his ideas came from, how he uses and discards peer remarks, how he actually changes lines or titles, and eventually, how he comes to trust his own judgment as much as or more than the judgment of others.

In *Revising Fiction,* David Madden (1988) offers these levels of revision fluency:

> In his or her development, the writer goes through four stages in the matter of revision, and you may recognize where you are:
>
> 1. He makes a mistake but fails to see it.
> 2. He makes a mistake, he sees it, but doesn't know how to fix it—or reimagine it. He hasn't learned enough about the techniques of fiction.
> 3. He makes a mistake, he sees it, he has learned how to fix it, because he has learned some of the techniques of fiction, but he just can't do it.
> 4. He makes a mistake, he sees it, he knows how to fix it, he fixes it—and by now he has learned that solving technical

> problems in the creative process is just as exciting as writing the first draft. (11)

In Madden's sequence, I would replace the word choice of *mistake* with, perhaps, *exploration* or *wrong turning* (something less overtly wrong and more nearly *not sufficient to a writer's purposes*).

I think John's journal provides a remarkable illustration of Madden's revision sequence: John learns to identify, fix, talk about, and tinker with problems and solutions to problems. He is engaged with writing *and* with revision. My own reading of the complete journal shows me John has advanced, at times, through all the levels of revision awareness and has in this way shown that he has learned technical aspects—line, stanza, and so on—as well as explored topics and writing opportunities of interest to him. Journals, when they accomplish all this, are invaluable, for they allow students to self-evaluate and teachers to track growth and achievement of writing workshop goals.

Groups: The Dialogue with Others

> In composing, as a general rule, run your pen through every other word you have written; you have no idea what vigor it will give your style.
>
> —Sydney Smith, quoted in *A Writer Teaches Writing,* by Donald Murray, 1969

> Read over your compositions, and when you meet with a passage you think is particularly fine, strike it out.
>
> —Samuel Johnson, quoted in *A Writer Teaches Writing*

> Criticism is knowing what you're doing and thereby how to do it. Criticism is method; it is practicing what you preach.
>
> —Anne Berthoff, *The Making of Meaning,* 1981

Writers as dissimilar as Samuel Johnson and Sydney Smith agree that pruning a work after generating the rough draft is essential. But novice writers do not have the highly developed critical abilities that allow them to take advantage of this sage advice; they do not know, as Ann Berthoff points out, that criticism is method. They do not realize that the portions of their writing they most admire might well appear to be clumsy, out of place, or clichéd to their readers. More important, novice writers often do not know who their readers are.

As I pointed out in chapter 1, students enroll in creative writing courses for many reasons, and they are often surprised at the demands of producing work for imagined or real audiences, particularly the audience of their teacher, who is much more widely read in the conventions and history of literature than they are. The long-term strength of creative writing workshops has always been the audience they provide and the training in criticism and reading. Hans Ostrom (1989) explains: "Ultimately, the workshop process itself lets students participate in a community of 'writer-critics,' respondents who take part in a special discourse. This participation builds confidence and refines the ability to talk about literature as well as about writing-in-progress. In several ways, then, creative-writing classes are also critical-thinking classes" (60).

In the creative writing workshop, students write, copy their writing, and submit it to class members who respond orally, and often in writing, on the copied text, suggesting changes, offering interpretations of and responses to the piece. This response business is conducted under the direction of the teacher who mediates the discussion, sometimes by focusing response to a certain point he wants to make (point of view, line length), and sometimes by offering only opening or summarizing remarks. Often the teacher is also the timekeeper with the power to linger over texts that interest him or to speed up discussion so that all members get "workshopped."

A good simulation of this traditional workshop response format can be found in Alberta Turner's *Poets Teaching: The Creative Process* (1980). Turner asked groups of teacher-poets to discuss selected student poems and explain how they would conduct a workshop and/or critique the poem. Overall, these poets guided and structured the response to the point, often, of showing how they might rewrite sample sections of the poem to model the revision process. Additionally, Turner, in her introduction, noted that teachers had developed a particular workshop vocabulary, some of which might be confusing or opaque to novice writers. In fact, some teachers intentionally seemed to choose terms that prevented them from offering clear statements of value or direction on student work:

> Perhaps because of their predominantly inductive teaching method, their need for a comfortable relationship with the students, or perhaps because of postmodernism's distrust of academic labels, these poets seem almost deliberately to avoid using many of the standard critical terms. For *theme* they tend to say *center* or *impulse*. For *persona* or *point of view* or *tone* they tend to say *voice*. They use colloquial and slang terms, such as *gut, cute, quirky, schmaltz;* moral terms, such as *self-indulgent, earned, committed;* metaphors

> such as the poem that *disintegrates*, the *view that takes breath;* euphemisms, such as *this bothers me*, instead of *this is cacophonous* or *this is a mixed metaphor*. They use abstractions which have been worn smooth in lay language to perform some very important value judgments—for example, *interesting* to mean *significant* or even *profound; surprise* to mean the effect produced by the most skillful fusion of theme, image, rhythm, and diction. Only rarely do they speak of *tension* or *texture* or *irony*. (5)

From my viewpoint, the traditional workshop format is to be praised for the long-term salutary effect it has had on developing the idea of a writers' community and in the equally salutary effect it has had on composition classes. Teachers in composition have been prompted by the workshop model to explore collaborative response in all writing classes. At the same time, the traditional creative writing workshop has, in my opinion, become unimodal. That is, students are encouraged to rely too heavily on the mediation of the teacher: "Too often, we instructors develop pseudo-workshop situations. Our comments are directive, whether given orally or when written in the form of editing imperatives on student work. Writing assignments can appear gratuitously experimental. Many texts are form and style-centered" (Bishop 1988b, 86).

Developing Group Work

To avoid static, teacher-centered workshops, we can and should explore alternative forms of collaborative response. This is accomplished when teachers visualize the place of peer writing groups in their entire curriculum. Because group work is based on a theory of learning that students may not be familiar with, the teacher will need to acquaint students with concepts of collaborative learning through prepared handouts, class discussion, and continual monitoring of group work.

In small groups, as I have shown in chapter 3, certain students feel free to respond and to learn from their peers. When forming peer groups, teachers may divide a class into sets of four to five students, or students may start working together in pairs and then pairs may be joined. Early writings may be used by the teacher to organize groups with a mix of strong and weak writers. Students may rate themselves on matters such as ability to lead, to help, to take risks, and so on, and groups may be formed with a member who is strong in each area. In addition, I try to balance groups by gender and by age; groups work best when they are balanced, focused, and comfortable.

The more groups are used, the more adept a teacher becomes in divining group personalities. Sometimes a teacher needs to intervene and change group membership (placing an overly dominant member in another, more challenging group, and so on), but often it is wiser to let the group itself solve group problems. Ideally, groups that stay together over a long period develop a strong group identity and sense of shared community. Equally, groups that change membership, either partially or wholly, are often revitalized and ready to undertake new class challenges with greater enthusiasm. Depending on my course goals, I try to let groups work together for at least four sessions, yet I rarely leave a group together for an entire semester. If immediate change is needed, I ask for one volunteer from each group to "travel" to another group or ask two smaller groups to join and work together.

Ordering and clarifying group members' roles, such as *monitor* (timekeeper) and *historian* (secretary) and *general member,* also assures that group work will be carried on in an orderly manner. Groups are formed to work together, so group activities should be clearly articulated in handout form or as directions on the chalkboard, and group work should be *real* work, contributing to each member's writing and reading development.

Group members should be encouraged to talk freely about their creative writing or about a reading. This talk will reflect the critical vocabulary of the class if it has been initiated by the teacher, reinforced by reference to the class textbooks, and nurtured by whole-class discussion. In this effort, the teacher functions as the conduit linking the class to the academic writing community. She may begin by teaching the class necessary terminology like cliché and point of view—as those issues arise naturally in response to a piece of class writing—and by training readers and writers to work together through guided discussion, role playing, a review of sample student writing, and so on (see chapter 3). Alberta Turner's observations, quoted above, remind a teacher that students will pick up her vocabulary: if a teacher responds to student writing by saying "it doesn't seem to have a center" and "this bothers me" and "this is interesting," she should not be surprised to hear her students using the same imprecise response vocabulary.

In their initial critique sessions, groups can work to answer limited questions (What is the most effective section of this writing and why? What four things would you suggest the writer change in the next draft?) and critical concerns can be added (for instance, questions about clichéd language or successful closure or plot can be added *after* problems arise or questions develop in those areas). Students can be encouraged to develop their own priority of concerns and list of review questions. At the end of each class meeting, groups can share their work, conclusions, and progress with the whole class; this sharing supports the class as a larger community and keeps groups from becoming too isolated (see Bishop 1988a and 1987a).

Guided Response

As I pointed out in chapter 3, *Sharing and Responding* by Peter Elbow and Pat Belanoff (1989) is one the most innovative discussions of response and sharing. Elbow and Belanoff suggest a developmental progress for response which moves from simple sharing (reading out loud with no response) to descriptive sharing in which the listener tries to "sayback" to the writer what he or she heard. Next, they suggest analytic responding (particularly for persuasion), or reader-based response (reader says what she is thinking and feeling), and, finally, criterion-based or judgment-based response in which some criteria are applied to the work, which may or may not match up to those criteria and reader expectations. Alan Zeigler (1989) has developed similar response categories and discusses their use in "'Mid-Wifing the Craft'" (1989).

Additionally, teachers will want to help students understand that different types of response are appropriate for different points in writing development. For instance, criterion-based response is *not* appropriate for an early draft nor is "sayback" response particularly useful for a writer who is trying to make last revisions before editing. Students need to learn to move along a no-evaluation to detailed-evaluation continuum as well as an early-to-late draft continuum.

In my own classes, I use the discussion of draft levels in figure 15. I will be discussing writing portfolios in more detail in chapter 8. However, in figure 15, I define portfolio drafts to show the ongoing nature of revision. Other teachers call early drafts zero drafts, discovery drafts, and so on, and then simply number drafts. I have used draft levels in an effort to avoid the idea that all pieces go through one, two, three drafts; for instance, John, in his journal quoted earlier, mentioned some poems requiring many drafts and one poem that he wrote in thirty minutes. In *Revising Fiction,* David Madden includes a quip from writer S. J. Perelman to point out the foolishness of offering draft *formulas*: "How many revisions are necessary really to finish a story? Thirty-seven, S. J. Perelman replied promptly when asked. 'I once tried doing thirty-three, but something was lacking . . .' " (11). Clearly, no set number of drafts assures writing will work. Other professional writers agree emphatically. Says James A. Michener: "You write the first draft really to see how it's going to come out." And Jules Renard claims that: "Talent is a question of quantity. Talent does not write one page: it writes 300" (both quoted in Murray 1968). These observations remind writers that drafting is discovery and drafting is development.

Peer response gives students ideas for the ways they can develop their ideas. I have worked most extensively with guided response sheets or protocols in introductory writing workshops for several reasons. First, they take the burden of direction off the teacher; the response sheets and the discussions they engender guide the small or large workshop response. Second, they make good use of always limited workshop time. Third, they train students by offering a response focus and by providing vocabulary for critical review of other students' writing. Hans Ostrom (1989) reviews the benefits of guided response:

> Workgroups, especially those guided by a carefully conceived protocol, allow students to write, think, talk, and read in one of the most challenging and least artificial situations in the university. One result I have begun to notice in all of my creative-writing courses is that in fifteen weeks most of the students become remarkably more poised, articulate, and confident about discussing their own and others' work. They usually become less defensive and less arrogant (as Newlin suggests), and they become better listeners and readers with more to say. (61)

These are large claims. What do these "carefully conceived protocols" look like? Many composition books now offer review protocols for student essays, and these can be adapted to writing workshops. In *Sharing and Responding*, Elbow and Belanoff (1989) offer lists of response questions and situations that teachers can also adapt. Figure 16 provides a sample of written responses to a draft of my muse poem, included in chapter 4. These responses were generated during a creative writing pedagogy seminar; we were exploring Elbow and Belanoff's descriptive response techniques by reading each other's rough or professional drafts and then having listeners "sayback" what they heard (in this instance, we used brief written notes to aid our oral response).

I found the activity revealing, particularly in the way listeners could tell me what they thought I wanted to say and for the lively metaphorical description of a child in a yellow slicker and the writer in a mix of yesterday's clothes. This response did not lead me directly to revision, but it did allow me to *confirm* a draft, to find out if readers would actually read a poem in the spirit I hoped they would.

In the same seminar, we devised a set of creative writing response protocols. The questions writers and readers ask about pieces clearly change when the draft designation changes (early to late). Additionally, response questions seem to include craft or drafting issues that those who devise the protocols are most interested in (an unquestionable interest in image, point of view, and cliché) and leave out other issues. After developing and using such sheets, teachers would be well advised to "read themselves," asking whether there are revision foci they are avoiding or missing when they use such sheets. Because the response protocol is a powerful teacher, prepared protocols are particularly useful when training students to critique. Later in the term, it may be more instructive to ask student writers to construct their own protocols, protocols which emphasize their own needs and interests, their own writerly questions. In so doing, novice writers learn to become their own best audience.

Figures 17 and 18 show one set of early and late response sheets that we developed for multigenre writing critiques. The complete set of response protocol sheets can be found in appendix A. To use versions of the sheets I have provided, teachers would want to leave adequate room for response on the page (often our sheets proved to have too many questions) and also decide if they want students to respond by writing on the writer's text.

The response sheet in figure 19 is an early draft of the response protocol found in figure 18. Interestingly, the group that was developing this sheet used food metaphors, which seem effective in the first section (higher-order concerns), and less so in the second section (lower-order concerns). Because they thought I, as teacher, did not like the early version, they sanitized it and made it more generic. Thinking about my response, I realized I had cut off a particularly useful exploration (I had frowned, I think, because their response sheet did not look like the others!). As I have shown in chapters 2 and 3, writers do look at writing as a metaphorical process. It may be that metaphor-based response sheets like this one could prove very engaging for students. I plan to try a version of this metaphor-based protocol and to ask student writers to devise others with me in my next workshop.

Figures 20 and 21 show two, completed, response sheets. A graduate student, Carolyn, and I responded to a poem by another graduate student, Peg Peoples. I have not included Peg's poem. Rather, I include the two responses to show how rich the response trail can be—the two responders *do* agree on sections and do offer individual readings of the poem. Also, the responses focus on the positive directions that Peg can take and assume that she is interested in revision.

Graduate students like these balked a bit about offering protocol-guided responses, especially since I stipulated that I would rather have them *not* comment on the text (poem) itself. They were used to and enjoyed having "other people scribbling on [their] work," but they were developed writers who were experienced in interpreting "scribbled" responses. Chapter 8 addresses problems of student interpretation of teacher response. Composition research shows that many writers experience difficulty when trying to decipher on-text response and that such response tends to focus on grammar and usage rather than on writing content (see Knoblauch and Brannon 1981). Scribbled responses can quickly become formulaic, bland, or obscure.

To review, in developing alternatives to the large-group workshop, teachers will want to explore the use of small response groups. Additionally, when using any groups of any size, small or large, teachers of transactional creative writing workshops will want to consider response sequencing (non-evaluative to evaluative) and draft sequencing (rough to professional to portfolio) and response protocols (designed to focus discussion and train writers to develop response skills). When students in a creative writing workshop consider these issues, they are already deeply involved in the drafting process. They can fruitfully ask: What do I say to someone about her writing? When is my writing done? What should I look for and work on in my writing? They are working to understand and improve their own texts and the texts of their peers.

At this point, certain in-class activities may also help students gain a deeper understanding of the ways writers revise. For instance, composition researchers have found that basic writers tend to revise primarily at the word level, adding or subtracting a word and checking their spelling over and over or avoiding a rich vocabulary choice and choosing, instead, a word that is easy to spell. Expert writers, on the other hand, both add and subtract but also rearrange and expand their writing, and they perform these changes at the word, sentence, paragraph, and whole-text levels.

Revision Activities

Students can learn about revision through various group activities. Traditionally, apprentice writers learned about such changes by *reading* variorum editions of writers' revisions (Yeats's, for instance) or through being informed about famous moments of literary editing (Pound and Eliot collaborating on "The Wasteland"). Equally, they can read collections of writers' retrospective accounts like those found in Alberta

Turner's *Fifty Contemporary Poets* (1977) or Lee Bartlett's *Talking Poetry* (1987) or Steven Berg's *Singular Voices* (1985).

Reading about revision can be productive for the avid literary writer, but I think *practicing* revision and doing so with a partner or group can make revision more meaningful to students. Sometimes I ask students to draft a better version of a less than successful student work that I have saved (with the student's permission). I bring in many copies of the now-anonymous piece and ask students to supply scissors, tape, marking pens, etc. We work all period to make a poor piece more effective. Usually we fail, but we have fine arguments and discussions as students negotiate purpose and word choice, add to plots, change line lengths and stanzas, develop new characters, and so on.

To discuss word choice, teachers can provide cloze versions of prose or poetry. In the cloze technique, every fifth word is left out and readers (traditionally speakers of second languages) are asked to use sentence structure and context to supply the missing words, thus exhibiting their comprehension and vocabulary. For creative writing classes, cloze-type structures can be developed in which writers' adjectives or adverbs are removed and students work to suggest vivid, tonally consistent alternatives. By negotiating such choices and then comparing them to the original, students learn about artistic possibilities *and* coherence.

In his book *Teaching Poetry Writing to Adolescents,* Joseph Tsujimoto (1988) suggests what he calls "circle revision," in which a student tapes a spare piece of paper to the side of her poem after numbering the poem's lines. Other writers then suggest line-by-line changes and pass the poem to the next reader, who can agree or disagree with the suggested changes and then make his own suggestions. I found that the circle response (which I have also explored with sections of prose) led more directly to editing concerns—punctuation, word choice, line breaks, paragraphing—than it did to whole-text response.

Over time, teachers can collect lists of revision exercises and activities, gleaned from their own writing experiences, from those they find in textbooks, and from those they learn from colleagues. For poetry they might ask students at one point to:

1. Experiment with adjectives: remove all the adjectives (or adverbs, or both) from the poem. Or, for students who do not use them enough, try using more, or using modifiers in pairs, etc.
2. Rearrange a poem so that the line breaks come at the end of sentences. Then arrange the same poem in ten-syllable lines. Try

it in two- or four-word lines. Finally, space it by phrases and move the lines across the white space. Read all versions aloud and try to explain how each works or does not work.

3. Remove all *and*'s, *the*'s, and prepositional phrases from the poem.
4. Cut the poem in half (half as many lines) while trying to maintain the original intensity.
5. Try turning an unmetered poem into iambic pentameter (or vice versa).
6. Write a paragraph description of what you intended to say in the poem without the poem in front of you. Compare the description to the poem. How successful were you?
7. Write some poems as spontaneously as possible (perhaps one each morning for a week). Do not revise them at the time. Then, a week later, look carefully at the faults and strengths of each, and revise them if you wish. (This is useful for prose writers also.)

For prose, students might want to work through a transformational sequence:

1. Write a dialogue between two characters without using names or identifying tags. The dialogue should present a scene already in progress, and during the course of the dialogue, the scene should reach a resolution.
2. Write a sketch based on one of the characters in the dialogue, keeping in mind the personality developed in the dialogue.
3. Write a one-paragraph setting for the characters.
4. Write a plot for a story that would incorporate the dialogue.
5. Write the story or play *or* give these materials to another student and have him or her write the story or play.

Or:

1. Rewrite a scene from an existing story in first-person point of view, then in second-person point of view, then in third-person point of view.
2. Change a portion of an existing prose piece from past tense to continuous present tense.

Or:

1. Ask prose writers to explore "poetic" techniques in their writings by including or leaving out adjectives, using clichés or dialect to

develop characters, reparagraphing, highlighting repetition, etc. (Adapted, in part, from Zender et al. 1979).

Many of these activities can be completed in pairs or groups, at home or in the classroom. Students can also learn about revising on their own by completing response protocols for their own writing or by answering response questions, such as the many detailed ones found in David Madden's *Revising Fiction*. Self-analysis can be a one-time exercise or can be set up as an ongoing set of journal entries. Most craft textbooks, like Stephen Minot's *Three Genres* (1982), offer some writer's self-review questions regarding the effectiveness of a piece of writing. Minot includes questions for fiction, poetry, and drama. Li Min Hua's (1989) writing protocol questions ask writers to examine their decision-making process in unusual ways (for instance, "How my personality did or did not affect or effect one choice" and "Where I broke a rule on purpose" and "How I tried to offend/confuse/intimidate/trounce the reader and still get away with it").

Revision activities like these can be ordered by the writing teacher to offer students insights into the revision process. However, all such exercises should be used sparingly, after the experience of revision in context: students working to improve their own meaningful texts.

Providing response is a primary function of the writing workshop. The transactional workshop can offer a writer readers' responses in a variety of formats (small and large group and during teacher conference), a written record of suggested change in the form of completed response protocol sheets, and an impulse to revise because students have a class audience who wants to read more. In addition, teachers may want to require a certain number of revisions, or ask a writer to collect revisions in a response folder for an end-of-semester review of the writer's progress. This review can allow teacher and students to examine the entire writing history (process) for at least one piece of writing. Equally, teachers may collect and grade a mid-semester and/or end-of-semester writing portfolio.

By engaging in a writer's cycle of response and revision, novice writers will develop the ability to use *first-* and *second*-order thinking. They will also develop the ability to use criticism as a *method,* one that lets them, as Ann Berthoff suggests, practice what they preach.

Rough Draft:

Written for student as she generates her ideas.

Also written for the student's peer group.

Must be legible to writer for oral sharing with peers in order to receive verbal critiques.

Sometimes written during in-class invention exercises and shared with classmates.

Professional Draft:

Written for student as she reviews, revises, and refines her ideas.

Also written for the student's peer group, the teacher, friends, writing center tutors, etc.

Drafts must be legible to other readers (*preferably* typed).

When shared with peer group, copies are provided for all group members who respond with oral critiques and/or written critiques.

When shared with teacher, teacher responds with written or oral (conference) critiques to discuss revision directions.

Portfolio Draft:

Written for the public—including student, teacher, and interested readers—after incorporating earlier revision suggestions.

Typed and then presented with *rough* and *professional* draft versions in mid-semester and end-of-semester portfolios.

Fig. 15. Overview of portfolio draft levels. (Adapted from: Bishop, Wendy. 1990a. "Designing a Writing Portfolio Evaluation System." *The English Record* 40 (2): 21–25. Used with permission.)

Response 1

Pointing: Grovelling, get it right this time, electrical circuit problems, read *Curious George* aloud tomorrow night, hold books right-side up.

Summary: [Couldn't list one from an oral reading.]

What is almost said or implied: Outside distractions to my writing—please take pity on me.

Center of Gravity: Let me sleep nights, relax, not worry, get it down in print.

Weather: Wants sunshine, waiting for weather change.

Clothing: Little kid's yellow slicker and rain-hat and umbrella.

What author really wanted to say (substitution): Would actually like to scream with frustration.

Response 2

Pointing: Germs of dreams.

Summary: Muse give me a break (but doesn't mean it).

Center of Gravity: [Didn't list one]

What is almost said or implied: Love/hate w/muse and writing.

Weather: Grey, storm on the horizon and could blow over or blow in, but it doesn't matter.

Clothing: Yesterday's clothes—slippers, sweatshirt with coffee stain over a $25.00 button down and gold slacks.

Substitutes: [Didn't list one.]

(Note: poem referred to is "Groveling" by Wendy Bishop)

Figure 16. Responses to poem using Elbow and Belanoff's techniques for guided descriptive response.

Writer:__________________

Title:____________________

Please use this sheet to respond to another writer's work. Remember, the writer is in an *early draft stage* and will expect to use your comments to help improve his/her writing for a future draft.

1. Find several words, lines, or passages that stand out in this piece of writing. Underline/highlight them on the paper or list them in the space below. Is each one effective? Distracting? Out of place? Unusual? Interesting? Explain for each example that you choose.
2. After reading this piece, what did you still want to find out? Why?
3. For you as reader, were there any words, lines, or passages that left you unsure or confused? If so, find several and explain what you felt unsure about.
4. How do you feel about the writer's use of language in this piece? Give some examples, using page numbers and sentences or by quoting lines:
   a. Examples of fresh, interesting, and/or appropriate language—language that you especially liked
   b. Examples of clichéd, too familiar, and/or out of place language—language that you think could be rewritten more effectively.
5. Suggest the most important change(s) you feel the writer could make to improve this piece while redrafting.

Your name:____________________ Date:____________________

Fig. 17. Response sheet for early peer response: multigenre (poetry, fiction, nonfiction, or drama).

Your name:____________________

Title of the work being critiqued:____________________

Author's name:____________________

Higher-Order Concerns

1. Describe how you felt after you finished reading this piece. What impressions did you leave with?
2. List three places where the author could streamline this piece by trimming certain words, lines, or passages.
3. List three places where the author could improve the piece by adding more information.
4. Do you feel this piece is complete? If yes, why? If not, what is missing?

Lower-Order Concerns

1. Did the author use punctuation in any way that concerns you? If so, where and why?
2. Were there any places in the piece where you were dissatisfied with the author's choice of words? Where and why?
3. What do you think of the title? Does it suit the piece? Why or why not?

Fig. 18. Response sheet for late peer response: multigenre (poetry, fiction, nonfiction, or drama).

Higher-Order Concerns

1. Describe the taste in your mouth when you finish reading this piece.
2. List three words/lines/passages where the author can trim the flab.
3. List three words/lines/passages where the author could put a little meat on the bones.
4. Was the meal complete? In other words, when you finished this piece, were you still hungry for more information? Why or why not?

Lower-Order Concerns

1. Was there the proper amount of space between the main courses? In other words, did the author use punctuation in any way that confused you? If so, where and why?
2. Was the table setting complete? In other words, did the author use sentence fragments in any way that confused you? If so, where and why?
3. What about the menu? What do you think of the title and why?

Fig. 19. Early draft—metaphorical response sheet for late shaping of multigenre writing.

Name of Writer: Peg

Name of Responder: Carolyn

Date: 4-13-89

Early Poem Critique

What are the strongest images in the poem? Write them below.

—the metal washtub/catching it w/a/ racket

—the hired boys

—my braid unfurls under pressure

—as if the men could see her

—fields . . . fields of corn

—blouse & Howie

—the boys & strawberries

—girl & Mom

—chamomile & silt

What does this poem make you think of? How does it make you feel?

This poem makes me think of growing up as a female. It doesn't give me any *strong* feelings yet, but it has the potential to make me feel stirings, hot summer and coming of age.

Is there surprise in this poem? Where? What's the surprise?

I was surprised by the blouse & Howie, the mother's line about the land, & the beautiful last line.

Where could the poem expand? Give two or three places if possible.

I'd like to know more about just what Howie did (or didn't) do, how light "the world" *could* be, why the mother said the line about the land, why the narrator raises her hand to her sternum.

Are there rhymes in this poem? Where do they work well? Are there places the rhymes draw attention to themselves—distract the reader? List the lines and words.

I don't see rhymes, exactly, but there are many *sounding* words that I like. For instance:

—weeks . . . heat

—catching . . . racket

—wait . . . shade

—other voices

—shuffling chairs

If there are clichés in the poem, list them below. Also write some examples of fresh and interesting language.

"the world"
"that other world"

Fig. 20. Completed early poem response sheet: Carolyn on Peg's poem.

Name of Writer: Peg

Name of Responder: Wendy

Date: 4-13-89

Early Poem Critique

What are the strongest images in the poem? Write them below.

"voices familiar by their weight"

"as if the men could see her see/through walls and the rough mirror"

"hoisting six at a time—how light/the world could be."

What does this poem make you think of? How does it make you feel?

It's sensual, mysterious, slightly confusing—particularly in some tone shifts. I wonder at the girl's age & relationship with her mother. "the guys" and "Howie" seem discordant, slight compared to lusher passages like "The smell of drying cornsilk . . . the way my blouse opened . . ." I wonder too about the import of the mother's speech about the father.

Is there surprise in this poem? Where? What's the surprise?

lots—this sounds like her 1st shower in weeks—why? If not, "for weeks" section leads me astray. Scene of making love at the lake floats up unexpectedly—surprising way narrator looks *out* the window & mother senses others looking *in* through the wall & mirror/mother keeping the water—chamomile? Comes from water? Mother's hair??

Where could the poem expand? Give two or three places if possible.

As above—familial relationships heavy with import that's not delivered esp. mother's mention of father. I think it's long enough for this vivid scene/moment but needs some simplifying, becoming less ornate but not necessarily less sensual and *somewhat* mysterious

Are there rhymes in this poem? Where do they work well? Are there places the rhymes draw attention to themselves—distract the reader? List the lines and words.

door/floor and skin/cottons/wind of first two stanzas almost had me looking for internal rhyme between lines 2/3 in each stanza—drops off though w/more reliance on repetition & alliteration/assonance

If there are clichés in the poem, list them below. Also write some examples of fresh and interesting language.

cliches: possibly "catching it with a racket"
"voices . . . drift from the kitchen"

interesting: "winds raising cottons on the lines"

Fig. 21. Completed early poem response sheet: Wendy on Peg's poem.

8 Evaluating and Responding

> Most of us learned how to comment on papers by first surviving and then imitating the responses of teachers to our work.
>
> —Erika Lindemann, *A Rhetoric for Writing Teachers,* 1982

> It's not a question of whether we like evaluation. When a teacher sees student work he almost invariably has an evaluative reaction. Even if he doesn't, the student almost invariably infers one. Even tone of voice and facial expression play a role here. Besides, we couldn't learn without feedback. Therefore, the only real question is what sort of evaluation to have. We decide best if we figure out what evaluation ought to do.
>
> —Peter Elbow, "Trustworthiness in Evaluation," 1986

Creative writing teachers tend to finesse the issue of grading student work by saying it cannot be done, by putting it off, or by developing an idiosyncratic evaluation method. From a historical perspective, creative writing teachers over the last sixty years have explored innovative writing evaluation methods, including evaluation by class consensus and grading by contract or portfolio. Creative writing teachers are also prone to some of the primary self-deceptions common to all writing teachers. Like their colleagues in composition and literature, creative writing teachers may focus on error and stifle writing discovery. They may respond to student writing in a personal, jargon-filled or vague, noninformational language, as observed by Alberta Turner in her study of contemporary writers. They may also withhold response for unproductive periods of time, sometimes for an entire semester. They may deny writing students input into the evaluation process or apply an unarticulated and privileged best reading (theirs) to in-process student work.

As Peter Elbow points out, writing teachers may *imply* evaluation

---

Portions of this chapter appeared in somewhat different form in Bishop, Wendy. 1990. "Designing a Writing Portfolio Evaluation System." *The English Record* 40 (2):21–25. Used with permission.

through negative personal reactions to difficult or different students; they allow these students to *infer* their disapprobation. For some teachers, such implication is a natural and easy means of separating "wheat from chaff," and "real" writers from "dilettantes." For novice writers, unarticulated evaluation can prove devastating.

In short, creative writing teachers may claim the texts they deal with are "different" from all other written texts and allow the classes that they teach to be evaluated in a social vacuum. These teachers apply their own standards yet appear to misunderstand how variable evaluation can be. They forget to acknowledge that, if texts are socially constructed, writing evaluation might also be subject to social construction.

Problems: Traditional Ideas about Writing Evaluation

Usually, the evaluative responses of creative writing teachers are not discussed. Most available anecdotes and research concern the responses of composition teachers to student texts. Composition teachers are famous for their abilities to wash a page with red ink. However, many creative writing instructors intervene just as dramatically on their students' drafts and may make unproductive or destructive comments. Since little research considers the effectiveness or ineffectiveness of teacher response to "creative" writing, Alberta Turner's (1980) book, *Poets Teaching: The Creative Process,* is all the more valuable for the way it illuminates the preferences and habits of some creative writers when they intervene as teachers on student texts. M.F.A. graduate students I have worked with indicate they are used to giving and receiving copious on-text response. But no one has really analyzed type, focus, or effectiveness of the responses made by creative writing teachers.

It would seem, then, that the research of C. H. Knoblauch and Lil Brannon on student response to teacher commentary may be useful reading for creative writing teachers. In "Teacher Commentary on Student Writing: The State of the Art," Knoblauch and Brannon (1981) explain that students often ignore or misunderstand teacher commentary. In "A Curious Case of Our Responding Habits," David Fuller (1988) gave two groups of seven teachers each a copy of the same piece of prose. One group received a typed copy and one group received a handwritten copy. Asked to evaluate the paragraph, writing teachers responded poorly to the handwritten version, giving it lower grades and less supportive remarks than did teachers who responded to the typed version. The paragraph (taken from Ernest Hemingway's

The Sun Also Rises) received teachers' grades ranging from A to D, averaging C-. Fuller suggests that teachers should become more aware of their biases toward "student" work.

Maxine Hairston (1986) details the problems a writer may encounter when she tries to understand teacher response to her writing. There may be too much information, creating cognitive overload. Too many items may be marked, discouraging the writer and causing her to ignore all comments. The comments may not indicate ways to improve or may offer contradictory advice. Hairston explains that negative messages may show that teachers do not care *what* students say but *how* they say things. Finally, through their responses, teachers may show that they view teaching writing as a burden (120–21).

Edward White (1988) discusses the research of Nancy Sommers (1980) on teacher response to student writing (again this research was based on composition and writing response but may prove true for creative writers and writing response). White explains:

> Sommers caustically deplores the confusion she has found in her study of routine paper markings by college writing teachers. These markings almost universally treat the student text as simultaneously a finished product with editing faults and an unfinished part of the writing and thinking process. It is as if our confusion about evaluation is somehow bound up with a confusion about the nature of the student text, an odd form of literature created for the sole purpose of being criticized. Sommers finds that *writing teachers tend to say the same things about student writing even though the texts in front of them change, as do the writers* [emphasis mine]. (95)

White hopes some of this confusion—of text, teacher, and student—can be mediated and clarified if teachers gain an understanding of new (post-structural) theories of reading. These theories are leading to new understandings of how writers and readers construct texts, and, hence, how texts need to be evaluated. White explains the problems that arise when we reconsider evaluation *as a reading problem*:

> In short, these [post-structuralist] theories of reading have brought a new liberation—some would call it anarchy—into the reading process and placed on the reader a much heavier responsibility to actually create meanings that may or may not be present on the page for other readers. The writer is not relieved of responsibility by this process but rather now must assume a new responsibility: to create the kind of reader he or she needs for the text being produced. The teacher is also not free to abandon texts to naive readers, although we are forbidden to declare that some misreadings are wrong. Our obligation is to help our students see

> what other, highly sophisticated readers have made of the text so that they can enrich the text with various readings. (95)

White suggests teachers need to understand that the writing student has valid but as-yet-unrealized insights that we as teachers must seek to identify and discuss as we respond. This means that "we can respond to early drafts with questions rather than with judgment (or invective!), since our aim is to urge the student back into 'the chaotic process of textuality' (that is the flux of ideas behind writing) where revision occurs" (White 1988, 94). Equally, he advocates holistic evaluation of writing as a grading procedure (evaluating the overall effect) rather than analytical evaluation which focuses on parts and errors. White and many other writers support revision as an integral part of the evaluation process, particularly as it provides formative response (what should be done) rather than summative response (what has been accomplished now that the writer is finished).

In considering the collaborative classroom, Peter Elbow (1986c) explores issues of evaluation, and he comes to some sensible conclusions. First, Elbow asserts that evaluation occurs whether we want it to or not. Second, he finds that teachers often become confused over the meaning of the term "Evaluation [which] refers to two very different activities: *measurement* (or grading or ranking) and *commentary* (or feedback)" (231). Third, he feels that few things are "more untrustworthy than conventional grading." In explaining why he feels this is so, Elbow lists several problems with traditional grading. Elbow finds conventional grading problematic because:

- It is almost invariably performed by only one person.
- It encourages confusion between measurement and commentary.
- It disguises the many diverse features of any important performance into a single number.
- As a result it is maximally misleading both to students and outside readers.
- As a further result it encourages students and the rest of the community in the myth that a person's intelligence or learning can be summed up on one dimension. (232)

Elbow's list prompts me to consider these issues by reversing his list, transforming it into a series of assertions about creative writing evaluation. To be preferable to traditional grading, then, evaluation in the transactional creative writing workshop should:

- become multimodal and include evaluation and even grading by teacher, peer, and writer;
- include both commentary and measurement;
- clarify and discuss the features of a writer's performance that are being evaluated and offer multiple ways of reporting such evaluation;
- be comprehensible (and usable) to the writer; and
- be understood and applied in light of the evaluation method's actual and real limitations.

Clearly, there is a need for research into evaluation issues in creative writing. Creative writing teachers will want to develop methods of evaluation that are consistent with the goals of their creative writing workshop. Until research findings become available, teachers may choose to borrow from the most applicable developments in critical theory and composition studies.

Suggestions: New Directions in Creative Writing Evaluation

Writing evaluation should be multimodal and include both commentary and measurement. Writing evaluation becomes multimodal when the writing teacher considers different evaluators, evaluation methods, and evaluation sequences. First, teachers may allow for individual goal-setting which is structured by the teacher, or they may ask students to contract for a certain amount of required writing. The contract grade places the emphasis on adequate completion of *amounts* of work rather than on the *quality* of finished products; therefore, contract grading may be particularly appropriate for novice writers.

In individualized goal setting, the following steps allow a teacher to adapt evaluation on a student-by-student basis.

1. The teacher models appropriate responses to student writing.
2. The teacher reads student work and uses commentary that supports the writer.
3. The teacher reads student writing and offers one positive response.
4. The teacher establishes a goal for the writer to work toward (using positive language).
5. The teacher evaluates the next piece of writing according to the goal(s) set in the previous response session.

6. Additional goals are added only as the writer is ready to take on new challenges.
7. Every several weeks, the student revises one piece more thoroughly for more extensive evaluation. (Adapted from Beavan 1977, 140–41; see her article for a thorough discussion of this and other methods of evaluation.)

It is worth noting the limitations of this method. Individualized goal setting proves useful at the beginning of a creative writing class since the technique develops trust between teacher and writer and offers a highly structured sequence that utilizes a teacher's experience. However, individualized goal setting almost assures that students remain dependent on the teacher's experience and criteria, as in other methods of traditional teacher response. Patrick Bizarro (1990) solves some of those problems by asking students to *participate* in individualized goal setting. Students learn to analyze their own poems with the teacher, to prioritize revision concerns, and to agree to write the next work with those priorities in mind. Bizarro suggests students can contract to have the teacher evaluate their forthcoming work according to *class-negotiated* priorities.

Self-evaluation allows students to participate in developing and monitoring instructional goals. Self-evaluation solves some of the problems of individualized goal setting. Writer self-evaluation occurs whenever a writer formally (or even informally) reflects upon his progress. Self-evaluation can take the form of a journal entry, a completed writing response protocol like the ones discussed in chapter 7 and found in appendix A. Although intended for guiding groups, these protocol sheets can easily be adapted by a writer for self-evaluation purposes. Other self-evaluation occurs when a writer participates in metacognitive review by evaluating a changed writing process or a draft sequence or by comparing his work to work he has imitated, and so on.

Mary Beavan's (1977) guide for self-evaluation asks students to consider the following issues regarding their piece of writing:

1. How much time did I spend on this piece of writing?
2. After the draft or evaluation, what did I try to improve and how successful was I?
3. What are the strengths of my paper? (Indicate these sections with a squiggly line or highlighting.)
4. What are the weaknesses of my piece of writing? (Put an X near sections where a peer or teacher may help you.)

5. What single thing will I do to improve my next piece of writing? What experimentation will I try?
6. Optional—what grade would I give myself on this piece? (Justify it.) (adapted from pages 142–43)

In a very similar way, I ask writers to provide what I call a writing process cover sheet, a written narrative that traces the generation, revision, and development of that piece of writing over the time period when it is composed. This response can be guided by protocol questions or can be modeled by the teacher (she can share a copy of her work and drafts and a sample cover sheet which narrates the history of a piece of writing). Peter Elbow's book, *Writing with Power*, includes two chapters of writers' questions that can be fashioned into self-evaluation prompts: chapter 22, "A Catalogue of Criterion-Based Questions"—includes questions that address quality, organization, language and usage; chapter 23, "A Catalogue of Reader-Based Questions"—includes questions that address a reader's moment-by-moment feelings, ask readers to summarize their feelings, and ask readers to create images of their responses.

Peer evaluation has been discussed in chapter 6. Peer response can result in both a commentary and an evaluation. Peers help writers "create the kind of reader [they need] for the text being produced" (White 1988, 92). Peers, like teachers, illuminate the vagaries of evaluation and response when they, like teachers, respond to nontext factors such as a writer's appearance, moral stance, experimental style, or social role. Peers, of course, also, and primarily, respond to the writer's text. Patrick Bizarro (1989) sees the peer role as particularly useful for helping to develop community-specific evaluation criteria. Student writers can be asked to read and respond to published creative writing and to negotiate and refine their definitions of adequate, good, and superior writing which then become part of the writing class evaluation criteria.

Writing evaluation should include both commentary and measurement, and it should clarify and discuss the features of a writer's performance that are being evaluated and offer multiple ways of reporting such evaluation. If they use portfolio evaluation, writing teachers resolve many problems raised in evaluating "creative" works. As I mentioned earlier, portfolios have long been the evaluation procedure most often mentioned by teachers of creative writing. However, the portfolio evaluation method I advocate for the transactional creative writing workshop is more analytical than the one found in the traditional workshop. Certainly it is more comprehensive than portfolio evaluation as I experienced it as an undergraduate creative writing student. When I turned in my undergraduate portfolios, they were no more than a collection of the required number of poems or stories, final drafts only, with no attached writer's meditation as to how those end results were achieved. Additionally, I often received my work back with little or no teacher commentary. In other words, the folders and collections were simply an administrative device. As writer, I was held responsible for keeping track of work, and the teacher was interested only in *finished* products.

Writing portfolios, however, have much more potential. Portfolios can allow writer and teacher to review classroom growth and to agree upon the worth of the semester's work. They can also mobilize all of the evaluation possibilities I have reviewed so far. Portfolios can include goal setting and contract evaluation, for a certain number of writings *and drafts*. Rough- to professional- to portfolio-quality drafts can be required. Portfolios may include self-evaluation. Writers participate in process self-analysis when they compose process cover sheets or complete self-evaluation protocols. Portfolios can include peer-evaluation. Writers collect and analyze peer responses in journal entries—like those of John included in chapter 7, where he traces his reactions to group work. Or writers compile, consider, and respond to completed response sheets from class members. Finally, portfolios include traditional teacher evaluation in the form of mid- or end-of-semester grades. At this point, teachers may grade selected pieces of writing or the entire portfolio (see Bishop 1990a and 1990c; Burnham 1986; Elbow and Belanoff 1986; and "Portfolio Assessment," 1988).

Why Choose Writing Portfolios?

I use writing portfolios because I agree with Edward White when he observes that "the most effective teachers of writing are traditionally those who are the most human and the most demanding of their students. Whatever their curriculum, they establish themselves or other defined audiences as live and sympathetic readers willing to participate in the quest for meaning that is writing" (95). Writing portfolios allow for the development of such an audience and demand that a student develop his own high standards for his own writing.

When compiling a creative writing portfolio, student writers learn that revision is a long-term, recursive process. As they share drafts with peers, tutors, and their teacher, these writers become aware of audience needs. Through reflection on and response to such conversations, students revise their work into a portfolio representative of their best writing. The teacher works as both advocate *and* evaluator, helping writers select and present work for end-of-semester evaluation in the portfolio. And when student work is "published" in this manner, writers can take pride in their own maturity of expression. Surveying a completed portfolio, they realize that they *have* written a lot and that they *did* grow as writers from the first day to the last day of the class. Using portfolios, novice writing students, literally, become practicing writers.

When starting to use portfolios, a writing teacher might find it useful to consider the following issues and suggestions.

Writing portfolios utilize drafts. Since portfolios present students' best work, submitted after work has been discussed and improved, generally, all portfolio pieces will have gone through drafts. Depending on the teacher's class organization, drafts may have been thoroughly critiqued in peer-response groups, in student/teacher conferences, and in tutoring sessions. The draft levels I use are described in chapter 7. In any event, portfolio presentation requires some version of a planned drafting cycle. Students generate, participate in, and later complete invention exercises and draft their own, out-of-class pieces. They share writing during a draft cycle, rough to professional to portfolio quality.

A writing portfolio may be evaluated at mid-semester and/or at the end of the semester. Having students collect all classroom writing at mid-semester to submit in a writing portfolio can lead to a productive student-teacher dialogue. Mid-semester portfolio evaluation allows teachers to talk to creative writing students about where they have been and where they are going. At mid-semester, teachers may ask students to place their writing in a two-pocket portfolio folder. In one pocket are *rough* and *professional* drafts for each piece of required writing and possibly a writing process journal. In the other pocket are *portfolio*-quality drafts of required work and, possibly, a *letter of self-evaluation*. For each student, a teacher will read the portfolio drafts carefully, review other portfolio materials briefly, and respond (a) to the portfolio as a whole and (b) to the writer's letter of self-evaluation, if used.

It is possible to write long and effective mid-semester responses to student portfolios, but such an activity will overtax most writing teachers. There is also the possibility of allocating evaluation time unfairly as a teacher lingers over some portfolios and speeds through others. Evaluation sessions that fluctuate with stamina may become less than fair.

Designing a one-page response sheet for each class can regularize a teacher's response time, allowing her to check off class requirements—thereby making sure the writing portfolio is complete—and to respond briefly in writing to portfolio content across three categories:

1. an overall response to writing development (what is successful?);
2. suggestions for improving writing during the second half of the semester (suggestions at this time are particularly important as they may refer to the student's self-evaluation. If teacher and student estimations exhibit great variance, the teacher will want to describe what changes will help the student progress more successfully); and
3. a mid-semester grade-in-progress with a sentence or two of explanation.

End-of-semester evaluation echoes mid-semester evaluation, but it is summative in nature rather than formative. Because this is the last time a teacher can respond to students, the response sheet may include only numbers 1 and 3, above. Figure 22 shows a sample evaluation sheet designed *to be adapted* for a creative writing course; figures 23 and 24 are copies of actual evaluation sheets (my responses on the originals were handwritten rather than typed).

Consider fairness in grading. Evaluating portfolios on their own, teachers may develop grading concerns that parallel the concerns they have had when grading individual student pieces. For instance, what constitutes an A-, B-, or C-level creative writing portfolio? How does a teacher assure that she is fair in her evaluations, not awarding a "fat" ineffective portfolio more credit than a "thin" focused portfolio, and so on? These concerns are central for any teacher instituting a portfolio system. Several practices can help:

1. Begin a portfolio system by outlining goals for portfolios *as used in that class*, and write a guide that details what is expected from a portfolio in each grading category (A, B, C, etc.).
2. Share this guide (or concepts from the guide) with students during class discussion, in conferences, and in mid-semester evaluation commentary.
3. Use a formalized response sheet (like the one in figure 22) for critiquing. By checking off materials received and recording responses *in categories*, teachers are forced to look up from the mass of writing collected and evaluate it as a whole effort. The checklist can include an "improvement" category or a "participation" credit as well as an evaluation of portfolio draft quality.

Remember that portfolio evaluation does not take less time. Portfolios do not provide a grading panacea. Writing portfolios change the quality of the time and the pacing of the time demands. To share the evaluation process with writers, teachers can ask class members to review portions of writing students' mid-semester and final portfolios to provide another "publishing" opportunity for writers. I often ask class members to exchange portfolios with another writer during the class when the portfolios are due. Each student reads through another writer's (at that moment) final drafts and compares what she has read with her memory of earlier workshop versions or with her own portfolio. Three sample responses follow. In this class, students were asked to look at six portfolio draft poems at the end of the semester.

> Karina responding to Tonie's portfolio:
>
> Tonie's last 6 poems show improvement especially from their drafts I saw earlier in the semester.
>
> I really liked "One of these Days," the cliche poem—it shows a child very well, & is funny too. "Going Home" was my favorite—I got such a clear image that I felt like *I* was the narrator, going home. Her poem "The Moose Ate My Dreams" was a very good attempt at fixed form—better than I could do that's for sure.
>
> Tonie's thing poem about staples was obviously hard, but I think I liked it more when it was in earlier stages. I know how hard these poems are to write especially when the object becomes almost human.
>
> I've noticed that both of us write about the same kinds of things—kids, memories, etc. I really like Tonie's style of writing—whether it's serious or funny, it always gets my mind going.

> Tonie responding to Karina's portfolio:
>
> —America poem as political statement works real well, poignant.
> —changes, job at Gary's in 1st floor apartment make time element cohere. Good revision.
> —love fingerprint on glass in Spring poem! and the dandelions yearly quest to overrun the back yard.
>
> Karina has chosen many of the same subjects I chose to write about. [Her] Bird in the tree like [my] squirrel poem. she ends her poems well and has good images. First Floor Apt. & America will stay with me for a long time. The form of paperclips is wonderful.

> Mark responding to Pamela's portfolio:
>
> I looked at Pamela's poems at mid-semester when we did the same thing we are doing now. I enjoy reading her poems and feel I have got to know her through her poetry. Particular poems that I liked were the [poem name—handwriting obscure]. I also

> like the poem "Toaster from a Former Marriage" in particular I like the honesty and I also finished this poem with a feeling that this mundane toaster has meaning. Most of all I like the situation (a woman cooking breakfast—for a man she does not seem to love.) I like the poem "Tragic" I had read a very different version on practically the first day of class.
>
> Pamela has developed noticeable since mid-semester. She has come to grips with titles and has harnessed her poetry much more. I enjoy the honesty of her love poems and I like her vocabulary and sense of humor. All her poems have a quality (not sure what it is) that pleases me.

And obviously, student's mid-semester and final self-evaluation letters allow both the creative writer and the creative writing teacher to better understand class members' growth and development. Here are three representative student self-evaluations.

> Self-evaluation 1: Introduction to Fiction Writing
>
> I think that I am doing much better in this class now. I'm enjoying writing a lot more and I am able to relate to my stories more.
>
> My favorite piece that I wrote was the one about my sister and I running the car into the ceramic shop. I really enjoyed writing that piece a lot. (The one from my point of view, not [the one] from my mother's [point of view]).
>
> "Naked Fear" is my second favorite piece also because I could relate to it well. However, the short story "The Wedding Threshold" no matter how I tried, I could not make work. the characters were flat and the plot was boring. I tried to make it work several times, but to no avail. Suggestions on the story to help?
>
> My attendance has improved. I missed one day because I was sick, but that was it. Also, I tried very hard not to come in late and was successful. I also think that my class participation has improved. I feel more comfortable critiquing (sp.?) other people. I even enjoy giving my opinion and accepting them.
>
> I enjoyed this class. I especially liked it when we did the in class writings (The shoes and hats). They were really interesting.
>
> [semester grade estimate] B− or C+
>
> Thanks,

> Self-evaluation 2: Introduction to Poetry Writing
>
> I hate judging anybody, especially myself so I will have, another, hard time evaluating myself. It is hard to avoid comparisons. I think that not as much improvement was made this half of the semester as was last half of the semester, but I think that I matured a little as a poet. I still do not think I have found the right voice,

my first drafts often have two voices in them and my final drafts—I think—show a poet who is in search of the right voice.

I did not utilize the Writing Center as much this half of the semester as last, which I think hurt me much more than helped me. But I also think that I did not need it as much this half since I have come to grips—not completely—with revision much more than early in the semester. I went to see you as much in the second half as in the first half of the semester; it is easier for me to go to you than to go to the Writing Center.

As a critiquer I think I became a little more vocal in group workshops than earlier. For some strange reason I really enjoy critiquing poems in workshop, in small group workshops I am usually quiet. My critiquing ability improved as much as I did as a poet, they reflect each other.

If I were to give myself a grade I would give myself a B+—I gave myself a B at midsemester. I hate any kind of grade though and have learned a lot, enjoyed doing it, and am sorry to see that this class has to end.

Self-evaluation 3: Introduction to Fiction Writing

In discussing my growth, change, and improvements as a writer, I feel that this class is where most of my development occurred. The English classes I had taken prior to this one dealt mostly with literature readings, and term paper style writing. I feel everyone can write a good term paper, but not everyone can write a good short, creative story. In this class I felt my style and desire to write had increased greatly. The pieces I want to focus on are, "Dead End", "Misconception", my mid-semester short story, "Kauffman's", and my semester short story "Partings".

As I mentioned in my last letter, I had a bit of trouble mixing thought, dialogue and action, mainly in the stories "Dead End" and "Misconception". I also mentioned that I had problems ending my stories, and in turn left readers feeling cut off. The story "Kauffman's" is where I felt that all of my problems started to iron themselves out. My dialogue flowed better, and I felt that Mary Dooley's actions fit the character well. My mid semester short story needed more description, and less telling. That story gave me some problems. By the time I started writing "Partings" I felt confident with my characters, plot, and actions that the characters were to take on. The dialogue came easy for me. I feel that this is my best piece. Eventually I would like to make some revisions, and make it longer.

In evaluating myself in attendance, participation, and my ability to critique others, I would have to mark myself highly. I rarely ever missed a class. I felt it was important to have the students present when critiquing my papers, so in return I tried to do the same for them. I even feel that my ability to critique has improved throughout the semester.

My outside reading done for this class has been limited to our

> text, and the other students papers. Keeping up with the text book readings in my other classes has deprived me of pleasure reading. I love to read, but find little time to read for pleasure. However, I did enjoy reading the other's work.
>
> I feel that the most valuable aspect of this class was the workshops themselves. I liked hearing what others thought about my work, and the students have given me alot of great tips. The only thing I disagree with is the reading log. I really feel that the log did not do me any good, as far as the class goes. If I were a full time writer I might feel differently, but I felt that it had no significance to the class. This is the main reason my log is lacking.
>
> Overall, I found the class fun and enjoyable. I especially liked the in class writing assignments such as the postcards, and writing a character with the hat and shoes. I developed the characters in "Partings" from the hat and shoes we worked with. They have undergone some major changes, but the assignment helped me to get started.
>
> The self grade is always a hard thing to do. I am basing my grade completely on my improvement and growth in my writing throughout the semester. I felt that this was the main emphasis of the class. I am not comparing myself to other writers in the class because we are all at different levels of writing. This in a way was good, because I learned alot from those who write exceptionally well. As I mentioned at the beginning of this letter, I honestly feel that my development has improved greatly, therefore I give myself an A. Have a nice summer. Sincerely,

A teacher with the not unusual teaching load of three to five classes will, reasonably, find the portfolio reading period daunting. When instituting the portfolio method and tailoring it to his classroom needs, this teacher will have to start with what works. Although it seems likely that a mid- and end-of-semester full reading of each student's work is the fairest possible evaluative review, teachers may not always be able to devote as much time as they would like to each creative writing portfolio and still submit grades on time. One of several possible modifications of the full-semester portfolio system may help.

1. Teachers can divide a portfolio evaluation period into two equal parts and evaluate the first half of the semester's work and then "retire" this work before going on to evaluate the the second half of the semester's work. Teachers who do this may wish to weigh the second half of the semester's grade slightly (60 percent), expecting writing to improve more impressively the longer students work at developing their writing process. This choice, a two-part portfolio review, while less than optimal in that it reduces formative evaluation, still allows students involved in such a class to participate in two process-oriented, grade-in-

progress drafting cycles. The teacher benefits by not having to read too many full-length, full-semester portfolios in a three-day grading period.

2. Teachers can have students submit a smaller number of "best" pieces from the semester for portfolio evaluation. This can be a timesaving device for the teacher, assuring her that portfolios will never include more than, say, three already familiar writings and a student's self-evaluation. Additionally, students learn to weigh and evaluate their own writing ever more objectively, working with the teacher, class peers, or writing center staff to decide which of their drafts are most effective from a reader's viewpoint.

   Additionally, the opportunity to choose and focus on selected "best" pieces of prose or poetry may support a teacher's end-of-semester transition from revision to editing and proofreading. Students have more incentive to edit *portfolio*-quality drafts than rough or professional drafts and may have greater success learning to edit and proofread when working with a limited number of pieces.

3. Teachers can collect portfolios up to two weeks before the end of the semester, offering the teacher more review time under less pressure. During the final week or two of class, students can be refining their work for the class book and then "publishing" their photocopied "class anthology" of peer chosen and edited writing from each student (described in chapter 3). Additionally, if the teacher's institution allows for such a substitution, conferencing time can be scheduled for the last week of class so that teachers can return the portfolio to each student and come to a satisfying sense of class closure. This slightly earlier due date can also assure that students are not trying to make extensive and often unsuccessful revisions while cramming for botany or calculus exams.

Portfolios help students and teachers better respect a student writer's progress and effort while engaging in necessary evaluation of her final class products. That is why, of course, portfolios support the transactional creative writing workshop. They provide a necessary, wide focus—on the writer of effective texts, on the developing texts, and on the readers of those texts (adapted from Bishop 1990a).

This review of evaluation and response shows the creative writing teacher taking on many roles. Teachers are coaches *and* evaluators. Some prefer the terms senior learner or mentor. Whatever the name, creative writing teachers need to remember that all students have potential as writers and as members of a writing community. Often, the creative writing teacher needs to monitor his classroom persona and his position in the classroom hierarchy. Current writing research suggests successful teachers learn to move themselves from the center of the room to the sidelines (see Bishop 1990g; Perl and Wilson 1986). These teachers are demanding individuals who also know the value of nurturing, collaborating, coaching, and facilitating.

There is immense value in the communities that these creative writing teachers develop. Karen Burke LeFevre (1987) describes how creative, inventive thinkers—what some people call geniuses—become noticeable in *clusters,* achieving prominence during certain time periods and in certain geographic locations. LeFevre claims that clusters occur due to *resonance,* and she observes this about resonance and resonators:

> When individuals collaborate to invent, new ideas arise in part because of a quality that I will call "resonance," a term used by Harold Lasswell. Lasswell notes that successful innovators often maintain "resonant relationships" with certain people in their social sphere. Those who are less successful innovators perhaps lack such "resonators" and may thus be more likely to succumb to the "dampening influence" of their environment. . . . Resonators might be groups of students or colleagues, accepting "apostles" who allow a person to investigate ideas in a safe place without the harsh evaluation that outsiders might make. . . . Resonance comes about when an individual act—a "vibration"—is intensified and prolonged by sympathetic vibrations. It may occur when someone acts as a facilitator to assist or extend what is regarded as primarily another's invention, or when people are mutual collaborators on a task. Resonance also occurs indirectly when people provide a supportive social and intellectual environment that nurtures thought and enables ideas to be received, thus completing the inventive act. (65)

For me, resonation seems a metaphorically satisfying term when it is applied to the transactional creative writing workshop. The transactional workshop allows for the development of resonant relationships. Individual development is intensified and prolonged by appropriate support. In this classroom writers are writing, and creative writing teachers dismantle unproductive hierarchies, allowing all class members to be resonators, sympathetic sharers in the intricate development of writing facility that results in poems, prose poems, novels, epics, screenplays, farces, journals, sermons, satires, stories, dreams, dialogs, and other discourses we care about. Then, creative writing students are released into language—for life.

Mid-semester Evaluation Sheet

________ In-class writing 1 ____________________

________ In-class writing 2 ____________________

________ In-class writing 3 ____________________

________ Out-of-class writing 1 ____________________

________ Out-of-class writing 2 ____________________

________ Out-of-class writing 3 ____________________

________ Optional writing (sometimes students like to add work they have done on their own or in other classes—I usually limit the amount I will read to one piece each half of the semester)

________ Craft-presentation (when students present talks, I have each listener write a comment and rate the presentation on a scale of check, check-minus or check-plus or 1–10, and the class average is the final evaluation for this activity) ____________________

________ Letter of Self-Evaluation ____________________

________ Class Journal or Learning Log ____________________

General response to the portfolio:

Suggestions for the second half of the semester: ____________________

Evaluation summary:

Journal (10%) ________

Class Participation (20%) ________
(includes attendance,
group work, readings, etc.)

Writing Portfolio (70%) ________

Mid-semester grade in progress: ________

Fig. 22. Sample mid-semester evaluation sheet for writing portfolios.

English 272 Spring 1988 Final portfolio evaluation for: Paul K.

Completeness:

__X__ 6 in-class poems ____________________

__X__ 6 out-of-class poems ____________________

__X__ learning log ____________________

__X__ letter of self-evaluation ____________________

optional poems ____________________

General remarks:

I'm going to note the most successful: "Sunrise" "Overridden" "Names" "Moss" (lots of potential but needs work) "Milkshake" (fun & different)

Evaluation

Learning Log (20%) A—lot of good self-analysis, self-critique & growth

Writing Portfolio (60%) __B+__
(final copies class poems)

Attendance/Participation (20%) __A/B__

Final Class Grade: __B+__

Suggestions for future writing: I agree that the poems during the second 1/2 [of the semester] are more ambitious & more interesting but also less finished—wish you had brought some by for conferencing. Your strengths are your willingness to engage w/new forms & explore intellectual/philosophical problems but the latter also leads you into confusing imagery and register shifts (sometimes archaic or overly gothic language). Developing more awareness of readers was of tremendous importance this semester & will help both your poetry and your fiction Hope I have you in future writing classes. Wendy

Good luck with your future writing projects: invent, revise, revise, revise, edit, enjoy, submit, publish and enjoy again.

Feel free to share some work with me or with writing center tutors next fall.

Fig. 23. Portfolio response sheet for Paul K.

English 272 Spring 1988 Final portfolio evaluation for: Donna S.

Completeness:

__X__ 6 in-class poems __________

__X__ 6 out-of class poems __________

__X__ learning log __________

__X__ letter of self-evaluation Thanks—although I didn't agree with all the self-evaluation I appreciated having your views

optional poems __________

General remarks:

I think some of the poems from the first 1/2 of the semester could have benefitted from revision. My favorite as yours is, is still "Cortez." I'll list the most successful in my view from the last 6: "Frozen" (I think says a lot with a little); "Timeclocks" (well-revised). "Purse & House" (needs more time from you) and your cliche poem is fun but could use a title to go to work for it.

Evaluation

Learning Log (20%) C—still not as useful as it could be—you don't write at any length or discuss readings from anthology, etc.

Writing Portfolio (60%) __B__
(final copies class poems)

Attendance/Participation (20%) A—it was enjoyable having your voice in class

Final Class Grade: __B__

Suggestions for future writing: I think there's been important growth here. Now you need to discipline yourself to longer/more revision & better proofing. Keep writing and exploring these important relationships and working out new ways to express these universal themes. Hope to have you in class again. Wendy

Good luck with your future writing projects: invent, revise, revise, revise, edit, enjoy, submit, publish and enjoy again.

Feel free to share some work with me or with writing center tutors next fall.

Fig. 24. Portfolio response sheet for Donna S.

Appendix A: Response Protocol Sheets

These protocol sheets were designed to help students complete productive critique sessions for fiction, poetry, and nonfiction. Two multigenre response sheets are also included; the generic protocols can be used to respond to experimental *or* to traditional writing. Although each sheet was designed for eliciting either early or late responses to a piece of writing, teachers and students will want to experiment with the protocols, altering them to suit each response situation; often questions will need to be added or deleted. In their current form, the sheets *can* train writers to respond and *will* help guide peer group work. However, the sheets will become even more useful if they are continually adapted by members of a particular writing community.

Writer's name: ____________________

Responder's name: ____________________

Answer any five of the following questions:

1. What part of the essay do you remember best?
2. Be nosey. What do you want to know more about? Think of three questions to ask the writer about his or her piece.
3. Was there anything that you didn't understand? If so, what part?
4. Which sensory details were most effective?
5. What do you wish the writer would leave out in the next draft?
6. Suggest some aspects for the writer to experiment with. (Examples: past to present tense, change point of view, serious to sarcastic tone, first to third person, move ending scene to the beginning, emphasize a different theme.)
7. If you could have lunch with one of the characters in the essay, which one would it be? What would you talk about?
8. What do you think about the beginning? What made you keep reading? What did you think of the end? Did you wish it had continued? Ended sooner? Or was it just right?
9. If this were your paper, what would you do next?
10. Tell the writer what he or she does best and encourage her to do it some more.

App. A-1. Response sheet for early response: nonfiction.

Feel free to write on the student's draft and/or on the back of this sheet, besides in the blanks. To save time, refer to sentences or sections by page number, paragraph, and line number, or use a highlighter.

1. Why do you think the writer wrote this piece?
2. Why could or couldn't/should or shouldn't this piece be a short story?
3. What do you like best about this piece?
4. What other titles might be good, or is this title the best one you can think of (and why)?
5. Which sentences or paragraphs did you have to reread in order to understand?
6. Which sentences sound especially good out loud?
7. Which sentences sound awkward, too slow, too long, too heavy, or out of tune?
8. Which words or sentences need more spice(!)?
9. Where could dialogue be added, or is there enough?
10. On the writer's paper, mark all the mechanical errors (syntax, grammar, spelling, punctuation, typing format) that bugged you or distracted you, or that you'd just like to point out to the writer. Use editing/proofreading marks if you wish.
11. Is there anything else you'd like to tell the writer?

Peer responder's name ____________________
Writer's name ____________________
Title of nonfiction piece ____________________
Date ____________________

App. A-2. Response sheet for late peer response: polishing nonfiction.

Name of Writer: ____________________
Date: ____________________

1. What are the strongest images in the poem? Write them below.
2. What does this poem make you think of? How does it make you feel?
3. Is there a surprise in this poem? Where? What's the surprise?
4. Where could the poem expand? Give two or three places if possible.
5. Are there rhymes in this poem? Where do they work well? Are there places the rhymes draw attention to themselves—distract the reader? Write down some samples, lines and words.
6. If there are clichés in this poem list them below. Also write some examples of the writer's use of fresh and interesting language.

App. A-3. Response sheet for early peer response: poems.

Name of Writer: ____________________

Date: ____________________

1. What are the strongest images in the poem? Write them below.
2. Is there a main emotion in this poem? If so, what? Are there other emotions that also work in this poem?
3. Is there tension, surprise, or conflict in this poem? Where? Does it work for you? If so, how?
4. Does the poem have a sense of closure? How does the writer achieve that effect? Or do you still expect more from the poem? If you expect more, what do you expect?
5. Where do the poem's rhythms work best? Where do they work the least? Is there rhyme, alliteration, assonance? Do they contribute to the effectiveness of the poem?
6. What are some of the words this poem doesn't need? Write down the word and what line it appears in.
7. Mark the clichés in the poem with an asterisk. List examples of fresh and interesting language here.

App. A-4. Response sheet for late peer response: poems.

Student Name ____________________

Title ____________________ Date ____________________

1. What is the best part of this story? Why?
2. Does the story have an understandable structure? How would you describe it?
3. Are the characters developed well enough? Which characters are most believable? Which could be improved?
4. Do you have a sense of the story's setting? What is it? How might it be improved?
5. Does the story have a clear point of view? What (whose) is it?
6. Are there problems with verb tense shifts? Sentence structure? Syntax? Grammar? If so, please note here and mark them on the draft.
7. Has the writer avoided clichés? Where could the writer be more careful about word choice?
8. Try to sum up what happens in this story in one sentence.

App. A-5. Response sheet for early peer response: fiction.

Student Name ______________________

Title ______________________ Date ______________________

1. (a) Do the characters' actions and the progress of the story (the plot) make sense to you? Why or why not?
   (b) Is the tension sustained? How?
2. Is *everything* in the story *essential* to the story's success? What could be deleted?
3. Are the characters developed (i.e., do they seem like real people to you)? How are the main characters different from each other? Consider dialogue, physical gestures, description.
4. Where is the language most vivid, or à la Pound, "charged with meaning"? Where does it go flat?
5. What is the story's point of view? Is it consistent? How is it *appropriate* for the story's purposes? Could a different point of view improve the story? How?
6. If you described the story's *texture* (i.e., the way it feels), what would it be? Why? Does the story seem three-dimensional? Where could that quality be improved?
7. Could the sentence variations be improved (i.e., do the rhythms vary sufficiently)? Where?
8. Does the story's pace fit its content? How?
9. Is the story's ending satisfying? Why or why not?
10. Why does the story fit its title?
11. What did you like most about the story?

App. A-6. Response sheet for late peer response: fiction.

Writer ____________________
Title ____________________

Please use this sheet to respond to another writer's work. Remember, the writer is in an *early draft stage* and will expect to use your comments to help improve his/her writing for a future draft.

1. Find several words, lines, or passages that stand out in this piece of writing. Underline/highlight them on the paper or list them in the space below. Is each one effective? Distracting? Out of place? Unusual? Interesting? Explain for each example that you choose.
2. After reading this piece, what did you still want to find out? Why?
3. For you as reader, were there any words, lines, or passages that left you unsure or confused? If so, find several and explain what you felt unsure about.
4. How do you feel about the writer's use of language in this piece? Give some examples, using page numbers and sentences or by quoting lines:
   (a) Examples of fresh, interesting, and/or appropriate language—language that you especially liked.
   (b) Examples of clichéd, too familiar, and/or out of place language—language that you think could be rewritten more effectively.
5. Suggest the most important change(s) you feel the writer could make to improve this piece while redrafting.

Your name: ____________________ Date: ____________________

App. A-7. Response sheet for early peer response: multigenre (poetry, fiction, nonfiction, or drama).

Your name: ____________________

Title of the work being critiqued: ____________________

Author's name: ____________________

Higher-Order Concerns

1. Describe how you felt after you finished reading this piece. What impressions did you leave with?
2. List three places where the author could streamline this piece by trimming certain words, lines, or passages.
3. List three places where the author could improve the piece by adding more information.
4. Do you feel this piece is complete? If yes, why? If not, what is missing?

Lower-Order Concerns

1. Did the author use punctuation in any way that concerns you? If so, where and why?
2. Were there any places in the piece where you were dissatisfied with the author's choice of words? Where and why?
3. What do you think of the title? Does it suit the piece? Why or why not?

App. A-8. Response sheet for late peer response: multigenre (poetry, fiction, nonfiction, or drama).

Appendix B: Teaching Creative Writing—A Selected, Annotated Bibliography

This bibliography selects out books and articles that are useful for new or continuing teachers of creative writing and concentrates, particularly, on invention techniques, classroom activities, and the intersection of creative writing and composition pedagogy. Some of the annotations were supplied by the following individuals: Steve Bailey (SB), Scott Herzer (SH), Carolyn Kremers (SK), Trecie Melnick (TM), Peg Peoples (PP), Jill Robinson (JR), and Terence Wike (TW).

Adams, James L. 1986. The Care and Feeding of Ideas: A Guide to Encouraging Creativity. Reading, Mass.: Addison-Wesley.

In this book on change and creativity and their elusiveness, Adams claims that ideas can be cultivated, for a wide variety of purposes, including financial gain. Part One of the book discusses "Thinking," in depth, and includes exercises on, for example, thinking in three different styles. Part Two, called "Doing," also involves comprehensive discussion, and includes a variety of exercises. The thrust of the book is expository, and the exercises serve more to illustrate points than to carry the text, but the exercises look useful. [Academic; Craft Mixed Genre; Non-specialized] (JR)

Armstrong, Cheryl. 1984. "A Process Perspective on Poetic Discourse." Paper presented at the Annual Meeting of the Conference on College Composition and Communication. New York, New York, March 29–31. [ERIC Document Reproduction Service No. ED 243 108.]

Over the course of six interviews, a novice poet revealed his revision process as being significantly different from that of professional poets. The novice poet altered little in his draft, had few audience influences besides himself and an occasional friend, and felt his poem was complete when he had satisfied himself. He also felt that a poem should look and sound like a poem but was unfamiliar with other poets' work or working methods. This poet also wrote only when "moved" to write. Armstrong suggests that developing poets must write not only for themselves but for others. [Academic; Research on Writing/Literature; College]

Bartel, Roland. 1983. *Metaphors and Symbols: Forays into Language.* Urbana: National Council of Teachers of English.

Concentrates exclusively on the metaphor, including discussions of origins, riddles, proverbs, and slang. Both poetry and prose are taken into consideration. Bartel also discusses "worn-out metaphors," clichés. Pedagogical use is limited because the sparse teaching exercises don't venture far beyond discussion. [Academic; Craft Mixed Genre; College] (TM)

Baumbach, Jonathan. 1970. *Writers as Teachers/Teachers as Writers.* New York: Holt, Rinehart and Winston.

Essays by different writers about writing. Topics vary but include advice to creative writing teachers, personal essays about how the writer writes, essays about experiences teaching in the high schools and colleges, and philosophies. Some of the essays include specific craft and invention exercises. Several of the writers deal with the question of whether creative writing can be taught and how/whether creativity is stifled by the nature of the American educational system. [Academic; Essays on Writing; Non-specialized] (TM)

Berenson, Sheila K. 1988. "Judy Blumes and Ray Bradburys Galore: Novelists in the Making." *English Journal* 77: 177–86.

The author's high school class wrote a novel in a collaborative effort. Berenson provides guidelines for instructors who want to attempt the exercise, which is designed to improve both composition and creative writing skills. [Academic; Craft Fiction; Secondary and College] (SB)

Bernstein, Bonnie. 1983. *Writing Crafts Workshop.* Belmont, Calif.: Pitman Learning.

A collection of thirty-four art projects that either incorporate or encourage young people's creative writing. The book includes directions for making a Victorian lap desk, quill pen, berry ink, marbled paper, a writer's portfolio, a folded book, stitched book, hornbook, linoleum block prints, a rolling pin press, paper stencils, a cipher slide, poetry grilles, ghostwriter's ink, rebus, among many other items. Another section presents homemade games that involve writing. Scattered throughout the book are "Writer's Gallery" pages, which feature facts about writers and writing in various historic and cultural periods. There is also a list of places that publish young people's writing, and a collection of decorative alphabets and "clip-art." [Non-academic; How-to General; Elementary and Secondary] (CK)

Betts, Doris. 1984. "Undergraduate Creative Writing Courses." *ADE Bulletin* 79: 34–36.

Betts argues against the idea that creative writing is taught to find "great writers" and advocates teaching as a way to form excellent readers. She suggests teaching grammar and mechanics and then discusses undergraduate teaching according to two models. In the first, large-scale teaching avoids line by line criticism and requires that students write a lot before looking at particular craft issues. In the second, instruction moves from parts to whole, i.e., scene to story. Teaching success, she feels, depends not on method, though, but on teacher/student seriousness of undertaking. [Academic; Essays on Writing; College]

Bishop, Wendy. "The 15 Sentence Portrait." *Exercise Exchange* 35 (2): 5–8.

An in-class invention exercise that allows students to find new ways to look at individuals for whom they feel powerful emotions. [Academic; Craft Mixed Genre; Secondary and College]

———. 1990. "Poetry Parodies." *Teaching English in the Two-Year College* 17 (February): 40–44.

Parody writing, as a college literature or writing class activity, can help students understand writers' decisions and may focus on the student's analysis of her parody as much as on the result or product—the parody. [Academic; Literature with Writing; College]

———. 1988. "Teaching Undergraduate Creative Writing: Myths, Mentors, and Metaphors." *Journal of Teaching Writing* 7: 83–102.

This article examines three myths about creative writing: (1) that it can't be taught; (2) that creative writing students have attitudes about reading and writing that are radically different than those of composition students; and (3) that a collaborative workshop situation is used successfully in the creative writing class. Bishop suggests that the mentor model of teaching writing is elitist, often sexist, and falsely collaborative, and that the division in American universities between literature and composition, fiction and poetry, creative and "noncreative" writing, is artificial and detrimental. The article encourages creative writing instructors to push for more departmental cooperation and more attention to relevant research and theory in the fields of criticism, composition, rhetoric, reading, linguistics, and psychology. Bishop also advocates seeking out or developing textbooks that include writers on writing and more material by women writers. [Academic; Essays on Writing; College] (CK)

———. 1989. "Using Postcards for Invention." *Exercise Exchange* 35 (1): 27–31.

Postcards can provide a powerful invention heuristic for writers at any level; several in-class writing activities will involve students in literal and figurative description, group writing, and so on. [Academic; Craft Mixed Genre; Secondary and College]

Bizzaro, Patrick. 1990. "Evaluating Student Poetry Writing: A Primary Trait Scoring Model." *Teaching English in the Two-Year College* 17: 54–61.

Bizzaro discusses the lack of criteria or discussions available to creative instructors for evaluating student writing and suggests utilizing text-specific primary trait scoring. During conferences, student and teacher prioritize revising concerns and negotiate an informal revision contract. In evaluating the next draft, the teacher will consider growth in agreed-upon areas, respecting the writer and the poem in progress. Includes a sample student poem and overview of the method. [Academic; Essays on Writing; Secondary or College]

———. 1983. "Teacher as Writer and Researcher: The Poetry Dilemma." *Language Arts* (October): 851–859.

Bizarro reviewed articles on teaching poetry and found few were available. He details the "models approach, activities approach, and models and activities approach," noting benefits and drawbacks of each and then advocates that teachers as writers should substantiate theory. Bizarro looks at several drafts of one of his own poems to illustrate and concludes that rather than following an "approach" he teaches writing "consistent with the way I compose." He advocates a teacher-as-writer-as-self-researcher stance for those interested in improving their own teaching. [Academic; Writers on Writing; Secondary and College]

Bogan, Don. 1981. "Beyond the Workshop: Some Alternatives for the Undergraduate Creative Writing Course." Paper presented at the Annual Convention of the Modern Language Association. New York, December 27–30. [ERIC Document Reproduction Service No. ED 233 342; also available as "Beyond the Workshop: Suggestions for a Process-Oriented Creative Writing Course." *Journal of Advanced Composition* 5 (1984): 149–62.]

Suggests, in detail, an alternative workshop format for undergraduate writers—with emphasis on reading like a writer and giving attention to process over product—using imitation, guided assignments, and exploring writers' potential through generation, arrangements, and revision. Bogan cites many writers on writing, and his appendix includes useful examples of exercises. A well-supported argument for an alternative yet cohesive instructional model. [Academic; Essays on Writing; College]

Brooks, Cora Vail. 1987. *The Sky Blew Blue*. Norwich, V.T.: New Victoria Publishers.

Brooks presents a clear, simple set of invention suggestions for poem making with preschool or elementary children. Although it contains the expected variations on thing or dream poems, Brooks also gets her young writers *moving* (poem after spinning, after drinking water, name chanting, etc.). [Non-academic; How-to Poetry; Preschool and/or Elementary]

Brooks, Gwendolyn, Keorepetse Kgositsile, Haki R. Madhubuti, and Dudley Randall. 1975. *A Capsule Course in Black Poetry Writing*. Detroit: Broadside Press.

Articles by four published writers which search for the essence of black writers' craft. Brook's essay offers a manifesto/definition of black poetry writing and eight writing hints which review traditional concerns of diction and style; Kgositsile offers a looser "how I write" essay; Madhubuti defines terms like "originality" and discusses writing aims from a black perspective and then reviews why poems go awry (triteness, too many words, etc.); Randall offers personal opinions about black poetry today (1975). The volume contains poem drafts by the writers. [Academic; Craft Poetry and Essays on Writing; College]

Brostowin, P. R. 1980. "Poetry by Seduction." *English Journal* 69 (6): 59–61.

Brostowin describes a collaborative poem writing activity designed to encourage beginning writers to create and share their poems. [Academic; Craft Poetry; Secondary and College]

Brown, Clarence. 1978. *Writing Short Stories, Plays, and Poems*. New York: American.

An introduction to creative writing geared towards beginners and high-school-age students. The first few chapters concentrate on getting a student used to writing creatively with suggestions on how to keep a journal and how to think about the writing process. Chapters advance to more craft instruction such as words, sentences, and plot development. Includes writing exercises and explains specific terminology such as onomatopoeia and alliteration. [Academic; Craft Mixed Genre; Secondary] (TM)

Bunge, Nancy. 1985. *Finding the Words: Conversations with Writers Who Teach.* Athens: Ohio University Press.

Bunge interviewed sixteen writers and discussed their attitudes about teaching writing and found that the writers appeared less interested in teaching techniques than in enabling student writers to accept themselves and to explore. Interesting contrasts developed, from Kelley Cherry, who believes all students have talent and genius potential; to Diane Wakowski, who claims teachers must teach students how to learn to hate their writing (to eventually produce better writing); to Ginsberg, who poses an extension of the mentor model of teaching to include love relationships between student and teacher; to William Stafford, who struggled to find ways to be a peer to students; to several others who believe writers are harmed by being teachers. These illuminating, short interviews stray from but ultimately center on pedagogical issues. [Academic; Writers on Writing; College]

Burack, Sylvia K., ed. 1986. *The Writer's Handbook.* Boston: The Writer, Inc.

This 787-page guidebook contains a staggering amount of material designed to help authors write marketable work. It is organized into four separate sections, the first three of which are filled with essays on the craft and business of writing by such bestselling authors as Isaac Asimov, John D. MacDonald, Sidney Sheldon, Stephen King, and Ken Follet. The first section deals with background for writers; the second contains essays on the writing of specialized fiction, nonfiction, poetry, drama, and juvenile works; and the third section provides valuable information on how to deal with editors, agents, and the business of writing in general. The fourth section of the work is composed of a list of potential markets. [Non-academic; How-to General; College and Older Writers]. (TW)

Burroway, Janet. 1987. *Writing Fiction.* 2nd ed. Boston: Little, Brown. [A third edition is in progress.]

This well-known text reviews all traditional aspects of craft and illustrates points using a variety of stories; it has provided a strong grounding in writing fiction for numbers of student writers. The ten chapters include discussions of story and plot, revision, use of detail, point of view, metaphor and simile, and theme. The second edition includes a chapter on writing process and the appendices include editing symbols and books for further reading. Burroway uses her personal experiences as a novelist to inform her discussions. [Academic; Craft Fiction; Advanced Secondary and College]

Carter, John Marshall. 1984. "Transforming the Self through Poetry: A Six Weeks' Project." *Illinois Schools Journal* 64 (1): 56–64.

Carter argues that a poetry project in which students immerse themselves in poetry—reading it, developing craft vocabulary, creating their own anthologies of their favorite poets' work as well as their own, and so on—transforms both students and teachers. He lists numerous responses by student writers to support his claim, ranging from "I don't think it really changed my life but it did make me understand my life" to "The study of poetry changed my whole life—it made me feel like a real person for the first time." [Academic; Craft Poetry; Primary and Secondary]

Chestek, Virginia L. 1986. "Teaching Creative Writing: An Emphasis on Preparation." *Freshman English News* 15: 16–19.

Chestek argues that instructors of creative writing can better prepare for teaching such classes by borrowing from pedagogical developments in composition studies. Four elements can help teachers to prepare students to write—recognizing the use of emotion in writing and defining audience (i.e., student investment in writing equals better writing); teaching students to control such emotions by focusing on a question that personally relevant writing raises; utilizing research; and working with analogy. Suggested activities include guided freewriting, question-heuristics that focus on conflict, finding personal symbolic analogies, and so on. A provocative article based on the premise that all students can be taught "to structure their own interesting perceptions of contemporary life into poetry or fiction that is worth reading." [Academic; Essays on Writing; College]

Collum, Jack. 1985. "Evaluating the Poetry Children Write." *Teachers and Writers Magazine* 17 (2): 1–9.

A rather general article that describes how Collum would discuss a student's poem and then offers statements about evaluation, personal anecdote, and so on, without really developing a clear-cut set of alternatives for teachers. [Academic; Craft Poetry; Elementary]

Cooke, John, and Jeanie Thompson. 1980. "Three Poets on the Teaching of Poetry." *College English* 42 (2): 133–41.

Writers Tess Gallagher, Sandra McPherson, and Galway Kinnell, share their ideas on teaching poetry—methods and activities—during interviews. [Academic; Writers on Writing; College]

Cornish, Roger N. 1983. "Five Finger Exercises for the Novice Playwright." Paper presented at the Annual Meeting of the American Theatre Association. Minneapolis, August 7–10. [ERIC Document Reproduction Service No. ED 235 538.]

Cornish feels the craft of playwriting can be taught and is aided by in-class writing assignments which include "finger exercises" such as writing down uses for a common object in a brainstorming session, incorporating "given" dialogue into an episode, etc. Invention helps students move from teacher lecture to skills development. [Academic; Craft Drama; College]

Duke, Charles R., and Sally A. Jacobsen. 1983. *Reading and Writing Poetry: Successful Approaches for the Student and Teacher*. Phoenix: Oryx Press.

Divided into three sections, perspectives, applications, and resources, this anthology offers students and teachers the thoughts of publishing writers and teachers of writers. These essays were gathered to broaden classroom creative writing experiences available to students, and range from X. J. Kennedy's discussion of "The Usefulness of Poetry" to Diane Wakoski's "Color Is a Poet's Tool" to Donald Murray's "Listening to Writing." The applications section focuses on language and composing, and the resources section includes information on ethnic and multimedia poetry. The volume is eclectic yet thought-provoking. [Academic; Craft Mixed Genre; Non-specialized]

Elbow, Peter, and Pat Belanoff. 1989. *Sharing and Responding*. New York: Random House.

This seventy-page booklet offers innovative and alternative response methods for composition or creative writing workshops and includes suggestions for helping students to share work, perform descriptive response (sayback, center of gravity, metaphorical description, etc.), analytic response (believing and doubting, skeleton feedback), reader-based response, and criterion-based response. An excellent and concise overview of response options for writers and teachers. [Academic; Craft Mixed Genre; Secondary and College]

Fitz-Randolph, Jane. 1980. *How to Write for Children and Young Adults—A Handbook.* New York: Barnes and Noble.

Intended to introduce writers to some common techniques of writing children's books and articles, both fiction and nonfiction, this guide presents and outlines basic story structures, such as wish fulfillment stories and stories of decision, which the author has found to have a good record of success with editors of children's books and magazines. Fitz-Randolph includes chapters dealing with the craft of writing children's fiction, with practical advice on the creation of characters and the use of point of view and dialogue. She also offers advice for nonfiction writers, suggesting topics for children's nonfiction articles, books, TV scripts and plays. [Non-academic; How-to Special Genre—Writing for Children; College and Older Writers] (TW)

Frank, Marjorie. 1979. *If You're Trying to Teach Kids to Write, You've Gotta Have This Book!* Nashville: Incentive Publications.

A giant toy box of ideas and projects to encourage writing, this book is aimed at children's creative processes and writing, but much of what is said and suggested is applicable to older beginning writers as well. Chock full of energy and options for all stages of writing, Frank ensures that the teacher will never run out of ideas or approaches. [Non-academic; How-to General; Elementary and Secondary] (JR)

Freisinger, Randall R. 1978. "Creative Writing and Creative Composition." *College English* 40: 283–87.

Freisinger suggests that composition classrooms should borrow techniques from the collaborative, writers' workshop class model favored by creative writing teachers, suggesting that in such a classroom, process is more important than product, student writing is never really finished, problems along the way are the focus of attention—themes, stylistic effects, etc.—and the teacher is a writer/friend, not a dictator. [Academic; Essays on Writing; College]

Frey, James N. 1987. *How to Write a Damn Good Novel.* New York: St. Martins.

In this nonacademic version of a traditional academic craft book, Frey takes his tone from Hemingway ("a damn good novel") and talks brusquely to novice writers about the basics, as in chapter 4, "The ABCs of Storytelling," where he offers hints, advice, rules, and brief examples. [Non-academic; How-to Fiction; Non-specialized]

Fuller, David. 1988. "A Curious Case of Our Responding Habits: What Do We Respond to and Why?" *Journal of Advanced Composition* 8: 88–96.

To further understand teachers' response habits, the author gave two groups of seven teachers each a copy of the same piece of prose. One group received a typed copy and the other group received a handwritten copy. Asked to evaluate the paragraph, teachers responded poorly to the handwritten version, giving it lower grades and less supportive remarks than did teachers who responded to the typed version. The paragraph (taken from Hemingway's *The Sun Also Rises*) received teachers' grades ranging from A to D, averaging C−. Fuller suggests that teachers should become more aware of their biases toward "student" work. [Academic; Essays on Writing; College]

Fulwiler, Toby, ed. 1987. *The Journal Book*. Portsmouth, N.H.: Boynton/Cook.

This book presents forty-two essays by as many authors. They discuss the nature of journals and their use in a variety of school settings, from first grade to college. The authors tell how they use journals in the teaching of English, history, art, music, philosophy, foreign language, physics, chemistry, mathematics, political science, sociology, and economics. The use of journaling to enhance speculation, exploration, discovery, critical independent thought, and other forms of creative thinking is affirmed. [Academic; Essays on Writing; Non-specialized] (CK)

Gallo, Donald R., ed. 1979. "Poetry: Reading, Writing, and Analyzing It." *Connecticut English Journal* 10 (2).

Over twenty-five essays and articles, most of them quite brief, that cover such topics as teaching poetry in junior high school, publishing student writing, using music and dance to teach poetry, and introducing poetic terminology. Especially helpful for teachers who may have anxieties about teaching poetry. See especially Thomas Devine's overview of the role of poetry in the English class. [Academic; Craft Poetry; Elementary and Secondary] (SH)

———. 1984. "Writing from Literature." In *Writing Exercises from Exercise Exchange*, vol. 2, edited by Charles R. Duke, 197–201. Urbana: National Council of Teachers of English.

Gallo suggests that writing from literature rather than about literature will engage students. He illustrates by describing a sequence where students write a Dear Abby type of letter from a character in a favorite novel which is answered by another student in class. Other activities include scripts, letters, obituaries, editorials, questionnaires, etc., to be used either singly or in a sequence to explore a piece of literature. [Academic; Literature with Writing; Secondary and College]

Gardner, John. 1984. *The Art of Fiction: Notes on Craft for Young Writers*. New York: Knopf.

Reading this now famous narrative discussion of fictional craft by experienced novelist Gardner is a bit like reading letters from a personal mentor. Gardner reviews his aesthetics and beliefs about writers and writing in the first part and moves on to practical discussions in the second part, including a review of common errors, technique, and plotting. He includes workshop exercises. [Academic and Non-academic; Craft Fiction; College or Older Writers]

Gebhardt, Richard C. 1988. "Fiction Writing in Literature Classes." *Rhetoric Review* 7 (1): 150–55.

Gebhardt argues that students in literature classes will become better readers of literature through creative writing "finger exercises" which allow them to experience "the subtlety and craft of the works they read." He suggests students can write new endings, rewrite sections of first-person stories in third-person point of view, create new dialogue between characters, and so on. [Academic; Literature with Writing; College]

Grossman, Florence. 1982. *Getting from Here to There*. Montclair, N.J.: Boynton/Cook.

Grossman's is essentially a book of invention techniques with lucid introductions to each activity and student and professional examples of poems that illustrate the techniques. Grossman covers lists, things, image, people, sound/silence, persona, dreams, and so on. [Academic; Craft Mixed Genre; Pre-college and College]

Haake, Katharine, Sandra Alcosser, and Wendy Bishop. 1989. *Teaching Creative Writing: A Feminist Critique*. Panel Presentation at the Annual Meeting of the Associated Writing Programs, Philadelphia, February 9–12. Also *AWP Chronicle*, 22, No. 2 (October/November 1989): 1–6.

Haake, Alcosser, and Bishop address issues and problems in creative writing instruction. Haake focuses on critical theory, women, and the writing classroom; Alcosser discusses women writers and voice, and polyphonic writing and other alternative forms; Bishop critiques current models of instruction at the undergraduate workshop level and discusses women, voice, and marginalized cultures. [Academic; Essays on Writing; College]

Hall, Donald, general editor. *Poets on Poetry: The Michigan Series.* [See entries for Hall's *Claims* and Stafford.]

The Michigan series was initiated to collect the prose pieces, interviews, and reviews of contemporary poets into book form. The books include those that concentrate on poetic influences, craft, criticism, living in the world as a poet, whether poetry can be taught, the writing process, and how to educate oneself as a poet, as well as thoughts on the arts, history, politics, and social issues. Recently, there has been another dimension added to the Michigan series: *The Writers Under Discussion* series—collections of critical articles on such poets as Elizabeth Bishop, Ann Sexton, and Richard Wilbur. [Academic; Writers on Writing; College and Older Writers] (PP)

Hall, Donald, ed. 1982. *Claims for Poetry.* Ann Arbor: University of Michigan Press.

Forty-three poets discuss a wide range of poetic concerns. Essays touch on the narrative form, prose poems, writing as re-vision, sound poetry, poem as time machine, images and the function of the line, plus many other elements of craft. Some of the poets included are Merwin, O'Hara, Bly, Hugo, Kennedy, Ostriker, Rich, Hall, Haines, Carruth, Hass, and many more. A book rich with possibilities for upper division craft courses or graduate level craft courses. [Academic; Craft Poetry; College] (PP)

Henkins, Kathryn. 1980. "Writing: Different Motivational Approaches." Paper presented at the Annual Convention of the National Council of Teachers of English. Cincinnati, Ohio, November 21–26. [ERIC Document Reproduction Service No. ED 199 695.]

Because students can teach each other, Henkins argues that creative writing instruction is most effective in heterogeneous classrooms. She suggests that a combination including this mixed audience, the use of anthology readings, the use of teacher's written comments on papers, and grades based on consistent participation and completion of assignments produces a strong, successful classroom. [Academic; Essays on Writing; Secondary and College]

Herzer, Scott, and Jill Robinson. 1989. "Your Ideas Are Unique." *Exercise Exchange* 35 (5): 43–45.

With this in-class invention activity and follow-up workshop, Herzer and Robinson show writing students how personal, individual writing can be generated from the same, basic, imagistic sentence or phrase; an illuminating and pleasurable sequence. [Academic; Craft Mixed Genre; High School and College]

Heynan, Jim. 1983. "Shimmering Chartreuse." In *Reading and Writing Poetry: Successful Approaches for the Student and Teacher,* edited by Charles R. Duke and Sally A. Jacobsen, 89–94. Phoenix: Oryx Press.

Heynan tells how he used word games and competition to engage a rather "frivolous" class of high school students in poetry writing and looks at issues of teaching poetry from the outside in versus the inside out. He concludes by advocating neither method, but rather "alertness and allegiance to the moment." [Academic; Writers on Writing; Secondary and College]

Hills, Rust. 1987. *Writing in General and the Short Story in Particular.* Boston: Houghton-Mifflin.

In this revised edition of a book originally published in 1977, Rust Hills provides a guide to the workings of short fiction. Hills, a fiction editor, claims not to be a fiction writer. He wrote the book with both the writer and the interested layperson in mind. Hills defines the various techniques used in a short story—suspense, point of view, plot, character, flashback, foreshadowing—and also explains how these techniques work. [Non-academic; How-to Fiction; College and Older Writers] (SB)

Hoberman, Ruth. 1986. "Writing Stories and Writing Skills." Paper presented at the Annual Meeting of the Conference on College Composition and Communication. New Orleans, Louisiana, March 13–15. [ERIC Document Reproduction Service No. ED 277 031.]

Suggests that students who write their own stories to study literary stories to learn literary terminology and understand writers' decisions. A second assignment asks for a one-page analysis of student stories to help students "recognize the dual role of their writing as at once something they did and the object of someone else's perception." A third assignment results in a critical paper. [Academic; Literature with Writing; College]

Hugo, Richard. 1979. *The Triggering Town: Lectures and Essays on Poetry and Writing*. New York: W. W. Norton.

Dedicated to student writers and their teachers, Hugo's essays are both satiric and serious discussions of writer's assumptions, the teaching of writing, and how poets write and live. The collection includes a memorial essay on Theodore Roethke as teacher. [Academic; Writers on Writing; College and Older Writers]

Kirby, David. 1989. *Writing Poetry: Where Poems Come From and How to Write Them*. Boston, Mass.: The Writer, Inc. [Enlarged edition of *Diving for Poems: Where Poetry Comes From and How to Write It*. Flagstaff: Word Beat Press, 1985.]

Beginning with a discussion of the nature of poetry and drafting, Kirby uses his own and student and professional writing to illustrate six poetry types (lists; marriages; reversals; speeches, letters, prayers; stories; and forms). An invention and process-oriented text, this one ends with suggestions for getting unstuck (alleviating writing block) and discusses beginning to publish. The current edition includes an extensive glossary of poetic terms and more writing samples. Overall, Kirby provides an honest, comfortable, and productive introduction for the writer who is new to the genre. [Academic; Craft Poetry; Secondary and College]

Koch, Kenneth. 1977. *I Never Told Anybody*. New York: Random House.

Koch taught poetry writing in a lower-class nursing home in New York, and this book records the astounding process. Koch planned as he went and made progress through trial and error: "It was starting from the beginning in every way." By emphasizing the close relationship between speaking and poetry, and by bringing in relatively unstructured poetry by authors such as Whitman, Williams, and Lawrence, for example, Koch enabled and encouraged the elderly and ailing "students" to write some superb poetry. [Non-academic; How-to Poetry; Older Writers] (JR)

———. 1970. *Wishes, Lies, and Dreams: Teaching Children to Write Poetry*. New York: Harper & Row.

In this classic "primer" for teaching young children methods for writing poems, Koch focuses on invention strategies for individual or class poems. Koch introduces a collaborative, in-class, invention-based writing workshop which has been highly influential. The strategies include wishes, lies, dreams, I used to/but now, I seem to be/but really am, and so on. Koch shares his teaching discoveries and many sample poems from students age three and up. [Academic; Craft Poetry; Primary and Secondary]

Koelling, Robert. 1983. "Market Analysis: Helping Creative Writing Students Publish." Paper presented at the Annual Meeting of the Wyoming Conference on Freshman and Sophomore English. Laramie, Wyoming, June 27–July 1. [ERIC Document Reproduction Service No. ED 234 424.]

Koelling suggests teachers can help beginning writers learn about publishing and professional writing by analyzing *Writer's Market* or other professional magazines together. [Academic essays on Writing; College]

Kremers, Carolyn. 1989. "Through the Eyes and Ears of Another Culture: Invention Activities and a Writers' Workshop." *Exercise Exchange* 35 (5): 3–11.

Kremers's multimedia invention activity and workshop helps student writers consider cultural diversity (and cultural prejudices) by responding to slides, tapes, photographs, and so on. Her sensitive sequence supports students' cultural explorations while enhancing traditional skills of description and dialogue writing and the study of effective images and ineffective clichés. [Academic; Essays on Writing; Secondary and College]

Krupa, Gene H., and Robert Tremmel. 1983. "Underground Writing." *Freshman English News* 12 (1): 12–14.

Survey and interview results show students at the college level are writing letters, journals, etc., to explore their own feelings and the ideas they are encountering, and suggests such self-sponsored personal writing provides a useful starting point for writing classrooms. [Academic; Research on Writing/Literature; College]

Lowey, Alva. 1981. "Consider, Watson, the Great Issues Which Hang from a Bootlace." *Illinois English Bulletin* 68 (3): 48–54.

Lowey stresses the importance of teaching use of detail to young poets, and then provides examples of how to help students remember and use detail. He includes invention techniques and a list of poems that provides examples of enumeration, sensory distortion, understatement, irony, meter, ellipsis, climax, metaphor, symbol, and other devices. He emphasizes the importance of a poetic "journal" and advocates the use of "model" poems. [Academic; Craft Poetry; Secondary] (SH)

Madden, David. 1980. *A Primer of the Novel for Readers and Writers.* Metuchen, N.J.: Scarecrow Press.

Madden's work is a useful reference tool. He offers sixty-eight categories of novel types (from "The Novel of Domestic Realism" to "The Anti-Hero Novel") with a brief discussion and lists sample titles. The book also contains an analysis of traditional fictional techniques (point of view to imagery) through close reading of well-known works. With several useful chronologies (development of the novel) and a selected critical bibliography, this text organizes a lot of information. [Academic; Craft Fiction; College]

———. 1988. *Revising Fiction: A Handbook for Fiction Writers.* New York: New American Library.

Based on his continuing interest in revision, fiction writing, and fiction writers, Madden offers 185 questions for self-critique and discussions of all aspects of technique from general considerations (unity, conception, autobiographicalsubjectivity) to specific questions on point of view, style, character, narrative, and so on. Although these questions would be dangerous if applied to a new writers' prose in the form of rules, each question is illuminated by a short discussion which refers to the work of well-known writers. Madden offers a final section which illustrates the revision process used in one of his own stories. [Academic; Craft Fiction; College]

Martin, Robert A., ed. 1982. *The Writer's Craft.* Ann Arbor: University of Michigan Press.

The sixteen essays in this volume of Hopwood lectures reflect concerns of poets, playwrights, novelists, editors, and critics. Their common theme is the craft of writing. The more practical or "how to" advice given in the essays occur in Joan Didion's "Making Up Stories." Didion illustrates how building or making uncharacteristic associations can help students carve out stories. Many of the other essays are highly literary. [Academic; Craft Mixed Genre; College and Older Writers] (PP)

Matthews, Dorothy, ed. 1981. "Producing Award Winning Poets: Tips from Successful Teachers." *The Illinois English Bulletin* 68 (3): [entire issue].

Ten articles that describe methods used by teachers and high school English departments to develop poets. The issue includes material on teaching the techniques of traditional and modern verse; teaching imagery; helping students understand the importance of rhythm over rhyme; providing accessible models for students to emulate; encouraging reluctant writers. It also shares guidelines from an English department renowned for its excellent student poets. [Academic; Craft Poetry; Secondary] (SH)

McKim, Elizabeth, and Judith W. Steinberg. 1983. *Beyond Words: Writing Poems with Children*. Green Harbor, Mass.: Wampeter Press.

These authors demonstrate their own class structure and lessons (essentially invention/exploration units) for teaching poetry and illustrate activities with student writings. McKim and Steinberg offer a good expansion of the basic Kenneth Koch scheme and also cover revision, although they offer little concrete direction in this area. The invention sequence moves from "What Is Poetry" to "Word Games," "Making Connections," "Listening," "Special Places," "Persona," "Instructions," and so on. [Academic; Craft Poetry; Elementary and Secondary]

McLaughlin, Gary L. 1988. "Patterns, Images, and Annotations: A Way into Poetry." *Exercise Exchange* 33 (2): 17–18.

McLaughlin offers an assignment sequence to interest secondary students in poem writing that includes reading and analysis of sample poems, and then writing thirty lines of poetry with a set pattern and number of required images but on open topics. On a separate sheet, the writer annotates the poem, describing what choices were made to achieve the final piece. The annotations are equally or more useful to student and teacher than the poems and spark class discussion. [Academic; Craft Poetry; Secondary]

Melton, David. 1986. *How to Capture Live Authors and Bring Them to Your Schools*. Kansas City, Mo.: Landmark Editions.

In this handbook for teachers and librarians, Melton discusses methods for setting up visits from writers and offers extensive quotes from visiting writers who recount successful or unsuccessful school interactions. Using a simple Question/Answer format, he helps readers define their own needs and discusses possible types of visits and how to contact authors, negotiate fees and responsibilities, and prepare students for author visits. A useful text for those setting up local, pre-college programs and visits. [Academic; Writers on Writing; Elementary and Secondary]

Meyer, Sam. 1988. "Prose by Any Other Name: A Context for Teaching the Rhetoric of Titles." *Journal of Advanced Composition* 8: 71–81.

From a text analysis of fiction and nonfiction titles, Meyer identifies four main types used by authors: (1) normative, (2) imagistic or figurative, (3) allusive, and (4) special effect. He illustrates each title type and suggests teachers may find it useful to "teach" titles and title analysis to enable students to understand how titles function in their own work. [Academic; Essays on Writing; College]

Mills, Ralph J., Jr., ed. 1965. *On the Poet and His Craft: Selected Prose of Theodore Roethke*. Seattle: University of Washington Press.

A revered teacher of poetry writing, Roethke's essays include his advice to instructors, memories of fellow poets, and selected reviews. [Academic; Writers on Writing; College]

Minot, Stephen. 1982. *Three Genres: The Writing of Poetry, Fiction, and Drama*. 3rd ed. Englewood Cliffs, N.J.: Prentice-Hall.

In this widely used creative writing text, Minot presents advice intended to be useful inside and outside of the classroom and for students of literature as well as for students of creative writing. The organization of the text allows Minot to explore the genres and include traditional craft discussions in each area as well as to include sample readings by professional writers and brief sets of invention suggestions and writing guidelines for each genre. [Academic; Craft Mixed Genre; Advanced Secondary and College or Older Writers]

Morgan, Jean. 1979. "The New Journalism: A Transition to Fiction Writing for Beginning Creative Writers." Paper presented at the Annual Meeting of the Popular Culture Association of the South. Louisville, Kentucky, October 18–20. [ERIC Document Reproduction Service No. ED 178 941.]

Morgan feels new journalism-type assignments—that tell a story by moving from scene to scene, record natural dialogue, use third-person point of view, utilize close detail of scene and person—can all help developing writers move from nonfiction to fiction writing. [Academic; Essays on Writing; Secondary and College]

Moxley, Joseph, ed. 1989. *Creative Writing in America: Theory and Pedagogy*. Urbana: National Council of Teachers of English.

Moxley's volume consists of 23 articles divided into the categories (1) Assumptions, Problems and Prospects [four articles on creative writing programs]; (2) Craft and the Creative Process [thirteen articles on making assignments, reading like a writer, teaching dialogue, etc.]; (3) Editing and Publishing [three articles]; (4) Maxims, Methods and Goals [two articles]. The volume includes "America's Master of Fine Arts Programs: Course Requirements" as an appendix. [Academic; Essays on Writing; College]

Muller, Lavonne, and Jerry D. Reynolds. 1977. *Creative Writing*. Irvine: California Laidlaw Brothers.

A detailed book that begins with basic writing techniques such as keeping a journal and developing a writing routine, and includes traditional information on techniques for writing poetry (rhyme and stanza forms) and fiction and plays (dialogue, diction, tags, and pacing). [Academic; Craft Mixed Genre; Pre-college] (TM)

Murray, Donald. 1982. *Learning by Teaching: Selected Articles on Writing and Teaching*. Upper Montclair, N.J.: Boynton/Cook. [Also, ERIC Document Reproduction Service No. ED 230 962.]

Throughout this collection of articles, Murray suggests teachers can learn from their own writing and apply that learning to the writing workshop. Articles cover writing process and teaching as a process, writing evaluation, and student/teacher interactions. See, especially, "Why Creative Writing Isn't or Is." [Academic; Writers on Writing; Secondary and College]

———. "Listening to Writing." In *Learning by Teaching: Selected Articles on Writing and Teaching*, 53–65. Portsmouth, NH.: Boynton/Cook, Heinemann.

In discussing writers' silences and the waiting and listening for inner voice that many writers seem to experience, Murray details his own revision and writing process, illustrating with samples of a poem in progress. He advocates listening, withholding early criticism, and asking questions about the poem in progress. His list of questions could be used for a student writer self-critique. [Academic; Writers on Writing; Secondary and College]

———. "Writing and Teaching for Surprise." *College English* 46 (1): 1–7.

In this personal essay, Murray explains the usefulness of training students to look for "surprise" in their writing by expecting it, getting in the habit of writing regularly, writing freely, and striving for recognition, pounceability, and acceptance; an alternative way to look at inspiration and writing. [Academic; Writers on Writing; Secondary and College]

Nims, John Frederick. 1983. *Western Wind: An Introduction to Poetry*. 2nd ed. New York: Random House.

A craft book with an anthology of 200 poems (the anthology is new to this edition), Nims organizes his detailed discussions of poetry, poetic techniques and effects, in sections entitled "The

Senses" (image, simile, metaphor, symbol, paradox), "The Emotions," "The Words," "The Sounds," "The Rhythms," and "The Mind," and ends with the anthology of poems. The discussions are heavily illustrated with exemplary poems and technique boxes (lists of examples of synecdoche, for instance). The exercises and diversions are more discussion prompts than invention exercises leading to student poems. This is one of the most vivacious (well formatted and packaged) of traditional craft texts and could also function as a text in an introduction to literature (poetry) course. [Academic; Craft Poetry; Advanced Secondary and College]

Ostrom, Hans. 1989. "Undergraduate Creative Writing: The Unexamined Subject." *Writing on the Edge* 1 (1): 55–64.

Ostrom details the prejudices that exist concerning undergraduate creative writing instruction, pointing out that the term "creative" irritates people and makes some English department members suspicious that such writing is just "therapy" or a less "real" activity than other academic endeavors. Ostrom explores such prejudices and argues that creative writing is an important, if not essential, component of English curriculums, that it can be taught, and that it is particularly valuable in training undergraduates to develop crucial critical and writing abilities. Overall, he stresses that a well-run creative writing workshop is not the "soft" course that many assume it is, since creative writing workshops allow students to assimilate other aspects of their learning and to improve the way they read. [Academic; Essays on Writing; College]

Otten, Nick, and Marjorie Stelmach. 1988. "Changing the Story That We All Know." *English Journal* 77: 67–68.

There is a long tradition of rewriting great literary works (*Romeo and Juliet* becomes *West Side Story*, for example), state the authors, and it is useful for students to explore this tradition. Rewrites are good ideas because students do not need to think about structure or come up with the plot, "but details are wide open possibilities and so the writers are free to make up anything they are creative enough to imagine." An exercise of this sort is a fun way to get students to study great literary works. [Academic; Literature with Writing; Secondary and College] (SB)

———. 1988. "Sight Versus Sound in Poetry." *English Journal* 77: 74–75.

Otten and Stelmach claim that "high school students tend to think poetry is something to read in print." Students need to be introduced to oral-based poetry and to understand the differences between visual and oral poetry. The authors provide four poems at the end of the article, which are to be used in an exercise where the instructor asks his/her students, "Does the poet want us to focus on the pictures or listen to the music?" [Academic; Craft Poetry; Secondary] (SB)

———. 1988. "A Writer Is Someone Who Can Do It Twice." *English Journal* 77: 92–93.

Otten and Stelmach provide two different beginnings to two different stories by the same author. Having students analyze the two beginnings for similarities and differences is a useful creative writing exercise. Students who do this exercise will learn to recognize that individual writers will repeat certain stylistic techniques, but that no two works by the same author are ever alike. This exercise shows that all good writers achieve a balance of style and repetition and variation. [Academic; Craft Fiction; Secondary and College] (SB)

Owens, Peter. 1984. "Creative Writing with Computers." *Popular Computing* 3 (3): 128–30, 132.

Owens reviews computer software packages that might be used for teaching creative writing including "Poetry Writing," "Story-Maker," and others, and suggests his own plan for instruction. [Academic; Essays on Writing; Secondary and College]

Packard, William, ed. 1987. *The Poet's Craft*. New York: Paragon House.

Packard, editor of *The New York Quarterly*, interviews twenty-five poets about their styles, techniques, habits, and beliefs about poetry and the writing and teaching of poetry. Among the poets are Snyder, Wilbur, Auden, Ashbery, Ginsberg, Shapiro, Levertov, and Rukeyser. While most of the questions center on the poet and his/her craft, some focus on teaching, the workshop, and advice to young poets. Those writers who talk most about teaching or the workshop are Leo Connellan, Amiri Baraka, Gary Snyder, Helen Adam, Richard Eberhart, W. D. Snodgrass, and Richard Wilbur. [Academic; Writers on Writing; College and Older Writers] (PP)

Parisi, Peter. 1979. "Close Reading, Creative Writing, and Cognitive Development." *College English* 41 (1): 57–67.

Parisi argues that the study of creative writing provides a transition into critical, expository writing and aids in the discussion and analysis of literary works. [Academic; Literature with Writing; College]

Parris, Peggy Baldwin. 1983. "Setting Free the Birds: Heuristic Approaches to the Teaching of Creative Writing at the College Level." Ph.D. Diss. Drake University. DA44: 2463A.

Parris studied the use of heuristics—tagmemic invention, Burke's pentad, freewriting—as adapted for beginning writers and found that students using heuristics generated more raw material at the prewriting stage, got started on writing projects, used concrete details, and continued to use heuristics on their own. Survey results showed students gained insight into and some control of their creativity. Parris claimed no current creative writing texts were adequately utilizing such heuristic techniques. [Academic; Research on Writing/Literature; Secondary and College]

Percy, Bernard. 1981. *The Power of Creative Writing: A Handbook of Insights, Activities, and Information to Get Your Students Involved.* Englewood Cliffs, N.J.: Prentice-Hall.

One author's effusions about the power of creative writing which is grounded neither in a literary tradition nor a firm psychological theory. Percy gives anecdotal witness to the effects of sensitive creative writing instruction on (primarily) young writers. In general, a compilation of aphorisms and questions: "Help students write toward a goal . . ." and "Is teaching creative writing impossible?" Often the observations or rules do seem accurate, based on writers' common sense, but the effect of the whole is disturbingly ungrounded. Perhaps the way in which author "talks down" to the elementary teacher, or perhaps the opening acknowledgment to L. Ron Hubbard, inclines the reviewer to skepticism. [Non-academic; General How-to; Elementary and Secondary]

Porosky, Peter. 1986. *How to Find Your Own Voice: A Guide to Literary Style*. Lanham, Md.: University Press of America.

Porosky offers a uniquely angled craft book based on close text analysis. He analyzes writers' styles for linguistic and tonal choices and then offers exercises for applying such analysis to a work in process. [Academic; Craft Fiction; College]

Powell, Brian S. 1973. *Making Poetry*. Ontario, Canada: Collier-Macmillan.

A teacher of young writers (nine to fourteen years of age), Powell intends to teach teachers how to introduce poetry into the classroom. He utilizes invention to illustrate form and content; discusses evaluation on the basis of word choice, structure, accuracy, appropriateness, simplicity; and offers impressionistic discussions/descriptions of good writing teachers and a small anthology of poems. Many of the invention techniques are worth looking at. [Academic; Craft Poetry; Elementary and Secondary]

Rainer, Tristine. 1978. *The New Diary*. Los Angeles: Jeremy P. Tarcher, Inc.

This book addresses topics of interest to people who already keep a journal, as well as to those who have never kept one before. It includes discussions of how to begin; whether to share or not to share; eleven "diary devices," including catharsis, description, free-intuitive writing, reflection, list, portrait, map of consciousness, guided imagery, altered point of view, unsent letter, and dialogue; and special topics such as transforming personal problems, discovering joy, dream work, eroticism, overcoming writing blocks, and making connections with the past and future. An extensive list of annotated "Readings of Interest to Diarists" is included at the end of the book. [Non-academic; How-to Special Genre—Journals; College and Older Writers] (CK)

Reed, Kit. 1982. *Story First: The Writer Inside*. Englewood Cliffs, N.J.: Prentice-Hall.

Reed stresses the need to learn to write fiction "from the inside." Elements of fiction such as theme and symbol cannot be imposed. The book is designed as a "partial map" of the inner, unfamiliar landscape of a writer's inner world, intended for beginning writers. But it is Reed's inner landscape, and the book is constituted more of advice-to-writers-based-on-my-own-experience, than of pedagogically useful information. Toward the end of the book, there are eight pages of exercises and assignments which might be consulted for ideas. [Academic; Craft Fiction; Non-specialized] (JR)

Regan, Sally, ed. 1987. "Special Issue: Teaching Creative Writing." *The Iowa English Bulletin* 35 (1).

A collection of twelve essays that discuss reasons for teaching creative writing; methods of instruction; theoretical comparisons between teaching poetry, music, and philosophy, and so on. Includes an article on the background of the historical poem, and helpful articles (including exercises) for beginning instructors of creative writing, and for instructors working with minority students whose English skills may be widely divergent. [Academic; Craft Mixed Genre; Secondary and College] (SH)

Renzulli, Joseph S. 1978. "What Makes Giftedness?" *Phi Delta Kappan*, November: 180–84, 261.

Renzulli analyzes and defines giftedness as the interaction of three ingredients: above average ability, creativity, and task commitment. He argues that it is easy to overemphasize superior abilities and not acknowledge the influence of creative thinking or task commitment. [Academic; Essays on Writing; Secondary or College]

Ridland, Muriel. 1988. "Group Presentations of Poetry." In *Focus on Collaborative Learning*, edited by Jeff Golub, 67–74. Urbana: National Council of Teachers of English.

Ridland suggests students benefit by performing oral class presentations of dramatic poetry which helps them analyze and understand the piece they are presenting. The exercise could be usefully adapted to the creative writing classroom. [Academic; Literature with Writing; Secondary or College]

Robinson, Jill. 1989. "Clichés: Finding Fresh Language." *Exercise Exchange* 2: 16–20.

Robinson provides an activity to sensitize students to the productive and nonproductive uses of clichés through identification, analysis, and sharing of regional clichés and sayings. [Academic; Craft Mixed Genre; Secondary or College]

Schwartz, Mimi. "Wearing the Shoe on the Other Foot: Teacher as Student Writer." *College Composition and Communication* 40 (2): 203–9. [Also available in Moxley's *Creative Writing in America*.]

Schwartz suggests teachers return to the classroom by enrolling in a creative writing course. This experience allowed Schwartz to understand her students better, experiment with a new genre, take chances with her writing, and take "creative writing"classes she hadn't been confident enough to take twenty years earlier. [Academic; Essays on Writing; College]

Scollon, Ron, and Suzanne B.K. Scollon. 1980. *Interethnic Communication*. Fairbanks: Alaska Native Language Center.

Useful for teachers with cross-cultural creative writing classrooms, this booklet was written to accompany a thirty-minute videotape by the same name, also available through the Alaska Native Language Center. It may be used, with or without the videotape, by individuals or in workshops/training sessions on cross-cultural and interethnic communication. Problems in Athabaskan-English interethnic communication are the focus of the text, but the examples and discussions are applicable to many other interethnic groups.

The Scollons cover basic principles of interethnic communication in Alaska, ethnic stereotyping, gate-keeping, communicative style, and conflicting styles of politeness. Three basic steps for improving interethnic communication are discussed: perception, acceptance, and repair. Their recommendations include (1) listen until the other person is finished, (2) allow extra time, (3) avoid "crowded" situations, (4) talk openly about communication, (5) talk openly about discrimination, (6) seek help, and (7) learn to expect and appreciate differences. [Academic; Research on Writing/Literature; Non-specialized] (CK)

Scott, Wilbur. 1977. *Skills of the Poet*. New York: Harper & Row.

In his skills approach to teaching craft, Scott uses word games (answers listed upside down) and an examination of sample poems. He provides exercises for diction (denotation and connotation) and so on which may be useful on occasion. His presentation of technical analyses of meter as games will have obvious drawbacks and could fragment a student's learning (if not applied to a student's own poems) and result in a type of poetic trivial pursuit; still, the games could engage some students and lead to real exploration. [Academic; Craft Poetry; Secondary and College]

Sears, Peter. 1981. "Teaching Poetry by Corruption." *Teachers and Writers Magazine* 13 (2): 6–9.

Suggests that students develop analysis and revision skills when they compare and contrast "corrupted" versions of exemplary poems. [Academic; Craft Poetry; Secondary and College]

———. 1985. "What Do You Say about a Terrible Poem?" *Teachers & Writers*, May-June: 1–3.

Essentially, Sears advocates careful conferencing to bring around writers of "terrible poems." Rather vaguely, he suggests asking students questions about the writing, which leads to analysis by getting the students talking. [Academic; Craft Poetry; Elementary and Secondary]

Shaughnessy, Shari E. 1987. "Creating Poetry." *Exercise Exchange* 32: 45–53.

Shaughnessy provides specific lessons and activities for students—that teach similes, and so on—geared toward writing finished poems, and includes samples of her class handouts. Her activities often teach appreciation of words, such as an exercise using the thesaurus, and are entertaining. [Academic; Craft Poetry; Elementary and Secondary] (TM)

Shelnutt, Eve. 1989. *The Writing Room: Keys to the Craft of Fiction and Poetry*. Marietta, Ga.: Longstreet Press.

Shelnutt discusses ways to generate fiction and develop point of view and describes the apprenticeship of a fiction writer, illustrating her points by describing the process of writing one of her own short stories. She includes several stories by (fellow) writers (sometimes former students) who also explore their writing processes for their included works. Author Herbert Scott introduces the art of writing poetry, covers invention and drafting, and overviews poetic terms and craft issues: metaphor, formal verse, symbol, and so on. He also illustrates with his own work, and then his section is followed by ten authors writing about their own poetic craft and process (one of the ten is Shelnutt). [Academic and Non-academic; How-to Fiction and Poetry; College and Older Writers]

Shiflett, Betty. 1973. "Story Workshop as a Method of Teaching Writing." *College English* 35: 141–60.

The Story Workshop is presented as an alternative method for teaching writing. Shiflett teaches students how to visually perceive the images they read and to transfer their own images onto paper without outside interference. The Story Workshop de-emphasizes the importance of grades and classifies grammar, punctuation, and syntax as secondary concerns. Instead, it stresses the importance of the rewriting process and is designed to guide students toward self-discovery of the secrets of writing. Telling, reading, and writing exercises are used to teach the student how to put his/her perceptions on paper and how to write in his/her own voice. [Academic; Essays on Writing; College] (TW)

Sommers, Jeffrey. 1980. "Multiple-Choice Story Writing: An Approach to Teaching Characterization." *Teaching English in the Two-Year College* 6 (2): 113–16.

Sommers offers an invention activity for teaching characterization where students choose from a set of personality characteristics, dialogue lines, and action possibilities; this develops students' ability to name literary devices and perform critical reading. [Academic; Writing with Literature; College]

Spacks, Barry. 1980. "Pogo's Bear." *College English* 42 (2): 130–32.

Spacks argues that the function of creative writing classrooms is as much to teach critical reading and appreciation of poetry as to teach writer's craft; this can be optimized by helping students make personal connections. [Academic; Essays on Writing; College]

St. Clair, Philip. 1987. "A Wilderness with a Map: Teaching the First Course in Creative Writing." *The Iowa English Bulletin* 35 (1): 43–55.

St. Clair suggests a flexible structure for the beginning creative writing instructor at the college level; he includes brief, clear discussions about creating class atmosphere (from both students' and instructors' perspectives), methods of teaching "texts, terms, and techniques," workshop approach, and evaluation. A comprehensive list of terms, a creative writing evaluation "rubric," and an adaptation of Della-Piana's circular model of the writing process are included. [Academic; Craft Mixed Genre; College] (SH)

Stafford, William. 1978. *Writing the Australian Crawl*. Ann Arbor: University of Michigan Press.

The essays in this collection concentrate on the writing process, discovering daily experience as poetic, where poems come from, the poetic voice, and "some arguments against good diction." Stafford's aim is to show that writing can be simple if we listen enough and let the material of the poem take us where it would like to go. He also concentrates on what makes a good poem and writing as a vocation. Some essays like "A Way of Writing" and "Writing the Australian Crawl" are useful to any process oriented writing class. [Academic; Craft Poetry; College and Non-specialized] (PP)

———. 1986. *You Must Revise Your Life*. Ann Arbor: University of Michigan Press.

Stafford centers on the writing process in a writerly manner. His book is divided into five sections: "Sources and Resources," "Poems on Writing," "Where Do Poems Come From?", "Glimpses of How It Is: Angles by Distinctive Interviewers," and "Teaching and Writing as Performing." There are useful essays for the teacher of poetry as well as essays for the beginning writer. While the essays offer information on craft, they also handle writing as process and inspiration. [Academic; Essays on Writing; College and Older Writers] (PP)

Stern, Jerome. 1990. *Making Shapely Fiction*. New York: W. W. Norton.

Stern gets readers writing and shaping fiction with activities that explore "The Shapes of Fiction" (examples: facades, icebergs, climbing the cliff) and that illustrate and lead to underlying principles of fictional composition. His accessible discussions cover subjects ("Write What You Know"), problems ("Don't Do This"), publishing, and resource books. Believing fiction writers need to know everything at once, yet also need continually to relearn aspects of craft, Stern provides an extensive, cross-referenced "Alphabet for Writers of Fiction" which allows "random access browsing" on many useful topics. [Academic and Non-academic; How-to Fiction; College and Older Writers]

Stoneham, Joyce Keever. 1986. "What Happens When Students Have a Real Audience?" *Journal of Teaching Writing* 5 (2): 281–87.

Stoneham developed a writing project that included eighth-grade students writing stories for a second-grade class. The eighth graders wrote letters to the second graders to find out their story preferences, reviewed books suitable for that age, wrote and revised stories with specific pen pals in mind, met with the second graders and read their stories to them, and then asked their "real" audiences for revision advice. [Academic; Craft Fiction; Elementary and Secondary]

Tomlinson, Barbara. 1986. "Cooking, Mining, Gardening, Hunting: Metaphorical Stories Writers Tell about Their Composing Processes." *Metaphor and Symbolic Activity* 1 (1): 57–79.

Analyzing the self-reports of writers from 2,000 published literary interviews, Tomlinson identified metaphors writers use to discuss their composing habits. She found cooking, mining, gardening, and hunting were the primary narratives used by writers to describe the act of writing. Tomlinson points out that each story about writing highlights some aspects of the process but hides other aspects; writers and teachers of writers will want to compare the metaphors to learn more about writers' processes and preconceptions concerning composing. [Academic; Research on Writing; College]

———. 1988. "Tuning, Tying, and Training Texts: Metaphors for Revision." *Written Communication* 5 (1): 58–81.

Analyzing the self-reports of writers from 2,000 published literary interviews, Tomlinson focused in this article on the metaphors writers use to discuss revision. This article discusses eight primary, metaphorical stories writers use to explain this part of their writing process: refining ore, casting and recasting, sculpting, painting, sewing and tailoring, tying things off, fixing things, and cutting. These revision stories can amplify our understanding of the writing process and add professional writers' intuitive insights to knowledge about the writing process that is being developed through cognitive research. [Academic; Research on Writing; College]

Torgersen, Eric. 1988. "Loving (Hating) the Messenger: Transference and Teaching." *AWP Newsletter* November: 1, 12, 14–15.

Torgersen argues for clarity in student-teacher relationships, warning that students undergo psychological transference (as in Freudian analysis) that can stunt their development. Such students expect teachers to turn them on to writers and to offer themselves as models and charismatic mentors. Students in such a relationship may fail to develop their own writing and identity. [Academic; Essays on Writing; College]

Treat, Lawrence, ed. 1976. *Mystery Writers Handbook.* Cincinnati: Writer's Digest.

Designed for the writer interested in the genre of the mystery novel, this collection consists of essays written by a variety of successful mystery writers and covers idea generation, development of plots, story structure, the use of outlines, authenticity, characterization, point of view, dialogue, style, and revision. Treat includes a number of surveys in which mystery writers reveal their writing habits and their tricks of the trade. [Non-academic; How-to Special Genre—Mystery Writing; Older Writers] (TW)

Trefethen, Florence. 1970. *Writing a Poem.* Boston: The Writer, Inc.

Trefethen discusses the progressive stages involved in writing a poem: planning, work with language and form, evaluation, and revision. She approaches problems that may be encountered in any of these stages, and provides examples of successful poems. The book contains many options and suggestions for every stage (which are helpful because they approach problems from a wide variety of possible angles), and journal projects at the end of chapters are based on chapter content, i.e., point of view, or finding fresh allusions for abstractions. [Academic; Craft Poetry; College] (JR)

Trepanier-Street, Mary L., and Jane A. Romatowski. 1986. "Sex and Age Differences in Children's Creative Writing." *Journal of Humanistic Education and Development* 25 (1): 18–27.

The researchers studied stories written by elementary school-age boys and girls for sex and developmental differences and found that female authors tended to assign emotional states and prosocial behaviors to their characters more often than did male writers, and male writers assigned aggressive behaviors to their story characters more often than did female writers. As age increased, children overall assigned more emotional states and prosocial and aggressive behaviors to characters, and female writers at fifth- and sixth-grade levels assigned more stereotypical feminine behaviors to female characters. Overall, the research found strong sex-typing characteristics in the children's writing. [Academic; Research on Writing/Literature; Elementary]

Tsujimoto, Joseph I. 1988. *Teaching Poetry Writing to Adolescents.* Urbana: National Council of Teachers of English.

A handbook that provides a step-by-step approach to designing the junior high school poetry writing classroom. Tsujimoto presents specific chapters on models and teaching designs, as well as many examples of assignments that range from "Found Poems" and "Two-word Poems" to "List Poems," "Bitterness," and "Paradox" poems. He illustrates his text with many examples of student writing and includes a helpful, if brief, bibliography. [Academic; Craft Poetry; Secondary and College] (SH)

Turner, Alberta. 1977. *Fifty Contemporary Poets.* New York: David McKay.

After Turner asked over 100 poets to choose a poem and explain how he/she wrote it, she received fifty responses which she collected in this volume. The questionnaire she uses is included and can function as a self-critique guide with questions such as "How did the poem start" or "Who do you visualize as your reader," and so on. Poets are arranged alphabetically and include Bell, Edson, Gluck, Haines, Kumin, etc. On the whole, poets were reluctant to explicate process but all exhibited a variety of invention/revision strategies. [Academic; Writers on Writing; College]

———. 1980. *Poets Teaching: The Creative Process.* New York: Longman.

Turner asked groups of poets to discuss selected (student) poems and explain how they would conduct a workshop and/or critique the poems. Some teacher-poets offer their own revisions, prioritize teaching concerns, and illustrate their own writing preferences. [Academic; Writers on Writing; College]

———. 1982. *To Make a Poem.* New York: Longman.

Turner assumes that poetry can be taught and taught to anyone. Her text is divided into four sections: (1) how to "invite" the raw material of poems, (2) how the student can "make" poems from raw material, (3) exercises and journal activities that help the writer move towards making poems alone, and (4) a collection of poems to be used for further discussion. A good half of the book is comprised of section 2—divided into subsections such as "concreteness and abstraction," "structure," "rhythm," "sound," "multiple meanings," and "metaphor." [Academic; Craft Poetry; Secondary and College] (PP)

Wallace, Robert. 1987. *Writing Poems*. 2nd ed. Boston: Little, Brown.

An exhaustive craft text with illustrations and anthology. Wallace divides his book into form, content, and process sections. Each section is further subdivided to cover, for example, types of free verse, types of meter, metaphor, revising (two chapters), and, finally, the odds and ends of writing such as poetic fashions, editing, publishing, etc. Each chapter ends with poems to consider, questions, and suggestions. The final chapter ends with a selection of poems about writers and writing. [Academic; Craft Poetry; Advanced Secondary and College]

West, William W. 1983. "Using Creative Writing to Teach Exposition/Artistic/Report Writing." Paper presented at the Annual Meeting of the Florida Council of Teachers of English. Fort Walton Beach, Florida, October 13–15, 1983. [ERIC Document Reproduction Service No. ED 236 696.]

West argues that aesthetic writing activities aid exposition and suggests teaching and using narration, chronological sequence, episodic rather than semantic memory, metaphors, conversations, visual concepts, and so on. [Academic; Essays on Writing; College]

Whitman, Ruth, and Harriet Feinberg. 1975. *Poemmaking: Poets in the Classrooms*. Lawrence: Massachusetts Council of Teachers of English.

A collection of essays by poets who worked in the Massachusetts public schools. These are personal "how I teach" discussions that include invention exercises and student samples (shaping poems—concrete poetry, bilingual poetry, taped poetry, etc.). [Academic; Craft Mixed Genre; Elementary and Secondary]

Wilhoit, Stephen. 1986. "Moffett and Point of View: A Creative Writing Assignment Sequence." *Journal of Teaching Writing* 5 (2): 297–305.

Wilhoit suggests that, after being trained in group work, students should follow a sequence of writing assignments based on the work of James Moffett to explore point of view. Wilhoit argues that the sequence offers an understanding based "not on difficulty or quality, but on increased distance between the major components of story telling: the narrator, narrative, and audience." The sequence begins with interior monologue and moves to correspondence, dramatic monologue, diary, detached autobiography, memoir or observed narration, and four types of biography with changing points of view. [Academic; Craft Fiction; College]

Willis, Meredith Sue. 1984. *Personal Fiction Writing*. New York: Teachers and Writers Collaborative.

An enormous collection of invention techniques for writing fiction, especially for writers at the precollege level but also adaptable for older writers. Willis divides her 355 ideas into six categories (describing place; describing people; describing action; writing dialogue; writing monologue; creating structure) and also includes a short revision discussion. She illustrates her techniques using student and professional samples; an excellent sourcebook. [Non-academic; How-to/Fiction; Elementary and Secondary]

Wyman, Linda, ed. 1984. "Poetry in the Classroom." *Missouri English Bulletin* 42 (6). [Also ERIC Document Reproduction Services No. ED 265 549.]

This collection of fourteen articles focuses on reading and writing poetry at all levels. Wyman has included articles by classroom teachers that cover a range of topics from "Teaching Poetry to College Freshmen: A Systematic Approach" to "Boredom, *Beowulf*, and Other Important Battles in Teaching Poetry." [Academic; Craft Mixed Genre; Secondary and College]

Zancanella, Don. 1988. "On the Nature of Fiction Writing." *Language Arts* 65: 238–44.

Zancanella evaluates fiction writing at the elementary level and argues that, for children, "fiction writing can be a kind of play;" such play should be encouraged. He also argues that standards for judging elementary-level fiction writing need to be re-examined. Teachers have inflated standards because they tend to compare their students' fiction with that of professional writers. Zancanella says teachers can help young fiction writers grow by exposing them to quality literature and by allowing them to write "personal fictions that may be of little interest to others." [Academic; Essays on Writing; Elementary and Secondary] (SB)

Zavatsky, Bill, and Rod Padgett, eds. 1977. *The Whole Word Catalogue 2*. New York: McGraw Hill.

Everyone will dip into this volume and come up with a different, favorite teaching activity or idea. The compendium starts out with short essays on teaching writing, moves to a large section on teaching ideas and activities, and finishes with a final section on drama, film, music, art, and publications—a great sourcebook. [Academic and Non-academic; Craft Mixed Genre; Pre-college and College]

Works Cited

Applebee, Arthur N. 1974. *Tradition and Reform in the Teaching of English: A History*. Urbana: National Council of Teachers of English.

Annas, Pamela J. 1987. "Silences: Feminist Language Research and the Teaching of Writing." In *Teaching Writing: Pedagogy, Gender, and Equity*, edited by Cynthia L. Caywood and Gillian Overing, 3–18. Albany: State University of New York Press.

Armstrong, Cheryl. 1984. "A Process Perspective on Poetic Discourse." Paper presented at the Annual Meeting of the Conference on College Composition and Communication. New York, New York, March 29–31. [ERIC Document Reproduction Service No. ED 243 108.]

Bartlett, Lee. 1987. *Talking Poetry: Conversations in the Workshop with Contemporary Poets*. Albuquerque: University of New Mexico Press.

Beaven, Mary H. 1977. "Individualized Goal Setting, Self-evaluation, and Peer Evaluation." In *Evaluating Writing: Describing, Measuring, Judging*, edited by Charles Cooper and Lee Odell, 135–56. Urbana: National Council of Teachers of English.

Berg, Stephen, ed. 1985. *Singular Voices: American Poetry Today*. New York: Avon.

Berlin, James A. 1987. *Rhetoric and Reality: Writing Instruction in American Colleges, 1900–1985*. Carbondale: Southern Illinois University Press.

———. 1984. *Writing Instruction in Nineteenth-Century American Colleges*. Carbondale: Southern Illinois University Press.

Berthoff, Ann E. 1981. *The Making of Meaning: Metaphors, Models, and Maxims for Writing Teachers*. Upper Montclair, N.J.: Boynton/Cook.

Betts, Doris. 1984. "Undergraduate Creative Writing Courses." *ADE Bulletin* 79: 34–36.

Bishop, Wendy. 1990a. "Designing a Writing Portfolio Evaluation System." *The English Record* 40 (2): 21–25.

———. 1987a. "Evaluating the Peer Group Process: The Group Folder." *Kentucky English Bulletin* 37 (1): 81–88.

———. 1990b. "The 15 Sentence Portrait." *Exercise Exchange* 35 (2): 5–8.

———. 1990c. "Going up the Creek without a Canoe: Using Writing Portfolios to Train New Teachers of College Writing." In *Portfolio Assessment*, edited by Pat Belanoff and Marcia Dickson. Portsmouth, N.H.: Boynton/Cook, Heinemann.

———. 1988a. "Helping Peer Writing Groups Succeed." *Teaching English in the Two-Year College* 15 (2): 120–25.

———. 1990d. "Learning about Invention by Calling on the Muse." *Arizona English Bulletin* 32 (2):7–10.

———. 1987b. "Planning for a Writing Across the Curriculum Program: Issues and Suggestions." *The English Record* 38 (1): 18–21.

———. 1990e. "The Poetry Class Writing Anthology—Why Process Should Turn into Product." *Western Ohio Journal* 11 (1): 94–95.

———. 1990f. "Poetry Parodies." *Teaching English in the Two-Year College* 17: 40–44.

———. 1989a. "Revising the Technical Writing Class: Peer Critiques, Self-Evaluation, and Portfolio Grading." *The Technical Writing Teacher* 16 (1): 13–25.

———. 1990g. *Something Old, Something New: College Writing Teachers and Classroom Change*. Carbondale: Southern Illinois University Press.

———. 1988b. "Teaching Undergraduate Creative Writing: Myths, Mentors, and Metaphors." *Journal of Teaching Writing* 7: 83–102.

———. 1989b. "Using Postcards for Invention." *Exercise Exchange* 35 (5): 27–31.

———. 1987c. "Writing Teachers and Writing Process: Combining Theory and Practice." *Arizona English Bulletin* 29 (3): 34–41.

Bizzaro, Patrick. 1990. "Evaluating Student Poetry Writing: A Primary Trait Scoring Model." *Teaching English in the Two-Year College* 17: 54–61.

———. 1989. "Interaction and Assessment: Some Uses of Reader-Response Criticism in the Evaluation of Student Writing in a Poetry Writing Class." In *The Writing Teacher as Researcher*, edited by Donald Daiker and Max Morenberg, 256–65. Portsmouth, N.H.: Boynton/Cook.

———. 1983. "Teacher as Writer and Researcher: The Poetry Dilemma." *Language Arts* 60: 851–59.

Bizzell, Patricia. 1984. "What Happens When Basic Writers Come to College?" Paper presented at the Annual Meeting of the Conference on College Composition and Communication. New Orleans, March.

Bogan, Don. 1984. "Beyond the Workshop: Some Alternatives for the Undergraduate Creative Writing Course." Paper presented at the Annual Convention of the Modern Language Association. New York, New York, December 27–30. [ERIC Document Reproduction Service No. ED 233 342; also available as "Beyond the Workshop: Suggestions for a Process-Oriented Creative Writing Course." *Journal of Advanced Composition* 5 (1984): 149–62.]

Boice, Robert. 1985. "Psychotherapies for Writing Blocks." In *When a Writer Can't Write: Studies in Writer's Block and Other Composing Process Problems*, edited by Mike Rose, 182–218. New York: Guilford.

Bridwell, Lillian S. 1980. "Revising Strategies in Twelfth-Grade Students' Transactional Writing." *Research in the Teaching of English* 14: 197–222.

Britton, James, Tony Burgess, Alexander McLeod, Nancy Martin, and Harold Rosen. 1975. *The Development of Writing Abilities (11–18)*. London: Macmillan Education.

Brodkey, L. 1987. "Modernism and the Scene(s) of Writing." *College Composition and Communication* 49: 396–418.

Brooke, Robert. 1988. "Modeling a Writer's Identity: Reading and Imitation in the Writing Classroom." *College Composition and Communication* 39: 23–41.

Brooks, Robert, and John Hendricks. 1989. *Audience Expectations and Teacher Demands*. Carbondale: Southern Illinois University Press.

Bruffee, Kenneth. 1984. "Collaborative Learning and the Conversation of Mankind." *College English* 46: 635–52.

Bunge, Nancy. 1985. *Finding the Words: Conversations with Writers Who Teach*. Athens: Ohio University Press.

Burke, Kenneth. 1945. *A Grammar of Motives*. New York: Prentice Hall.

Burnham, Christopher C. 1986. "Portfolio Evaluation: Room to Breathe and Grow." In *Training the New Teacher of College Composition*, edited by Charles Bridges, 125–38. Urbana: National Council of Teachers of English.

Burroway, Janet. 1987. *Writing Fiction*. 2nd ed. Boston: Little, Brown.

Calkins, Lucy McCormick. 1986. *The Art of Teaching Writing*. Portsmouth, N.H.: Heinemann.

Caywood, Cynthia L., and Gillian Overing, eds. 1987. *Teaching Writing: Pedagogy, Gender, and Equity*. Albany: State University of New York Press.

Cazden, Courtney B. 1988. *Classroom Discourse: The Language of Teaching and Learning*. Portsmouth, N.H.: Heinemann.

Chestek, Virginia L. 1986. "Teaching Creative Writing: An Emphasis on Preparation." *Freshman English News* 15: 16–19.

Churchman, Deborah. 1984. "Fertile Time for Creative Writing: More College Courses Every Year." *New York Times*, 8 January: 42–43.

Ciardi, John. 1974. *Teaching Creative Writing*. Proceedings of the Conference on Teaching Creative Writing. Washington, D.C., Library of Congress, January. [ERIC Document Reproduction Service No. ED 102 556.]

Clark, John R., and Anna Lydia Motto. 1986. "The Uses of Parody and Excess in Composition." *Exercise Exchange* 31 (2): 11–13.

Coe, Richard. 1988. *Toward a Grammar of Passages*. Carbondale: Southern Illinois University Press.

Connors, Robert. 1981. "The Rise and Fall of the Modes ofDiscourse." *College Composition and Communication* 32 (December): 444–55.

Cooper, Marilyn. 1986. "The Ecology of Writing." *College English* 31: 134–42.

Crowley, Sharon. 1989. *A Teacher's Introduction to Deconstruction*. Urbana: National Council of Teachers of English.

Dacy, Philip, and David Jauss, eds. 1986. *Strong Measures: Contemporary American Poetry in Traditional Forms*. New York: Harper & Row.

Daly, John A. 1985. "Writing Apprehension." In *When a Writer Can't Write*, edited by Mike Rose, 134–65. New York: Guilford Press.

Daly, John, and Michael Miller. 1975. "The Empirical Development of an Instrument to Measure Writing Apprehension." *Research in the Teaching of English* 9:242–49.

D'Angelo, Frank. 1975. *A Conceptual Theory of Rhetoric*. Cambridge, Mass.: Winthrop.

Daniels, Harvey, and Steven Zemelman. 1985. *A Writing Project: Training*

Teachers of Composition from Kindergarten to College. Portsmouth, N.H.: Heinemann.

Daumer, Elisabeth, and Sandra Runzo. 1987. "Transforming the Composition Classroom." In *Teaching Writing: Pedagogy, Gender, and Equity,* edited by Cynthia L. Caywood and Gillian R. Overing, 45–64. Albany: State University of New York Press.

Eagleton, Terry. 1983. *Literary Theory: An Introduction*. Minneapolis: University of Minnesota Press.

Elbow, Peter. 1986a. "Nondisciplinary Courses and the Two Roots of Real Learning." In *Embracing Contraries: Explorations in Learning and Teaching,* 5–37. New York: Oxford University Press.

———. 1986b. "Teaching Two Kinds of Thinking by Teaching Writing." In *Embracing Contraries,* 54–64.

———. 1986c. "Trustworthiness in Evaluation." In *Embracing Contraries,* 217–32.

———. 1981. *Writing with Power*. New York: Oxford University Press.

———. 1977. *Writing without Teachers*. New York: Oxford University Press.

Elbow, Peter, and Pat Belanoff. 1986. "Portfolios as a Substitute for Proficiency Examinations." *College Composition and Communication* 37: 336–39.

———. 1989. *Sharing and Responding*. New York: Random House.

Emig, Janet. 1971. *The Composing Processes of Twelfth Graders*. Urbana: National Council of Teachers of English.

———. 1983a. "Literacy and Freedom." In *The Web of Meaning: Essays on Writing, Teaching, Learning, and Thinking*. Upper Montclair, N.J.: Boynton/Cook.

———. 1983b. "Non-Magical Thinking: Presenting Writing Developmentally in School." In *The Web of Meaning*, edited by Dixie Goswami and Maureen Butler, 132–44. Upper Montclair, N.J.: Boynton/Cook.

Engle, Paul, ed. 1961. *Midland*. New York: Random House.

Faigley, Lester. 1986. "Competing Theories of Process." *College English* 48 (October): 527–42.

Flower, Linda. 1981. "Writer-Based Prose: A Cognitive Basis for Problems in Writing." *College English* 41: 19–37.

Flower, Linda, and John R. Hayes. 1981. "A Cognitive Process Theory of Writing." *College Composition and Communication* 32: 365–87.

Foerster, Norman, et al. 1941. *Literary Scholarship: Its Aims and Methods*. Chapel Hill: University of North Carolina Press.

Foster, David. 1983. *A Primer for Writing Teachers: Theories, Theorists, Issues, Problems*. Upper Montclair, N.J.: Boynton/Cook.

Frank, Francine Wattman, and Paula A. Treichler. 1989. *Language, Gender, and Professional Writing*. New York: Modern Language Association.

Freisinger, Randall R. 1978. "Creative Writing and Creative Composition." *College English* 40: 283–87.

Fuller, David. 1988. "A Curious Case of Our Responding Habits: What Do We Respond To and Why?" *Journal ofAdvanced Composition* 8: 88–96.

Fulwiler, Toby, ed. 1987. *The Journal Book*. Portsmouth, N.H.: Boynton/Cook.

Gardner, John. 1984. *The Art of Fiction: Notes on Craft for Young Writers*. New York: Knopf.

Garrett, George. 1989. "The Future of Creative Writing Programs." In *Creative Writing in America: Theory and Pedagogy*, edited by Joseph Moxley, 47–63. Urbana: National Council of Teachers of English.

———. 1974. *Teaching Creative Writing*. Proceedings of the Conference on Teaching Creative Writing. Washington, D.C., Library of Congress, January. [ERIC Document Reproduction Service No. ED 102 556.]

Gebhardt, Richard C. 1988. "Fiction Writing in Literature Classes." *Rhetoric Review* 7(1): 150–55.

Gere, Anne Ruggles. 1987. *Writing Groups: History, Theory, and Implications*. Carbondale: Southern Illinois University Press.

Graff, Gerald. 1987. *Professing Literature: An Institutional History*. Chicago: University of Chicago Press.

Grossman, Florence. 1982. *Getting from Here to There*. Upper Montclair, N.J.: Boynton/Cook.

Haake, Katharine, Sandra Alcosser, and Wendy Bishop. 1989. "Teaching Creative Writing: A Feminist Critique." *AWP Chronicle* 22 (October/November): 1–6.

Hairston, Maxine. 1986. "On Not Being a Composition Slave." In *Training the New Teacher of College Composition*, edited by Charles W. Bridges, 117–24. Urbana: National Council of Teachers of English.

Harris, Muriel. 1986. *Teaching One-to-One: The Writing Conference*. Urbana: National Council of Teachers of English.

Harste, J. C., V. A. Woodward, and C. L. Burke. 1984. *Language Stories and Literacy Lessons*. Portsmouth, N.H.: Heinemann.

Hawkins, Thom. 1976. *Group Inquiry Techniques in Teaching Writing*. Urbana: National Council of Teachers of English.

———. 1980. "Intimacy and Audience: The Relationship Between Revision and the Social Dimension of Peer Tutoring." *College English* 42: 64–68.

Heath, Shirley Brice. 1983. *Ways with Words: Language, Life, and Work in Communities and Classrooms*. New York: Cambridge University Press.

Herzer, Scott, and Jill Robinson. 1989. "Your Ideas Are Unique." *Exercise Exchange* 35 (5): 43–45.

Heynan, Jim. 1983. "Shimmering Chartreuse." In *Reading and Writing Poetry: Successful Approaches for the Student and Teacher*, edited by Charles R. Duke and Sally A. Jacobsen, 89–94. Phoenix: Oryx Press.

Hoffmann, Leonore, and Margo Culley. 1985. *Women's Personal Narratives: Essays in Criticism and Pedagogy*. New York: Modern Language Association.

Hua, Li Min. 1989. "Re-Mystifying Composition." *ATAC Newsletter* 1 (2): 12–13.

International Directory of Little Magazines and Small Presses. Edited by Len Fulton and Ellen Ferber. Paradise, Calif.: Dustbooks. [Published annually.]

Johnson, David W., and Roger T. Johnson. 1984. "Cooperative Small-Group Learning." *Curriculum Report* 14: 1–6. [ERIC Document Reproduction Service No. ED 249 625.]

———. 1975. *Learning Together and Alone: Cooperation, Competition, and Individualization*. Englewood Cliffs, N.J.: Prentice-Hall.

Kennedy, George A. 1980. *Classical Rhetoric and Its Christian and Secular Tradition from Ancient to Modern Times*. Chapel Hill: University of North Carolina Press.

Kinneavy, James. 1971. *A Theory of Discourse: The Aims of Discourse*. Englewood Cliffs, N.J.: Prentice-Hall.

Kirby, David. 1989. *Writing Poetry: Where Poems Come From and How to Write Them*. Boston: The Writer, Inc. [Enlarged edition of *Diving for Poems: Where Poetry Comes From and How to Write It*. Flagstaff: Word Beat Press, 1985.]

Koch, Kenneth. 1970. *Wishes, Lies, and Dreams: Teaching Children to Write Poetry*. New York: Harper & Row.

Knoblauch, C. H., and Lil Brannon. 1984. *Rhetorical Traditions and the Teaching of Writing*. Upper Montclair, N.J.: Boynton/Cook.

———. 1981. "Teacher Commentary on Student Writing: The State of the Art." *Freshman English News* 10 (Fall): 1–4.

Kremers, Carolyn. 1989. "Through the Eyes and Ears of Another Culture: Invention Activities and a Writer's Workshop." *Exercise Exchange* 35(5): 3–11.

Krupa, Gene H., and Robert Tremmel. 1983. "Underground Writing." *Freshman English News* 12 (1): 12–14.

Lakoff, George, and Mark Turner. 1989. *More than Cool Reason: A Field Guide to Poetic Metaphor*. Chicago: University of Chicago Press.

Lakoff, George, and Mark Johnson. 1980. *Metaphors We Live By*. Chicago: University of Chicago Press.

Larson, Richard L. 1986. "Making Assignments, Judging Writing, and Annotating Papers: Some Suggestions." In *Training the New Teacher of College Composition*, edited by Charles W. Bridges, 109–16. Urbana: National Council of Teachers of English.

Lavine, Ann. 1987. "Subject Matter and Gender." In *Teaching Writing: Pedagogy, Gender, and Equity*, edited by Cynthia L. Caywood and Gillian Overing, 135–43. Albany: State University of New York Press.

LeFevre, Karen Burke. 1986. *Invention as a Social Act*. Carbondale: Southern Illinois University Press.

Lindemann, Erika. 1982. *A Rhetoric for Writing Teachers*. New York: Oxford.

Lowenstein, Sharyn. 1987. "A Brief History of Journal Keeping." In *The Journal Book*, edited by Toby Fulwiler, 87–97. Portsmouth, N.H.: Boynton/Cook.

Lunsford, Andrea, Helene Moglen, and James F. Slevin, eds. 1989. *The Future of Doctoral Studies in English*. New York: Modern Language Association.

Madden, David. 1988. *Revising Fiction: A Handbook for Fiction Writers*. New York: New American Library.

Martin, Anne. 1989. "Allowing the Unconventional." *Teachers and Writers* 20 (5): 1–4.

Martin, Nancy, and others. 1975. *Why Write?* London: London University Schools Council. [ERIC Document Reproduction Service No. ED 177 555.]

McMillen, Liz. 1990. "Ken Kesey Weaves His Magic Spell, Turns Graduate

Students of Creative Writing at U. of Oregon into Published Novelists." *Chronicle of Higher Education* 17 January: A15, A22, A23.

Miner, Valerie. 1989. "The Book in the World." In *Creative Writing in America: Theory and Pedagogy,* edited by Joseph Moxley, 227–36. Urbana: National Council of Teachers of English.

Minot, Stephen. 1982. *Three Genres: The Writing of Poetry, Fiction, and Drama.* 3rd ed. Englewood Cliffs, N.J.: Prentice-Hall.

Moffett, James. 1968. *Teaching the Universe of Discourse.* Boston: Houghton Mifflin.

Moxley, Joseph, ed. 1989a. *Creative Writing in America: Theory and Pedagogy.* Urbana: National Council of Teachers of English.

———. 1989b. "Tearing Down the Walls: Engaging the Imagination." In *Creative Writing in America,* 25–46.

Murray, Donald. 1989. *Expecting the Unexpected: Teaching Myself—and Others—to Read and Write.* Portsmouth, N.H.: Boynton/Cook.

———. 1982a. *Learning by Teaching: Selected Articles on Writing and Teaching.* Upper Montclair, N.J.: Boynton/Cook. [Also, ERIC Document Reproduction Service No. ED 230 962.]

———. 1982b. "Why Creative Writing Is—Or Isn't." In *Learning by Teaching: Selected Articles on Writing and Teaching,* 135—38. Upper Montclair, N.J.: Boynton/Cook.

———. 1968. *A Writer Teaches Writing.* Boston: Houghton Mifflin.

———. 1984. "Writing and Teaching for Surprise." *College English* 46 (1): 1–7.

———. 1980. "Writing as Process: How Writing Finds Its Own Meaning." In *Eight Approaches to Teaching Composition,* edited by Timothy Donovan and Ben McClelland, 3–20. Urbana: National Council of Teachers of English.

Neeld, Elizabeth Cowan. 1990. *Writing.* 3rd ed. Glenview, Ill.: Scott Foresman.

Nelson, Jennie, and John R. Hayes. 1988. "How the Writing Context Shapes College Students' Strategies for Writing from Sources." Technical Report No. 16. Center for the Study of Writing. Berkeley, California.

Ostrom, Hans. 1989. "Undergraduate Creative Writing: The Unexamined Subject." *Writing on the Edge* 1 (1): 55–65.

Packard, William, ed. 1987. *The Poet's Craft.* New York: Paragon House.

Peoples, Peg. "Letters." Unpublished manuscript.

Perl, Sandra. 1979. "The Composing Process of Unskilled College Writers." *Research in the Teaching of English* 13: 317–36.

Perl, Sandra, and Nancy Wilson. 1986. *Through Teachers' Eyes.* Portsmouth, N.H.: Heinemann.

Plimpton, George, ed. 1967. *Writers at Work.* 3rd ser. New York: Viking.

———. 1976. *Writers at Work.* 4th ser. New York: Viking.

"Portfolio Assessment: An Annotated Bibliography." 1988. *The Quarterly* 10 (October): 23–24.

Preminger, Alex, ed. 1965. *Princeton Encyclopedia of Poetry and Poetics.* Enlg. ed. Princeton, N.J.: Princeton University Press.

Progoff, Ira. 1975. *At a Journal Workshop*. New York: Dialogue.

Rainer, Tristine. 1978. *The New Diary*. Los Angeles: Jeremy P. Tarcher, Inc.

Reigstad, Thomas, and Donald McAndrew. 1984. *Training Tutors for Writing Conferences*. Urbana: National Council of Teachers of English.

Rich, Adrienne. 1979a. *On Lies, Secrets, and Silence: Selected Prose 1966–1978*. New York: W. W. Norton.

———. 1979b. "Taking Women Students Seriously." In *On Lies, Secrets, and Silence*, 237–46.

———. 1979c. "Teaching Writing in Open Admissions." In *On Lies, Secrets, and Silence*, 51–68.

Robinson, Jill. 1989. "Clichés: Finding Fresh Language." *Exercise Exchange* 2: 16–20.

Rohman, D. Gordon, and Alfred O. Wlecke. 1964. "Pre-Writing: The Construction and Application of Models for Concept Formation in Writing." U.S. Department of Health, Education, and Welfare Cooperative Research Project No. 2174. East Lansing: Michigan State University.

Ronald, Kate, and John Volkmer. 1989. "Another Competing Theory of Process: The Students'." *Journal of Advanced Composition* 9: 81–96.

Rose, Mike. 1980. "Rigid Rules, Inflexible Plans, and the Stifling of Language: A Cognitivist Analysis of Writer's Block." *College Composition and Communication* 31: 389–401.

Scholes, Robert. 1985. *Textual Power: Literary Theory and the Teaching of English*. New Haven: Yale University Press.

Scholes, Robert, Nancy R. Comley, and Gregory L. Ulmer. 1988. *Textbook: An Introduction to Literary Language*. New York: St. Martins.

Schwartz, Mimi. 1989. "Wearing the Shoe on the Other Foot: Teacher as Student Writer." In *College Composition and Communication* 40 (2): 203–9. [Also available in Moxley's *Creative Writing in America*.]

Segedy, Michael. 1986. "Adapting the Courtroom Trial Format to Literature." In *Activities to Promote Critical Thinking*, edited by Jeff Golub, 88–92. Urbana: National Council of Teachers of English.

Shaughnessy, Mina P. 1977. *Errors and Expectations: A Guide for the Teacher of Basic Writing*. New York: Oxford University Press.

Shelnutt, Eve. 1989. "Notes from a Cell: Creative Writing Programs in Isolation." In *Creative Writing in America: Theory and Pedagogy*, edited by Joseph Moxley, 3–24. Urbana: National Council of Teachers of English.

Smelcer, John. 1989. "A Round-Robin Creative Writing Exercise." *Exercise Exchange* 34 (2): 8–9.

Smith, Barbara Herrnstein. 1988. *Contingencies of Value: Alternative Perspectives for Critical Theory*. Cambridge, Mass: Harvard University Press.

Smith, Frank. 1981. "Myths of Writing." *Language Arts* 58:792–98.

———. 1983. *Writing and the Writer*. New York: Holt, Rinehart and Winston.

Sommers, Nancy. 1980. "Revision Strategies of Student Writers and Experienced Adult Writers." *College Composition and Communication* 31: 378–88.

Stegner, Wallace. 1988. *On the Teaching of Creative Writing*. Hanover, N.H.: University of New England Press.

Stewart, Donald. 1989. "What Is an English Major, and What Should It Be?" *College Composition and Communication* 40: 188–202.

Stock, Gregory. 1985. *The Book of Questions.* New York: Workman Publishing.

Tobin, Lad. 1989. "Bridging Gaps: Analyzing Our Students' Metaphors for Composing." *College Composition and Communication* 40: 444–58.

Tomlinson, Barbara. 1986. "Cooking, Mining, Gardening, Hunting: Metaphorical Stories Writers Tell About Their Composing Processes." *Metaphor and Symbolic Activity* (1): 57–79.

———. 1988. "Tuning, Tying, and Training Texts: Metaphors for Revision." *Written Communication* 5(1): 58–81.

Tsujimoto, Joseph I. 1988. *Teaching Poetry Writing to Adolescents.* Urbana: National Council of Teachers of English.

Turner, Alberta. 1977. *Fifty Contemporary Poets.* New York: David McKay Co.

———. 1980. *Poets Teaching: The Creative Process.* New York: Longman.

———. 1982. *To Make a Poem.* New York: Longman.

Waldrup, Tom, ed. 1985. *Writers on Writing.* New York: Random House.

Wallace, Robert. 1987. *Writing Poems.* 2nd ed. Boston: Little, Brown.

Weddle, David. 1989. "Ken Kesey's Eclectic Writing Acid Test." *Rolling Stone* 5 October: 122, 123, 153.

Weiner, Harvey S. 1986. "Collaborative Learning in the Classroom: A Guide to Evaluation." *College English* 48: 52–61.

White, Edward. 1988. *Teaching and Assessing Writing.* San Francisco: Jossey-Bass.

Wike, Terence. "Using Auditory Scenes to Spark Creative Writing." Unpublished manuscript.

Wilbers, Stephen. 1981. *The Iowa Writers' Workshop: Origins, Emergence, and Growth.* Iowa City: University of Iowa Press.

Wilhoit, Stephen. 1986. "Moffett and Point of View: A Creative Writing Assignment Sequence." *Journal of Teaching Writing* 5 (2): 297–305.

Writers' Market. Cincinnati: Writer's Digest Books. [Published annually.]

Wyche-Smith, Susan. 1987. "Teaching Invention to Basic Writers." In *A Sourcebook for Basic Writing Teachers,* edited by Theresa Enos, 470–79. New York: Random House.

Ziegler, Alan. 1989. "'Midwifing the Craft'—Teaching Revision and Editing." In *Creative Writing in America: Theory and Pedagogy,* edited by Joseph Moxley, 209–26. Urbana: National Council of Teachers of English.

———. 1981. *The Writing Workshop.* Vol. 1. New York: Teachers and Writers Collaborative.

———. 1984. *The Writing Workshop.* Vol. 2. New York: Teachers and Writers Collaborative.

Zender, Karl, Wendy Bishop, Rex Burwell, Kevin Clark, Elin Diamond, Brent Duffin, Jeff Lipkis, Rod Moore, and Tom Venturino. 1979. *A Manual for English 5F and 5P.* Department of English, University of California–Davis.

Index

Adams, James, 183
Alcosser, Sandra, xvi, 51, 193, 221
Annas, Pamela, 26, 217
Applebee, Arthur, ix, 217
Armstrong, Cheryl, 27, 183, 217
Associated Writing Programs (AWP), xiv
Atwood, Margaret, 123
Auden, W. H., 18, 27
Audience, 7, 20, 22, 28, 29, 40, 141, 164
Autobiography, 103–108

Bartel, Roland, 184
Bartlett, Lee, 18, 30, 148, 217
Basic writers, 19, 21, 50
Baumbach, Jonathan, 184
Beattie, Anne, 69
Beavan, Mary, 53, 162, 217
Belanoff, Pat, 52, 144, 145, 152, 164, 190, 220
Bell, Marvin, 62
Berenson, Sheila, 184
Berg, Steven, 18, 217
Berlin, James, ix, xi, xv, 23, 217
Bernstein, Bonnie 184
Berryman, John, 16–17
Berthoff, Ann, 134, 140, 150, 217
Betts, Doris, 13, 185, 217
Bibliography for teaching creative writing, 183–218
Bishop, Wendy, xvi, 2, 15*n*, 32, 51, 53, 62*n*, 66, 68–69, 72–73, 84*n*, 87, 94, 96, 100, 115*n*, 116n, 122, 131*n*, 132, 142, 144, 151*n*, 152, 157*n*, 164, 171, 172, 185–186, 193, 217–218, 221, 225, 227
Bizarro, Patrick, 13, 162, 163, 186, 218
Bizzell, Pat, 23, 218
Bogan, Don, 13, 186, 218
Boice, Robert, 21, 218
Bowen, Elizabeth, 17
Bradbury, Ray, 17
Brannon, Lil, 22, 73, 147, 158, 222
Bratcher, Suzanne, vii
Bread Loaf Writers Conference, xii
Bridges, Charles, 219, 222, 222
Bridwell, Lillian, 20, 218
Britton, James, 27, 28, 29, 218
Brodkey, Linda, 2, 218
Brooke, Robert, 13, 23, 132, 219
Brooks, Cora Vail, 187
Brooks, Gwendolyn, 187
Brooks, Robert, 219
Brostowin, P. R., 187
Brown, Clarence, 187
Bruffee, Kenneth, 23, 53, 219
Bunge, Nancy, 18, 34, 39, 41, 42, 43, 90, 188, 219
Burak, Sylvia, 188
Burgess, Tony, 28
Burke, Carolyn, 23, 221
Burke, Kenneth, 27, 219
Burman, Ben, 21, 164
Burnham, Christopher, 219
Burroway, Janet, 25, 51, 62, 70, 188, 219
Burwell, Rex, 225
Butler, Maureen, 220

Calkins, Lucy, 46, 219
Canonical literature, x, 3
Carter, John Marshall, 189
Cary, Joyce, 17
Cassill, R. V., xiv
Caywood, Cynthia, 42, 217, 219, 220, 222
Cazden, Courtney, 44, 47, 219
Cherry, Kelley, 34, 42–43
Chestek, Virginia, 12, 13, 189, 219
Churchill, Winston, 17, 19
Churchman, Deborah, 52, 219
Ciardi, John, 11–12, 22, 219
Circle revision, 148
Clark, John, 124, 219
Clark, Kevin, 225
Classical college education, x–xi
Classroom discussion, 47–48
Classroom teaching modes, 44
Cliché writing, 85–88
Clusters, 172
Coe, Richard, 27, 219
Collaborative composing, 116–117

Collum, Jack, 189
Comley, Nancy, 14, 103, 119, 124, 224
Commissioned work, 69–70
Community, 7–8, 51, 142
Composition research
 cognitive research, 18-19, 22
 research on creative writers, 22–27
 and the writing process, 20–21
Composition studies, defined, 13–14
Conference on College Composition and Communication (CCCC), xiv
Connors, Robert, ix, 219
Conrad, Joseph, 21
Cooke, John, 190
Cooper, Charles, 217
Cooper, Marilyn, 23, 219
Coover, Robert, 126
Cornish, Roger, 190
Craft talks, 46
Creative writing in the precollege classroom, 10–12
Creative writing students
 compared to composition students, ix
Creativity, defined, 43
Crowley, Sharon, 2, 5, 15, 30, 219
Culhane, Alys, 133
Culley, Margo, 30, 221
cummings, e. e., 123

Dacy, Philip, 126, 219
D'Angelo, Frank, 27, 219
Daniels, Harvey, 11, 219
Daly, John, 21, 219
Daumer, Elisabeth, 220
De Fabio, Roseanne, vii
Devalorization, xi
Diamond, Elin, 225
Dickey, James, 25
Discourse theories, 27–28
Donovan, Timothy, 223
Duffin, Brent, 225
Duke, Charles, vii, viii, 190, 221
Dyadic critique, 52

Eagleton, Terry, ix, x, 220
Elbow, Peter, xv, 15, 27, 52, 53, 73, 101, 102, 131, 132, 144, 145, 152, 157, 160, 163, 164, 190, 220
Emig, Janet, 9, 11, 18, 220
Engle, Paul, xiii, 52, 220
English studies, ix
 and literary theory, xv–xvi
 and types of texts, xv
Epigraphs, 74–75

Evaluation
 draft levels for, 146, 147, 151, 165
 grading creative writing, 157, 160
 new directions in, 161–164
 by peers, 163, 167–168
 portfolio evaluation, 144, 151, 164–175
 self-evaluation, 150, 162–163, 165, 168–170
 teacher responses, 159–160, 174, 175
 timing of, 165–166
 traditional ideas about, 158–161
Exercises
 as class challenges, 117, 129
 fishbowl activity, 53
 muse activity, 64–69
 writing topics, 64, 82, 83
Expert writers. *See* Professional writers
Exploratory writing, 6, 36, 37
Expressive writing, 28, 29. *See also* Exploratory writing

Faigley, Lester, 23, 230
Faulkner, William, 20, 45
Feinberg, Harriet, 213
Felt sense, 20
First-order thinking, 131, 133, 150
Fishbowl activity, 53
Fitzgerald, F. Scott, 17
Fitz-Randolph, Jane, 191
Flower, Linda, 20–21, 22, 63, 220
Foerster, Norman, xii, xiii, 220
Foster, David, 27, 220
Frank, Francine Wattman, 48, 220
Frank, Marjorie, 191
Freewriting, 30, 31, 57, 65, 75, 85, 89
Freisinger, Randall, 12, 191, 220
Frey, James, 191
Frost, Robert, 122, 124, 125
Fuller, David, 158, 192, 220
Full-group critique, 52–55
Fulwiler, Toby, 133, 192, 220

Gallagher, Tess, 190
Gallo, Donald, 192
Gardner, John, 70, 193, 221
Garrett, George, ix, xii, xiv, xvii, 50, 221
Gebhardt, Richard, 124, 193, 221
Geisel, Theodor Seuss, 19
Generating writing, 62–63
Genius, 42–43
Genre, 7, 29, 30, 53, 71
Gere, Anne Ruggles, ix, xii, 221
Golub, Jeff, 224
Gonzalez, Ray, vii

Goswami, Dixie, 220
Grading, 157, 160
Graff, Gerald, ix, x, xi, xv, 9, 221
Grossman, Florence, 70, 126, 193, 221
Group models, 63, 81
Group writing. *See* Collaborative composing
Guided portraits, 98–101

Haake, Katharine, vii, xvi, 51, 107, 129, 193, 221
Hairston, Maxine, 159, 221
Hall, Donald, 194
Harris, Muriel, 56, 221
Harste, Jerome, 23, 221
Hawkins, Hunt, 126
Hawkins, Thom, 53, 56, 221
Hayes, John R., 20–21, 22, 23, 63, 220, 223
Hazlitt, William, 23
Heath, Shirley Brice, 23, 221
Hemingway, Ernest, 20, 123, 158
Hendricks, John, 23, 219
Henkins, Kathryn, 194
Herzer, Scott, vii, 94, 116*n*, 120, 195, 221
Heynan, Jim, 40, 42, 127, 195, 221
Hills, Rust, 195
Hoberman, Ruth, 195
Hoffmann, Leonore, 30, 221
Hua, Li Min, 150, 221
Hugo, Richard, 133, 196

Imaginative writing, x, xii, 11, 36, 37
Imitation, 119–120
  as guided invention, 122–129
Impersonation, 122
In-class writing, 18, 48–52
  freewriting, 30, 31, 57, 65, 75, 85, 89
  invention activities, 14, 29, 48–50, 69–76, 82, 85–115
Instrumental writing, 29, 36, 37
International Directory of Little Magazines and Small Presses, 59, 221
Intertextuality, 14
Invention techniques, 14, 29, 48–50, 64
  adapting and tailoring, 71–76
  connections to genre, 71
  designing, 69–71, 74
  types of, 71, 72, 82, 85–115
Iowa Writers' Workshop. *See* University of Iowa Writers' Workshop

Jacobson, Sally, 190, 221
Jauss, David, 126, 219
Johnson, David, 53, 221–222
Johnson, Mark, 25, 101, 222
Johnson, Roger, 53, 221–222
Johnson, Samuel, 140
Journal writing, 3–4, 18, 30, 31, 62, 132–140
Joyce, James, 17

Kennedy, George, 64, 222
Kennedy, X. J., 190
Kesey, Ken, 117, 222
Kgositsile, Keorepetse, 187
Kinneavy, James, 27, 222
Kinnell, Galway, 84, 190
Kirby, David, 25, 70, 90, 97, 109, 111, 126, 196, 222
Knoblauch, C. H., 22, 73, 90, 97, 109, 111, 126, 196, 222
Koch, Kenneth, 70, 196, 222
Koelling, Robert, 197
Kooser, Ted, 65
Kremers, Carolyn, vii, 73, 84*n*, 89–90, 96, 97, 197, 222
Krupa, Gene, 6, 13, 197, 222
Kunitz, Stanley, 21
Kusz, Natalie, 103

Lakoff, George, 25, 101, 222
Large-scale teaching, 13
Larson, Richard, 222
Lasswell, Harold, 172
Laughlin, James, 65
Lavine, Ann, 48, 222
LeFevre, Karen Burke, 172, 222
Letter forms, 108–111
Lewis, Sinclair, 17
Lindemann, Erika, 157, 222
Lipkis, Jeff, 225
London University Writing Across the Curriculum Project, 28
Lowell, Robert, 19
Lowenstein, Sharyn, 134, 222
Lowey, Alva, 197
Lunsford, Andrea, 222

Madden, David, 17, 131, 132, 139, 144, 197, 222
Madhubuti, Haki, 187
Mailer, Norman, 30
Major, Clarence, 42, 60
Martin, Anne, 15, 222
Martin, Nancy, 28, 29, 218, 222
Martin, Robert, 198
Mathews, Dorothy, 198

Maugham, W. Somerset, 17
McAndrew, Donald, 63, 224
McClelland, Ben, 223
McKim, Elizabeth, 199
McLaughlin, Gary, 199
McLeod, Alexander, 28, 218
McMillen, Liz, 117, 222
McPhee, John, 30
McPherson, Sandra, 190
Melton, David, 199
Memory, 20–21
Mentoring, 8, 10, 55
Metaphorical description, 101–103
Meyer, Sam, 199
M.F.A. programs in creative writing, ix, xii, 10, 11, 39
Michener, James, 20, 145
Miller, Michael, 21, 219
Mills, Ralph J., Jr., 200
Miner, Valerie, 3, 223
Minot, Stephen, 150, 200, 223
Moffett, James, 27, 28, 223
Moglin, Helene, 222
Moore, Ellen, vii
Moore, Rod, 225
Moravia, Alberto, 21
Morgan, Jean, 200
Motto, Ann, 124, 219
Moxley, Joseph, viii, xvi, 2, 9, 11, 43, 116, 200, 221, 223, 224
Muller, Lavonne, 201
Multimedia cross-cultural activity, 96–98
Murray, Donald, 1, 2, 16, 17, 18, 49, 63, 140, 145, 190, 201, 223
Muse activity, 64–69
Myths of writing, 5, 24

National Council of Teachers of English (NCTE), viii, xiv
Neeld, Elizabeth Cowan, 72, 73, 223
Nelson, Jennie, 23, 223
New Critical methodology, xv, 3
New Criticism, 5
Nietzche, Friedrich, 17, 20
Nims, John Frederick, 201

Odell, Lee, 217
Olson, Toby, 123
One-to-one conferences, 55–56
Ostrom, Hans, vii, xvi, 2, 9, 141, 145, 202, 223
Otten, Nick, 201
Out-of-class writing, 50
Overing, Gillian, 42, 217, 219, 220, 222
Owens, Peter, 203

Packard, William, 18, 19, 20, 21, 25, 27, 127, 203, 223
Padgett, Rod, 215
Parisi, Peter, 203
Parody, 122–123
Parris, Peggy Baldwin, 203
Peoples, Peg, vii, viii, 109, 146, 223
Percy, Bernard, 204
Perelman, S. J., 144
Performance, 14, 46, 56–58
Perl, Sondra, 19, 172, 223
Ph.D. programs in creative writing, ix, 11
Pickett, Nell Ann, vii
Pictures for description, 92–94
Plagiarism, 119–120
Plimpton, George, 18, 223
Poetic writing, 28–29. *See also* Imaginative writing
Portfolios. *See* Writing portfolios
Porosky, Peter, 204
Powell, Brian, 204
Preminger, Alex, 223
Professional writers
  defined, 1
  goals of, 21, 23
  habits of, 21–22
  as instructors, xiv, 9
  interviews with, 22, 24–25
  process of, 17–18, 20–21
  rituals of, 31, 49, 64
  self-reports by, 16–18, 19
Progroff, Ira, 134, 224
Projective structuring, 19
Publication, 14, 58–60
  class anthologies, 58–59
  contributor's notes, 59
  reference books for, 59

Rainer, Tristine, 134, 205, 224
Randall, Dudley, 187
Reader-based prose, 22, 24
Reed, Ishmael, 30
Reed, Kit, 205
Regan, Sally, 205
Reigstad, Thomas, 63, 224
Renard, Jules, 145
Renzulli, Joseph, 206
Research on writing. *See* Composition research
Resonance, 172

Response protocols, 145–146, 150, 153–156, 163, 177–182
Retrospective structuring, 19
Reversals, 111–113
Revision, 14, 25, 132–133
  activities, 147–156
  groups and, 140–144
  guided response, 144–147, 152
  levels of, 20, 139–140
  students' images of, 78
Reynolds, Jerry, 201
Rhetoric, xi, 36
Rich, Adrienne, xvi, 224
Ridland, Muriel, 206
Robinson, Jill, vii, 84*n*, 85, 88, 116*n*, 120, 195, 206, 221, 224
Rohman, Gordon, 18, 224
Romatowski, Jane, 211
Ronald, Kate, 23, 63, 224
Rose, Mike, 21, 224
Rosen, Harold, 28, 218
Runzo, Sandra, 220

St. Clair, Philip, 209
Scene of writing, 2, 16, 51
Scholes, Robert, ix, xv, 3, 9, 14, 103, 119, 124, 224
Schramm, Wilbur, xiii
Schumaker, Peggy, vii
Schwartz, Mimi, 57, 206, 224
Scollon, Ron, 206
Scollon, Suzanne, 206
Scott, Wilbur, 207
Sears, Peter, 207
Second-order thinking, 131–132
Segedy, Michael, 124, 224
Self-evaluation, 150, 162–163, 165, 168–170
Sestinas, 126–127
Sexton, Ann, 17, 19, 20
Shaughnessy, Mina, 19, 224
Shaughnessy, Shari, 207
Shelnutt, Eve, xvi, 10, 116, 208, 224
Shiflett, Betty, 208
Shonagan, Shei, 126
Slevin, James, 222
Small-group critique, 52–55, 57, 142, 147
Smart, Christopher, 126
Smelcer, John, 117, 224
Smith, Barbara Herrnstein, 131, 224
Smith, Frank, 2, 224
Smith, Sydney, 20, 159, 224
Sommers, Jerry, 208
Sommers, Nancy, 39, 41, 112, 113, 209
Sound activity, 94–96
Spacks, Barry, 208
Spooner, Michael, viii
Stafford, William, 39, 41, 112, 113, 209
Stark, Dave, 112
Stegner, Wallace, ix, 62, 224
Steinberg, Judith, 199
Stelmach, Marjorie, 202
Stern, Jerome, 209
Stevens, Wallace, 17, 72
Stewart, Donald, xvi, 225
Stock, Gregory, 133, 225
Stoneham, Joyce Keever, 210
Student lecture, 46
Subjective theory of writing instruction, xii

Talent, 42–43
Teacher lecture, 4–45
Teachers and Writers Collaborative, 210
Thompson, Jeanie, 190
Tobin, Lad, 63, 225
Tomlinson, Barbara, 24, 25, 26, 34, 64, 209, 210, 225
Torgersen, Eric, 211
Transactional creative writing workshop, xvii, 14, 29, 37
  goals of, 41, 42
  students' observations about, 61
Transactional theory of writing instruction, xii, xv, 40
Transactional writing, 28, 29
Treat, Lawrence, 211
Trefethen, Florence, 211
Treichler, Paula, 48, 220
Tremmel, Robert, 6, 13, 197, 222
Trepanier-Street, Mary, 211
Tsujimoto, Joseph, 70, 148, 212, 225
Turner, Alberta, 31, 49, 70, 101, 102, 141, 143, 147, 157, 158, 212, 225
Turner, Mark, 222

Ulmer, Gregory, 14, 103, 119, 124, 224
Undergraduate writing workshop
  departmental expectations of, 8–12
  history of, ix, xii
  pedagogical approaches to, xii, ix
  students' view of, 2–8
Underground writing, 6, 13
University of Iowa Writers' Workshop, xii–xiii
Updike, John, 20

Venturino, Tom, 225
Volkmer, John, 23, 63, 224

Wakowski, Diane, 127, 190
Waldman, Ann, 84, 90
Waldman, Ken, vii, viii, 86–87, 117, 118
Waldrup, Tom, 18, 225
Wallace, Robert, 65, 126
Weddle, David, 116, 117, 225
Weiner, Harvey, 53
West, Rebecca, 101
West, William, 213
White, Edward, 159, 160, 163, 164, 225
Whitman, Ruth, 213
Wike, Terence, vii, viii, 94, 225
Wilbers, Stephen, ix, xii, xiii, 225
Wilhoit, Stephen, 28, 213, 225
Willis, Meredith Sue, 214
Wilson, Nancy, 172, 223
Winterowd, W. Ross, 5
Wlecke, Alfred, 18, 224
Woodward, Virginia, 23, 221
Woolf, Virginia, 17
Writer-based prose, 22, 24
Writers
  and audience, 7, 20, 22, 28, 29, 40, 141, 164
  and community, 7–8, 51, 142
  and genius, 42–43
  and mentoring, 8, 10, 55
  and talent, 42–43
Writer's apprehension, 21
Writer's block, 21–22, 49, 50
Writers' Market, 225
Writer's metaphors, 24–27, 63, 65, 77
Writing about writing, 30, 31, 38
Writing centers, 8, 56, 118
Writing from objects, 89–92
Writing groups
  developing in the classroom, 23
  group roles, 142–144
  guided response, 144–147, 152
Writing portfolios, 82, 144, 151, 164–175
Writing process
  models of, 63, 79–81
  professional writers on, 17–18
  stages of, 18, 22
  among students, 23, 77
  in women, 26
Writing process cover sheets, 163, 164
Writing teachers, 1–2, 141–142
Writing theories, 27–35
Writing workshop models, 12–14, 23
Wyche-Smith, Susan, 31, 225
Wyman, Linda, 214

Yeats, William Butler, 69, 147

Zancanella, Don, 214
Zavatsky, Bill, 214
Zeigler, Alan, 70, 144, 225
Zemelman, Steve, 11, 219
Zender, Karl, 150, 225

Author

Wendy Bishop, Director of Freshman English at Florida State University, is the author of *Second Nature,* a chapbook of poems, and *Something Old, Something New: College Writing Teachers and Classroom Change,* a research monograph. She has won the Joseph Henry Jackson Award and published poetry and fiction in many magazines and journals including *The American Poetry Review, The Chronicle of Higher Education, College English, Permafrost, Prairie Schooner, Western Humanities Review,* and *The Yale Review.* Her articles on the teaching of writing appear regularly in composition journals.